ACCRINGTON STANLEY

The club that wouldn't die

ACCRINGTON STANLEY

The club that wouldn't die

Phil Whalley

SPORTS
BOOKS

Published in Great Britain by
SportsBooks Limited
PO Box 422Cheltenham
GL50 2YN

© Phil Whalley 2006
First Published September 2006

Front cover designed by Kath Northam.

Front cover photographs by Garth Dawson, Actionimages and
Getty Images.
Back cover photograph by Don McPhee/Guardian Newspapers
Ltd 2006

A catalogue record for this book is available from
the British Library.

ISBN 1 899807 47 0

Printed and bound in England by Cromwell Press

Dedication

For my Dad, Roy Whalley, who shivered alongside me in the Crown Ground shed for many a year; and for my Mum, Christine Whalley, who thought we were daft but didn't point it out too often.

Only those who will risk going too far can possibly find out how far one can go.

TS Eliot

Contents

Acknowledgements

FOR GIVING ME their time freely and willingly to talk about Accrington Stanley, sincere thanks to: Jack Barrett, Gerald Berry, Eric Bolton, Ian Brooks, Tony Clements, John Coleman, George Duffy, Mike Ferguson, Alex Hamilton, Geoff Heap, Rob Heys, Dave Hindle, Jimmy Hinksman, Jack Hudson, Rod Kenyon, Arthur McGilveray, Paul Mullin, Alan Parkinson, John Prescott, Rob Russell, Jim Spencer, Harry Stevenson, Terry Styring, Jack Tansey, Dave Thornley, Mark Turner and Eric Whalley.

In addition to patiently and frankly answering my questions, John Alty provided some valuable documents; Mary Andrews of the *Guardian* newspaper efficiently tracked down some long-forgotten photographs of Accrington Stanley; Joan Croasdale also discovered and copied some unseen photographs and gave me her collection of cuttings and papers; Catherine Duckworth of Accrington Library was always helpful and provided me with useful contacts and a photograph; Alison Gabryszak tolerated me setting up camp in her house while I went through her vast collection of Accrington Stanley photographs, and generously allowed me to use as many as I wanted; Tony Greenwood (www.kipax.com) kindly offered to reproduce any of his photographs for my use; Bernard and Kathleen Grimshaw trusted me with a prized photo of their son, Chris; David Hooley took the trouble to get in touch and allowed me to borrow his meticulous playing records of Accrington Stanley as well as providing a photograph of the famous Stanley milk T-shirt; Bert Johnson sent some unique photographs of Peel Park with the generous gesture that they could be used freely; Dave Mooney gave up most of an afternoon to talk to me about his years at Stanley and by loaning his scrapbooks saved me hours of work in the library;

Bryan Pemberton wrote down his vivid insights into the early years at the Crown and also provided feedback on a couple of draft chapters; Timothy Pond kindly sent me his surreal Accrington Stanley illustration that raised a smile in the clubhouse at Barnet; and Phil Terry provided me with the statistics that I needed and patiently answered my confused queries.

Behind the scenes, there are always people nudging the writing process along. Karen Neill as always provided unconditional support and encouragement, even when she caught me writing on the hotel PC when we were supposed to be on holiday. David Whalley, as he did with my other Accrington Stanley book, agreed to read the drafts and give me his thoughts, which were invariably helpful and encouraging. Thanks also to Randall Northam of SportsBooks for his patience and advice.

Introduction

The Power of Memory

ON SATURDAY APRIL 15th 2006, Accrington Stanley travelled to Woking and defeated their hosts 1-0, and in so doing completed a remarkable 36-year journey to the Football League. This famous football name had been re-established in 1968, five years after the original club had been wound up in the High Court, and had only started playing again in August 1970. They kicked off on a home ground that only the most optimistic of enthusiasts could ever envisage hosting League football, and for years toiled away at the lower end of northern non-league.

There was no historical process at work, nor any force of romantic inevitability. In fact, there are few reasons why Accrington Stanley should be in the Football League. Though the mayor might disagree, Accrington is a smallish and unremarkable town. It has never been a particularly big or expansive place; it has never been a hotbed of anything or excelled in any field; it does not attract visitors on the grounds of its architecture or ambience. The people are both modest and moderate, a combination that produces decency, friendliness and a degree of community attachment. Accrington is just an ordinary northern town really, and no more or less distinguished than dozens of other similar locations across the land.

But there is one thing: though Accrington is an entirely typical town, its name resonates atypically – far louder, far further than it ought to, and the reasons why have their roots in human tragedies with which anyone with a sense of empathy cannot fail to sympathise.

The first happened on July 1st 1916, when the Accrington Pals were sent to their graves on the first day of the Somme campaign. Many other Pals regiments from around the country suffered the same fate, but of them all, Accrington was the smallest town in which a full battalion of 1,000 men was based. Though not all of the men came from the town, the name of the Accrington Pals was distinctively local; it personified the concept behind the Pals – that communities took their collective spirit onto the battlefields of Europe. The human tragedy of the story, with hardly any of the 40,000 residents of the town escaping a family loss that day, has been captured and preserved in Peter Whelan's play *The Accrington Pals*, performed worldwide since its debut in 1981. Thus in theatres across the globe, the name of Accrington is invoked as a way of asking people to muse upon the consequences of war – not a bad legacy, some might say, for the 584 deceived Lancastrians who perished in the mud that day.

It seems inconsequential, next to the dark events of the Somme, to relate that devastating loss of human life with the death of a football club. But if the 20th century was the era in which war went global, then it was also the era in which one game went global – and that game was football.

For years, young men (and women) had been kicking footballs around fields, but it was in England that enthusiasts first made the effort to place the game in a framework so that some semblance of order and merit could allow teams to prosper. Their efforts bore fruit – not just in the very first Football League competition, but in starting a format that would spread rapidly and endure across the world. In this remarkably successful venture, Accrington was there from the start, one of the original 12 Northern and Midland towns to commit to this bold innovation, implemented in the empurpled face of a London elite – the Football Association.

That first team – 'Th'owd Reds' of Accrington FC – unfortunately did not live to the ripe old age that their wonderful nickname intimated. They lasted five years in the Football League before relegation heralded the end of the club, indebted and poorly supported. Even then, Accrington was the smallest town to support a Football League club, and only a few smaller localities have managed it since. But Th'owd Reds had secured Accrington's place in history, and another town team soon emerged. Accrington Stanley, with its origins in and around the Stanley Street area of the town and its first base in the Stanley Arms pub, rose to become one of the top non-league sides in the county. With perfect timing, Stanley won the Lancashire Junior Cup in 1921 and cemented their place in the Football League's new Third Division (North).

So, for the second time, Accrington ventured into the Football League, the competition it had helped to start more than 30 years before, but again the town's club struggled to survive. It was merely a bitter irony that Stanley resigned from the League only a few years after the most successful period in their history. Prior to this, the club had been on the brink of extinction on more than one occasion. Once more, Accrington's Football League club fell, indebted, and towards the end, unloved. What was different this time was the context.

By the 1960s, the global world was starting to emerge. Information was winging its way across the wires from one continent to the other in minutes, jet travel was dismantling the barriers of distance, and politicians were heralding a brave new world dominated by advances in science and technology. These developments made the story of Accrington Stanley what it is today.

The pictures taken outside Peel Park that chilly March morning in 1962 were seen around the world, but one in particular had a deep emotional resonance. It showed elderly groundsman Frank Nash and his dog trudging away from the camera, across the snowbound pitch, head bowed in a resigned sadness. It said everything about those times, as did the popular reaction in the national press. Frank represented the past, as did Accrington Stanley – an Edwardian relic of a football club that should have been cast adrift a long time ago. Even the very name implied a bygone era that had no place in the modern world. Accrington Stanley thus became a byword used in jest to ridicule anything perceived as too old, clapped out, laughably hopeless, on the way out (and good riddance).

Odd to recognise this now, but this harsh treatment probably did the town a favour. Other teams lost their League status around this time, such as Gateshead and Bradford Park Avenue, but no one kept mentioning them. Instead, the name of Accrington Stanley endured in the public consciousness and its role remained the same – to remind the country of the amateurish, old-fashioned way things once were.

However, the white heat of technology quickly cooled and tarnished in the face of the industrial strife and economic troubles of the 1970s, and Accrington Stanley started to mean something else – not just that old, moribund football club with the funny name, but also a reminder of an era that suddenly started to be reappraised for its qualities – when people were secure in a modest calling; when it was natural to support your local team; when the terraces were safe and good-natured; when it was a genuine community effort that gave in return a measure of civic pride and a sense of belonging. This uneasy realisation of what had been lost gave pause for thought to those all too ready to mock Accrington Stanley and the image it portrayed in the mind's eye of the nation. Their withdrawal from the Football League heralded the end of a particular way of life: a little insular perhaps, but comfortingly communal and fundamentally decent.

It is no coincidence that the people who founded the new Accrington Stanley came from the older generations within the town, those who had not given up on the idea of rallying round and pulling together. There were no more than a couple of dozen of them at the beginning, but it was in this very spirit that they created Accrington Stanley (1968).

This small group of citizens began with precisely nothing: no money, no ground, no manager or players. It was a football club born of old habits and out of memory – reflections on those years when the experience of pride and contentment was strong, strong enough to survive subsequent disillusionment and despair. Such experience left as its residue the idea not that the past could be recreated, but that it was worth trusting in life and having a go anyway. To reform the club was simply to do the right thing together; it was not an imposition.

Attitudes to the new Accrington Stanley were not uniform. For some, it was ultimately about finding a way back to the Football League berth that they had wrongly taken for granted. For others, it was simply about having a town team to watch on a Saturday afternoon. When, on the odd occasion, a decision had to be made about whether Stanley should stay put or move to another league in search of higher standards, the tension between these two perspectives would surface. The result, however, was always the same. The club moved on, driven by an instinctive sense of purpose.

Nothing illustrates this more than Accrington Stanley's new home, the Crown Ground. When Stanley competed in the Lancashire Combination through the 1970s, they travelled to grounds that looked very similar to the Crown. Most Combination grounds in those days consisted of little more than a pitch enclosed by a fence, or occasionally a concrete wall, with some covered standing space, often referred to as the scratting shed for obvious reasons. At the more opulent end of the spectrum, one might find a small wooden stand.

Some of those grounds remain today in virtually the same condition, while in the intervening period the Crown Ground has been transformed. This has not, however, been done via the chequebook of a loaded businessman. Instead, for many years and with formidable dedication, a small army of volunteers has scratched around the building projects and demolition sites of the area, recycling unwanted timber, brick and steel. Even today, when Accrington Stanley finds itself in a much stronger financial position, the volunteer spirit remains, ensuring that the club avoids the fees of builders and subcontractors wherever possible. In short, a small group of fans have built their team a Football League ground.

The dynamo at the heart of this remarkable story is memory, and its lesson is that the power of memory can endure the most distressing of experiences and confront the most overwhelming odds. In 1968 – and for some years thereafter – there was no such thing as promotion to the Football League, and yet the club chased that unlikely dream with a gentle but relentless insistence, aware that it played not just for the few hundred faithful but also for the memory of a grander tradition, one that not all around the Crown could remember.

The passage of time did not matter. In an age when even Andy Warhol's fifteen minutes feels indulgent, Accrington Stanley have gloriously shown that 44 years is nothing compared to a sense of shared injustice and the determination to right a deeply-felt wrong. The music hall jokes might remain, but the club and the town have had the last laugh and a defiant one at that, in the face of those who watched Stanley go under in 1962 and reasoned that it was a good thing for English football. It is that perspective that has proved to be the bankrupt one.

Chapter One

1962
An Irreplaceable Loss

THE SCENE WAS late on a Monday evening, March 5th 1962. Most of the townsfolk, resting after the first day of the working week, and looking forward perhaps to Easter's long weekend, were going through the well-worn, gentle routines of the quiet night in. An exception was the meeting taking place in the public library, for there a drama had ensued whose outcome would find the back pages of newspapers from Stockholm to Melbourne, and fleetingly place a small town in north-east Lancashire at the centre of the football world.

Accrington Stanley, a club with a history of both struggle and resilience, were, once again, in trouble both on and off the field. With a squad shorn of most of its talent, sold to pay the bills, the team lay at the bottom of the Fourth Division, watched by the remnants of what was once a vibrant and proud set of supporters that had numbered some thousands. As the unpaid invoices mounted, the board had called on an old hand to take the tiller and steady the ship. In February 1962, Sam Pilkington had emerged from retirement to oversee proceedings at Peel Park, the neat ground to the north of the town centre that had been Accrington Stanley's home since 1919.

Perhaps nothing underlined the extent of the crisis more than Pilkington's reaction, for here was a man who had been involved with Accrington Stanley for his entire adult life, serving as player, manager and chairman. Pilkington's reign in the chair had encompassed the difficult years in the 1950s that saw Stanley mired perennially at the wrong end of the

Third Division (North). Sam's masterful networking of the lower League boardrooms was the stuff of legend, vital husbandry that reaped a very necessary annual harvest of re-election votes to preserve Accrington's Football League status.

So it was no surprise, and something of a relief, when Pilkington answered the call to negotiate the club through its immediate uncertainties. Perhaps Sam was not aware of quite how stealthily the malaise had wound its way through every corner of Peel Park, but it is certainly no exaggeration to say that he was deeply shocked at the state of affairs he found. Few onlookers, however, expected Pilkington – the man dubbed 'Mr Accrington Stanley' – to walk sadly away, declaring that all was lost.

For all the years of accumulated experience that Pilkington brought to the table, he could not see a way out. On the evening of March 5th 1962, two weeks after he had returned to the club, Pilkington presided over a meeting of the club's creditors. It became clear during the course of the evening that Stanley had virtually exhausted the reserves of goodwill and understanding that small football clubs often need to survive periodic financial difficulties. Most of the creditors were prepared, wearily, to grant further leave of payment, but crucially the public utilities would not. Without the immediate payment of a £400 bill, energy supplies to Peel Park would be cut off. It was a few hundred quid that Accrington Stanley simply did not have.

As the meeting neared its conclusion, Pilkington resigned from the board for the final time. With Sam Pilkington gone, the four remaining directors were left adrift and very much alone, with a husk of an organisation that just a few years before had boasted one of the very best teams outside the top two divisions. Accrington Stanley had hardly any playing assets, there was no cash in the bank, and the support of the town itself – the most crucial factor – had been frittered away and then withdrawn. As the night drew in, the bedside lamps being switched off across Accrington made for an apt postscript as the light and heat of Football League competition was extinguished from the town. The four directors had made a fateful decision. There was nothing for it, they reasoned, but to resign.

A lot can happen to a football club in four years. Blackburn Rovers' metamorphosis in the 1990s was from a competitive Second Division team to Premiership champions. Burnley went the other way in the 1980s, as did Manchester United in the 1970s, relegated just six years after their first European Cup win. Wimbledon fans have had to start again from the lower end of the football pyramid, just a few years after two Cup semi-finals in one season. And, let it be said, today's Accrington Stanley has completed a remarkable journey under John Coleman, who arrived at the Crown Ground in 1999 to find the bare remnants of a team and a Unibond First Division club unsure and uncertain of itself after its first ever relegation.

Football clubs occasionally find that alchemy of the visionary manager and the responsive squad, and when it happens there's no guessing where the journey might end. But such meetings of mind and spirit are rare enough to tell us that the science of team-building is inexact, and to assume a position of unassailable dominance is merely to invite a fall. A wrong signing at the wrong time can undo the work of ten good recruits; a healthy, vigorous organisation at Christmas can wither with the first daffodils of spring.

So it need not be a shock to find that just four years before Accrington Stanley's demise in March 1962, the team was challenging strongly for promotion to the Second Division of the Football League. Stanley's manager, a young and charismatic Scot named Walter Galbraith, had just been the subject of yet another approach, this time by First Division Blackpool, then still a force in English football. The board, keen to retain Galbraith, had already laid in front of him a lavish £1,750 a year contract, First Division money at the time, and their plans to modernise Peel Park for Second Division football signalled their confidence in the manager and their ambition for Accrington Stanley. Careful management seemed to epitomise the club from top to bottom. The *Accrington Observer* reckoned that six reserve team youngsters would each command at least £2,000 on the transfer market, most of these youngsters being graduates of the 'A' team that had reached the final of the Lancashire League Cup the previous season, where they had lost narrowly to Manchester United. As the season drew to a close, the club announced the purchase of a grandstand, for which planning permission had already been obtained.

From this brief sketch alone, Accrington Stanley's rude health seemed destined to endure, but hindsight provides the historical X-ray that reveals the problems within. As was usual under Galbraith, Stanley were challenging at the top end of the Third Division (North) and would soon have a ground worthy of a higher league. But this investment in the infrastructure of Accrington Stanley had overplayed the hand that Galbraith's astuteness had provided. When Galbraith left for Bradford Park Avenue, Stanley quickly reverted to type as a struggling lower League club, and then found it impossible to recover. What had happened to precipitate such a cataclysmic decline?

Most Stanley followers regret with bitterness the purchase of a stand from the Aldershot Military Tattoo, which was dismantled and transported to the north-west where it became the Burnley Road stand. History has a way of taunting us with seemingly innocuous accidents of circumstance from which devastating consequences flow, and, in the best tradition of such things, the story goes that Stanley chairman Bob Moore only clapped eyes on the construction because a set of roadworks in Aldershot led to him taking a detour that passed the rural venue hosting the town's military show.

It was in this venue that the stand was located. It was an impressive edifice, reaching 80 feet in height and providing seating for 4,700 spectators. There was only one problem – its design was not anything like that of a typical football stadium stand. Photographs show the construction standing behind and above a large bank of terracing, with the seats some distance from the field and tiered at a shallow angle, especially the upper tier, which appeared oddly to contain fewer seats than the lower tier and was fronted by white, steel barriers. It was obvious that it would not fit into the limited confines of a typical British football ground.

What, therefore, could the chairman have been thinking when he decided, in April 1958, to commit the club to the expense of buying and relocating the Aldershot stand? It set the club – already indebted – on a path that would lead to financial ruin and extinction. Was Moore, and for that matter the other directors who sanctioned the purchase, guilty of the most irresponsible hubris?

It is easy to allocate blame after the event, so it is worth considering how Moore's rationale can be reasoned through. When the club purchased the stand, the seating capacity at Peel Park was just 776, and it was rudimentary at that, the wooden stand in the shadow of the Coppice having its foundations in the early 1920s when Stanley had first joined the Football League. For the visit of some of the top names in the Third Division (North), Stanley could expect gates close to 10,000, and attendances rarely fell below 6,000. It was undeniably true that the demand for seating far outstripped Stanley's modest supply, a problem that a new stand would solve at a stroke.

It was also the case that the board had not been previously remiss in the area of ground development. The director for whom the ground was a preoccupation was Charles Kilby. As a key figure in the Supporters' Club, Kilby had been instrumental in the extension of the terracing at the Huncoat end during the late 1940s, work which increased the capacity of Peel Park to a verified 24,500. In December 1953, and by this time on the board, Kilby had unveiled plans for a stand along the Burnley Road side of the ground which included the idea of creating a separate limited company to raise the £30,000 needed.

The years that followed were Stanley's most successful ever and saw some highly effective fundraising by supporters, but the plans for the Burnley Road stand stayed on the shelf, and by the end of the 1950s, the estimated cost of a new stand had risen to a prohibitive £40,000. Who, then, could blame the board for seeing in the Aldershot stand the opportunity to solve the club's seating shortage once and for all, and for a fraction of the cost of a new construction? Not the *Accrington Observer*, who warmly commended the board when the purchase of the stand for just £1,450 was made public. The local paper, always a considered barometer of mood and opinion among the Stanley faithful, saw in the purchase evidence of the club's ambition and enterprise. This impression was encouraged by Moore himself, who told the local paper:

"I have seen only one stand on a football ground like this, and that is at the Arsenal. We saw an opportunity to realise an ambition and save the club thousands of pounds in the future. The whole future of football is in the melting pot. There is a possibility of a European League, and we want to be in on the ground floor and make Accrington one of the centres of football."

However, this is where the questions start. With this statement, Moore was being disingenuous at best. The stand was not like Arsenal's, and the froth about Accrington Stanley in a European League struck a worryingly unrealistic note from a club that had yet to make it into the Second Division. Significant progress is never made without ambition, but there's always a line to be drawn between courage and recklessness.

It is true that some clubs had risen from the regional Third Divisions to make an impact on the national stage in the post-war era. Cardiff had gone all the way from the Third to the First Division, but they were a city club who had been there before. A better example was Rotherham, a club with more modest means. The Millers, Third Division (North) champions in 1951, missed out on promotion to the First Division only on goal average a few years later in 1955. If a town club like Rotherham could knock on the door of the top league, why not Stanley?

It was a fair enough question, but Rotherham's experience was not typical. Most Third Division (North) champions struggled to make an impact at the higher level. In the twelve post-war seasons of regional Third Division football, three Northern champions came straight back down, and most others managed only lower or mid-table positions. Even then, Accrington was one of the smallest towns to support a Football League club; the assertion of Stanley's place in the brave new world of European football could not be seen as anything other than egotism prevailing at the expense of a reasoned judgement of the club's circumstances.

Moore must also have known that the £10,000 budgeted to dismantle, transport and rebuild the stand was money the club did not have, and he may well have suspected that it might not prove to be enough. For Accrington Stanley had not bought an identikit football stand ready to go up once all the bits had arrived, as Moore had intimated to the press. Instead, the £1,450 had simply bought the raw materials from which a stand could be built, and there was no chance that the builders at the Accrington end could erect anything like the original version.

In the end, what eventually materialised had all the defects of the Aldershot stand but none of the benefits. The angle of the seating remained too shallow, giving restricted views for spectators at the back. Photographs show a construction with a very low roof that swooped down at an unusually steep angle over the heads of the spectators, quite unlike a typical football stadium stand. And not only had the operation gone over budget, but the end product was less than half the capacity of the original. The club had spent £15,000 for just 2,000 extra seats, each of which brought in the meagre sum of 25p per match, provided anyone sat in them.

Very quickly, those praiseworthy words bandied around in the *Accrington Observer* looked fanciful. Ringing uncomfortably closer to the truth were accusations that the board had been seduced by the size and scale of the stand to the point where hard-headed facts had been either ignored or dismissed far too easily. Neither was the whole operation free from talk of underhand goings-on, with one rumour suggesting that a middleman, in cahoots with the board, had sold the stand to the club for a fee.

It was all very wearing on the social fabric of the club, and as the saga of the stand finally ended in the close season of 1958–59, harsh realities hit home. Just days before the 1958–59 campaign kicked off, the directors summoned manager Galbraith to a board meeting. They told him that, in the light of the club's financial commitment to the stand, they had to redirect some of the club's funds from the playing staff. Moore's plan to pay for the stand by selling 400 four-year season tickets at a cost of £25 each had failed to bear fruit. Had he done his homework on this initiative? There was probably never much demand for such a package in the first place.

For Galbraith, the decision to prune his budget was the tipping point. The sums of money involved with the Burnley Road stand, which were being discussed openly in the media, had acutely irritated the manager, who thought that the club ought instead to be strengthening the squad in preparation for the new demands of the 1958–59 campaign, for this was to be the inaugural season of nationwide Third and Fourth Division football. As runners-up in the Third Division (North) the previous season, Stanley were in the nationwide Third Division on merit, but now they faced longer treks and bigger foes in the shape of city clubs like Norwich, Plymouth Argyle and Southampton. Galbraith knew that Stanley had a challenge on their hands to compete.

Jack Kirby, a Stanley fan helping out with the construction of the stand at Peel Park, witnessed Galbraith's scepticism for himself. As the manager monitored pre-season training one morning, he wandered over to the stand, where Jack made a comment to the effect that the stand was shaping up well. Galbraith's reply made no concession to Kirby's enthusiasm: "We'll never fill it, and I could have had three new players with the money."

Galbraith took his dark attitude into the board meeting and made it clear that he needed more resources if he was to continue his quest to guide Stanley into the Second Division. The manager fought his corner in the boardroom, but he could not wring from the directors money that simply was not there. Sensing that the club had taken a wrong and portentous turn, and perhaps with a mind on his future, Galbraith decided to resign.

In terms of possessing a manager who could find good players for modest fees and motivate them to play above themselves, Accrington Stanley would never replace Walter Galbraith. Judging that good semi-professionals playing in Scotland could make an impact south of the border, he invested in promising young Scots, and was able to offer them relatively good money and a homely community of expats in Huncoat's Within Grove.

It was an attractive proposition for them, and Galbraith's Caledonian imports played with the grateful eagerness of those given a chance to prove themselves. Schooled in the passing game, they immediately impressed with the vision and imagination of their football, the quality of which was a revelation to the Peel Park faithful.

On occasions, the manager unearthed a player that had the First Division scouts flocking. Defender John Ryden, for instance, arrived from Alloa for little more than £1,000 and left less than two seasons later for the bright lights of White Hart Lane, with Stanley pocketing ten times their investment. With these Scottish connections severed on Galbraith's departure, Stanley began instead to pick up the crumbs from beneath the tables of bigger clubs, but these men rarely acquitted themselves with enthusiasm or distinction.

As well as Galbraith's unrivalled eye for a player, he brought Accrington Stanley an unprecedented run of success: four consecutive top three finishes in the Third Division (North) including two runners-up spots. In today's money, Galbraith's record equates to two automatic promotions and two play-off places, a real achievement by anyone's standards.

But in those more elitist times, full membership of the Football League could be earned only by claiming a Third Division title, and it was this distinction alone that eluded Galbraith in his five memorable years at Peel Park.

So spectacular had been the rise of Stanley under Galbraith that it was tempting to forget from what depths the manager had dragged the club, and how easily it could sink back to those levels. Galbraith was the first Accrington Stanley manager to steer the team anywhere near promotion to the Second Division. In the seven post-war seasons prior to his arrival, Stanley had applied for re-election twice and achieved a top half finish just once. Upon Galbraith's departure, Stanley's fortunes quite rapidly returned to those that had been fairly typical of the club's experiences in the Football League.

Galbraith was a little fortunate also in that his arrival coincided with a wholesale renewal of personnel throughout the club. Inheriting few players, Galbraith was able to build his own team, and he was supported by new blood in the boardroom. Treasurer George Pratt, soon to be the new chairman, embarked on a speculative financial policy. In a short period of time, he extended the club's overdraft to £10,000, raised £7,000 through a debenture issue which the club had to repay at 5%, spent £9,500 on floodlights and bought property worth £3,720. To finance this expenditure, Pratt was banking on the activities of the Supporters' Club, which had started a football lottery that had quickly burgeoned into a seriously profitable operation.

The lottery, masterminded by Stanley stalwart Albert Lucas, was simple enough. A coupon listed 58 weekend fixtures, and if the three numbers you chose coincided with three home winners, you were in the hat for the cash prizes, which were won by the two people whose teams had in total scored the most goals. At its height, the lottery offered an eye-opening £200 first prize, and neither was the consolation prize of £125 to be sniffed at. A typical weekly wage at this time was around £10.

The money on offer attracted the stake of the seasoned punter, for the lottery allowed you to change your numbers weekly, but its simplicity also attracted those who saw the weekly flutter as merely a bit of fun. A team of agents, some door-to-door but many of them working in the major factories of the town, distributed the coupons and collected the money each week with admirable dedication, and their efforts quickly paid off. Lucas's lottery was a resounding success. There was only one problem: its legality was questionable.

Under the Betting and Gaming Act, an organisation could run a lottery only among its own members, and though Lucas's operation charged a nominal shilling membership fee each year, that was as far as they went to meet this legal technicality. Not that anyone thought the lottery underhand or fraudulent. It was common knowledge that the profits went to Accrington Stanley, and the townsfolk were happy to participate. They trusted Lucas and thought the lottery was harmless; it was only a shilling to play, might win them some extra cash and it made a bit for the local team.

Stanley supporters were not the only ones testing the legal boundaries of the Act. Similar supporters' club lotteries operated around the country; indeed, they were the most significant form of fundraising in football at the time. But the lottery eventually caused Accrington Stanley a real problem, not just because it was stopped and became the subject of a court case, but because the club had come to take for granted – and budget for – the significant amounts of cash the scheme raised.

When, in February 1955, the Supporters' Club opened new offices and social facilities in Stanley Street, George Pratt told the assembled members, "If you stop your activities now, I do not think you would have an Accrington Stanley Football Club in another six months."

It was quite a statement of how important the income of the Supporters' Club – and especially of their lottery scheme – had become to the functioning of the new, promotion-chasing Stanley, though not all of the club's financial muscle in this period was due to the lottery. The floodlights, though expensive, were also an astute investment and for a couple of years thereafter raised additional cash through midweek friendlies. Another financial boost was the renewed appetite for football shown by the Accrington people. Word of Galbraith's exciting new team quickly spread, and the crowds started to flock to Peel Park, with the average gate in 1954–55 just under 10,000.

It was unknown for Stanley to find themselves with three abundant sources of income at the same time, and to the club's credit, they and their supporters had made it happen through their own initiative. In Galbraith's first two seasons in charge – 1953–54 and 1954–55 – the Supporters' Club lottery raised £27,921 for the club, vital resources that allowed the manager to pay good money and maintain a squad with strength in depth. During the 1954–55 season, Stanley employed 24 professionals on £14 per week, with a £2 win bonus for the relevant first team players.

Even at this affluent point in time, the club owed £16,000 to creditors, around half a year's income. It was a burdensome debt, but a manageable one provided the lottery carried on delivering. And it was precisely at this moment, February 1955, with Stanley clear at the top of the Third Division (North), that the lottery bounty came to a sudden end.

The uncertainty surrounding the Betting and Gaming Act saw the law interpreted differently in various parts of the country. Most local police forces turned a blind eye to football club lotteries, but in Torquay the authorities had prosecuted the supporters' club over theirs, and in December 1954 the verdict came through that Torquay United's lottery was unlawful. This set a legal precedent applying to all such schemes, but Lucas decided to continue with Stanley's, on the grounds that since Torquay's supporters' club had appealed, the case was still ongoing.

When Torquay lost their appeal in January 1955, Lucas temporarily stopped his lottery, but by this time Accrington police had started to investigate. The following month, the entire committee of the Supporters' Club was summonsed to appear in court, charged with running an illegal gambling operation.

The trial revealed just how successful the lottery was. In three months between October 16th and January 15th, the lottery had brought in £10,882. A total of £4,400 had been distributed in prizes, and £6,194 had gone to Stanley, a weekly average of £442 – easily enough to cover the wage bill for the entire first team squad. A staggering 15,000 tickets had been sold on a weekly basis.

Even the prosecution marvelled at the energy and ingenuity of the Supporters' Club committee, and it was accepted that the lottery had been run entirely for the benefit of Accrington Stanley. But though the supporters argued their case strongly, they were found guilty as charged. Both Albert Lucas and Charles Kilby were given small fines, and all had to pay costs.

It is perhaps instructive that, shortly after the suspension of the lottery, chairman Pratt launched a share appeal. This probably did some damage as it gave the impression that, even with 10,000 home gates, Stanley still could not make ends meet. How could the club possibly survive in the Second Division, with a higher wage bill, if they could not manage in the Third? It was not an immaterial question, as Stanley entered the final stages of the season still atop the Third Division (North). Agonisingly, they were overhauled by Barnsley, who put together a freakish run of victories to clinch the title and promotion.

The sudden cutting off of the lottery money in 1955 was not the end of Galbraith's efforts to hoist the team into the Second Division, but from this point on Stanley found themselves struggling to meet the costs of their manager's ambition. The lottery scheme was, in time, modified and restarted, but it would never be as successful as it was in those years under Albert Lucas. The suspension of the lottery in this final part of the season, as Stanley pushed hard for promotion, drained the fund-raisers of the momentum they had generated. By the time of Galbraith's departure, Stanley had posted three consecutive financial year losses, amounting to something in the region of £17,000, an amount that the lottery would have covered had it been able to continue as before. As it was, not only did Stanley lose this abundant source of cash, but gates started to fall from the 10,000 peak of 1954–55.

If there was any one indication that Stanley's future might necessarily have to be more modest than the pipe dreams of Bob Moore, it was the gradual decline of support through the turnstiles during the Galbraith years. From 10,000 in 1954–55, average attendances slowly eroded: 8,967 in 1956, 7,045 in 1957, and then, in Galbraith's final season in charge, down again to 6,730. There was an even steeper fall in the number of season-ticket holders, from 5,220 for the 1955–56 season to 2,338 just two years later.

It seems almost shameful that Accrington people started to withdraw their support precisely when their team were making their hardiest efforts to achieve the goal of Second Division football. But in fact, these gates did reflect Stanley's elevation in the football world. Before the arrival of Galbraith, Accrington Stanley was not a well-supported club.

In 1953, Supporters' Club veteran and unofficial club cartoonist Tom Booth published a booklet, *75 Years in the Red*, commemorating this anniversary of Accrington football. He dedicated it to the "faithful 3,000", and this was indeed an indication of Stanley's core support during the social hardship of the 1930s and the team's struggles in the early 1950s.

From this perspective, for Stanley to average 10,000 during an entire season was unprecedented, and the 1957–58 average of 6,730 was still historically good, but inevitably viewed as disappointing in the light of what had gone immediately before. But why did Accrington Stanley suffer from declining gates at this most auspicious time in their history?

It is often thought that the upturn in the fortunes of Stanley's local rivals Blackburn Rovers and Burnley was a contributing factor, but this only happened towards the end of the decade. For most of the 1950s, Burnley were a solid, mid-table First Division team, while Blackburn were a good Second Division side who, rather like Stanley, found their annual assault on promotion just short of what was required.

It was, in fact, a slow start by Stanley to the 1957–58 season that saw the first significant erosion of attendances at Peel Park, this in the face of a strong and prolonged promotion challenge by Blackburn. As things turned out, Stanley pulled their season round and ended up challenging once more for promotion, attracting healthier gates by the end of the season. But Stanley missed out again, and the success of Blackburn in winning promotion to the First Division as runners-up to West Ham dashed long-held hopes of watching Stanley lock horns with Blackburn Rovers in a genuine local 'derby'.

There was another aspect of the failure to reach the Second Division, and this was Stanley's inability as an associate member of the Football League to influence the schedule of League fixtures. Each full member of the Football League can request some consideration from fixture compilers about avoiding clashes with the home fixtures of neighbouring teams. Naturally, Burnley and Blackburn ensured that their home games did not clash, the outcome being that a League game at Peel Park was almost always in direct competition with one at either Ewood Park or Turf Moor.

With East Lancashire now boasting two First Division clubs, the Accrington board approached their neighbours and asked for some consideration of their position. The rumours among the fans at this time was that Blackburn had been sympathetic, but Burnley less so, although precisely what help Blackburn were offering remains unclear.

In the event, gates remained reasonably healthy for most of the 1958–59 season. An experiment with Friday evening fixtures was successful, and the novelty of nationwide Third Division football, with the visit of many new teams to Peel Park, helped to bring people through the turnstiles.

But predictably, Stanley found nationwide football tougher than the regional variety. From competing with the likes of Southport, Barrow, Workington and Gateshead, Stanley found themselves in the company of Norwich, Southampton, Reading and QPR. Gate receipts held up reasonably well, but the additional travel and hotel expenses ensured that Stanley once more made an operating loss, the fourth consecutive year the club had lost money.

At this point, the loss of the lottery income was felt especially acutely. Try as they might, the Stanley board failed to increase the club's income through commercial operations. Just as the board had taken on a new and large debt for the Burnley Road stand, revenues from all sources were falling drastically. Even more galling was the volte-face of the football authorities, who, after years of resistance, had finally done a deal with the football pools companies to channel some of their profits into the game. In 1957, the regulations restricting football gambling were relaxed. Small lotteries run by football clubs were now allowed, but the reforms had come too late for Stanley. The Supporters' Club lottery continued, albeit modified and on a smaller scale than the great days of Lucas, but a row in June 1957 had led chairman Moore to publicly 'disown' the Supporters' Club. It was a rancorous and ridiculous state of affairs. The supporters, furious at their treatment, accused the directors of effectively seizing the fundraising operations for themselves. Actually running them was a task at which the directors proved mere amateurs compared to the dynamism of Lucas and his team.

If maintaining Stanley's status was the priority, then this moment was, as Galbraith had maintained, the least judicious time to start cutting the running costs of the team. But given that the club's financial commitment to the Burnley Road stand came in addition to the operating losses of the previous years, there was no other option. The club was forced to sell its top performers to reduce the wage bill and meet the payments for the stand. And it was one of Galbraith's major virtues, the ability to find good players for a modest outlay, that Stanley now needed more than anything else.

However, neither of Galbraith's immediate successors, George Eastham or Harold Bodle, seemed to have his knack of finding a cheap and effective solution to a positional problem. While Galbraith could scour the semi-professional Scottish leagues with an expert eye, Eastham and Bodle focused on the reserve teams of larger clubs. They rarely found anyone who relished the prospect of playing for Accrington Stanley.

The template was set for the calamitous few years that followed. From looking every bit the Second Division club-in-waiting just a few years previously, Stanley found themselves locked in a downward double-helix of debt and selling-to-survive.

In quick succession, Stanley cashed in on their most valuable players whilst minimising the outlay on replacements. Legendary striker George Stewart, scorer of more than 150 goals in little over 200 appearances, was the first to go, sold in November 1958 for £3,500 to Fourth Division Coventry City, a team with Stanley in their sights. Stalwarts like Bob McNichol and Wattie Dick were also traded in, and any emerging talent went the same way.

Stanley survived their first season of nationwide football, but after a bright start, the asset-stripping of the squad saw the team fall away alarmingly to finish in 19th position. There was no mistaking the gloom that enveloped the club as they struggled to compete. A 9-0 defeat at Tranmere as the season drew to a close was an embarrassment from which only one lesson could be taken – that Accrington Stanley needed to seriously invest in new players if they were to remain a Third Division club. Stanley vice-president Sam Pilkington went to the local press and warned that falling support at Peel Park would have disastrous consequences:

"Unless there is considerable improvement, Stanley will be in the gravest danger of sinking into the Fourth Division. I therefore appeal in the strongest possible way to the people of Accrington to rally round."

The final standings in the new Third Division illustrated starkly what the larger and richer southern teams had long complained of: that the Football League had been a northern cartel that prevented the rise of stronger southern teams. Hull City were the sole northern team to manage a top six finish, whereas only one southern team, Notts County, were in the bottom six. The reality was clear for all to see. The meritocracy of nationwide football would not immediately be kind to the small northern clubs.

Sam Pilkington argued that northern clubs had no option but to face up to the challenge of the south to improve standards, and that the fans had a role to play. He was clearly right, but the sudden departure of manager George Eastham in July 1959 did not help, reinforcing as it did the perception that the club was somehow in a chronic decline. Chairman Bob Moore also stood down at this point due to declining health.

Moore's place in the chair was taken by local solicitor Edwin Slinger, and the board wasted no time in installing ex-Stanley left-half Harold Bodle as Eastham's replacement. As captain of the great 1954–55 side, Bodle was a warm favourite at Peel Park and his appointment was welcomed all round. But Bodle was soon to learn that things had changed from those prosperous days under Galbraith.

He had hardly settled into the manager's chair before he lost forward Jimmy Mulkerrin, sold by the board to Tranmere Rovers for £3,000, and then suffered terrible luck in losing midfield prodigy Ian Gibson, lured to Bradford Park Avenue by none other than Walter Galbraith. Gibson was only 16, and though he had already made his first team debut, he was not old enough to sign as a full-time professional and thus be subject to a transfer fee. Stanley appealed to the League Management Committee, but were shocked to be told that Galbraith's actions had been deemed legal.

Things did not improve for poor Bodle. He was allocated a wholly inadequate transfer budget, leaving him with no margin of error when signing players, and no manager, however experienced, avoids the odd miscalculated recruit. With the Accrington squad having lost the attacking prowess of players such as Stewart, Mulkerrin, Dick, Scott and Gibson in the previous nine months, Bodle spent what little he had on forwards, including Jackie Keeley, signed from Everton. Keeley looked a good bet in the Third Division, but he made little impression.

Instead, two youngsters, Harvey McCreadie and Jackie Swindells, proceeded to form a forward partnership of some potential, but Bodle quickly discovered that his attempts to build a winning team would always be sacrificed for money.

Teenager McCreadie was hastily sold to Luton Town before Christmas, only weeks after having signed his first professional contract with Stanley. Luton's £5,500 offer might have been good money, but both Bodle and the Peel Park faithful found it intensely frustrating to watch the better members of the squad picked off by clubs able to proffer just a few thousand pounds. It was – and remains – the one thing guaranteed to drive away fans, so it was no surprise that in this disastrous season, 1959–60, Stanley's support crumbled to levels not seen since the barren days of the early 1950s. Gate receipts halved to just under £11,000, resulting in a crushing £9,000 deficit on the year.

Harold Bodle resigned just before the season's end in April 1960, only ten months into the job and with Accrington Stanley emphatically relegated to the Fourth Division. A few miles either side of Stanley, Burnley were parading the League Championship trophy round the streets, and Blackburn had enjoyed the prestige of an appearance in the FA Cup Final. Success for those two teams could not have come at a worse time for Stanley, still saddled as they were with monthly payments for a stand that hardly anyone sat in, and fewer playing resources than ever.

Defender Jimmy Harrower took the reigns as player-manager for Stanley's first season in Division Four, and for once Stanley had some good fortune when a 16-year-old called Mike Ferguson turned up at pre-season training. In March 1959, Stanley had played at Home Park, Plymouth, where it was Ferguson's job as an apprentice to clean the away team's dressing room after the game. A member of the Stanley entourage heard his accent, and, curious, found out that Ferguson was from Burnley, and invited the youngster to Peel Park the next time he was in the area. Ferguson did not forget the offer and clearly made an impression on Harrower, who quickly snapped up the young inside-forward after a short trial. Also joining the Peel Park ranks was striker George Hudson, generously given a free transfer by Blackburn Rovers.

Harrower was at least able to lead by example on the pitch, but a poor run of form in December 1960 saw gates slump to around the 2,000 mark, and not for the first time the club's leaders appealed to the public through the pages of the *Accrington Observer*. Said chairman Slinger:

> "We would like very much to go ahead and get new players, but we can only do that if we get increased gates, and we appeal to the public of Accrington to rally round and give us all the support and encouragement they possibly can."

It all sounded rather familiar, and it seemed obvious to the remaining Stanley loyalists that limp appeals to the public would have no effect on gates. What was needed was pro-active leadership, people who could innovate and put forward ideas that might at least get people talking about Stanley in pubs and workplaces – anything to reawaken interest in the club. The *Accrington Observer* itself voiced its doubts that the chairman's appeal, before a home game with Hartlepools, would have the deserters returning to the fold.

Stanley could no longer rely on the support of the townspeople simply because they lived in the town. It was a time of change in the way people spent their leisure time, and fewer people in general were attending football matches. From a peak in 1949 of 41 million attendees, the turnstiles would click fewer than 30 million times in the 1960–61 season. Football clubs used to having a monopoly on Saturday afternoon began to understand that they had to compete for custom.

In other ways too, football was opening up to the vicissitudes of the market. The Professional Footballers' Association, led by Jimmy Hill, succeeded in abolishing the maximum wage. A rise in wages, coupled with falling attendances, saw many clubs surviving only through fundraising by fans. Stanley were no exception, receiving more than £300 per week from the ever-industrious Supporters' Club, but only seven out of twenty-four Fourth Division clubs posted a profit in the 1960–61 season.

Harrower's Stanley battled spiritedly to stay out of the re-election places, and succeeded with a final placing of 18th. An unexpected run in the FA Cup brought some financial reward with two Third Round ties against First Division Preston, the first a highly creditable 1-1 draw at Deepdale in which Jackie Swindells missed a glorious last-minute chance to win the tie. Stanley were never in the replay, however, and ended the season playing in front of only 2,000 loyalists and with the bare bones of a competitive team. Only three years after the departure of Walter Galbraith, it represented a terrible withering on the vine for a club suddenly deprived of its brightest playing talents and the nourishment of financial support.

But if Stanley ended the season in a fragile condition, they were not alone. The end-of-season clear-out of May 1961 saw three clubs retain just nine professionals, and only two maintained squads of 20 or more. In total, the Fourth Division released 178 professionals on free transfers that summer, and put 69 others up for sale. Only 336 full-time professionals remained in the division, an average of just 14 per club, a figure only slightly higher than the 12 retained by Harrower at Peel Park. What Stanley's rivals did not have to contend with, though, was the need to find money to pay for a stand, the purchase of which now appeared a bitterly regrettable folly.

Such was the state of so many lower League clubs at this time that Football League secretary Alan Hardaker released a proposal for the re-organisation of English football. He suggested the expansion of the League to 100 clubs in five divisions of 20, with three nationwide divisions above two regional fourth divisions. Hardaker appeared to be conceding the argument that the costs of nationwide football could not realistically be met by all 92 clubs.

The proposals were to be debated for months thereafter, with most clubs unwilling to countenance a drop in the number of fixtures they were to play, but one proposal did meet with widespread approval – the institution of three up/three down for the higher divisions, and four up/four down between the two lowest divisions – reforms that in time were implemented, and would, of course, have seen Stanley reach the Second Division had they been in place earlier.

In the close season of 1961–62, manager Jimmy Harrower, now retired from playing, worked ceaselessly to add to his skeletal squad. There had been some disquiet at the release on free transfers of established performers such as goalkeeper Bill McInnes and centre-half Gordon Stones, and Harrower was further hampered by the sale of striker Jackie Swindells to Barnsley for a mere £750.

Working with hardly any resources, Harrower did a sterling job in constructing a first team squad of 17 players. If he could have kept this full group together, avoiding major injuries, he would have had a fighting chance of keeping Stanley out of the re-election places. Early season form indicated that Harrower's team was good enough to maintain Stanley's League status. Eight points after eight games, including victories over Darlington, Carlisle and Bradford City, saw Stanley in the comfort of mid-table, and in central defender Garbutt Richardson and goalkeeper Alex Smith, Harrower had discovered a couple of quality performers who made Stanley's defence one of the tougher propositions in the division.

What worried the fans more was the lack of firepower up front, George Hudson notwithstanding. Harrower agreed, and just five games into the season bought Jim Milner from Darlington to strengthen the forward line.

Events from this point on, however, were to cruelly expose the lack of depth at Harrower's disposal.

A bad knee injury in the game at Barrow on September 18th ended defender Garbutt Richardson's season, but far worse was the sale of striker George Hudson to Peterborough United just two weeks later. The decision to sell Hudson encapsulated the desperate position of Stanley's finances by this time, for his sale, although realising around £4,000, was absolutely the last resort for the team.

Stanley relied heavily on Hudson to score goals, which he did with remarkable proficiency. The previous year, in a struggling team, Hudson had equalled George Stewart's record of 35 League goals in a season. It was a dreadful decision to sell him, for though Stanley had some good, young forward players, none had Hudson's physical presence or striker's instinct. Youngsters like Mike Ferguson and Paddy Mulvey could do a decent job supporting Hudson, but they could not replace him. Harrower was given little of the Hudson money, and those he did bring in, such as Wrexham's Barry Smith, made little impression.

Without George Hudson, Stanley would score only eight more League goals in the remaining six months of the season. They were fortunate that two of the goals, both from Jim Milner, were enough to secure narrow victories at home to Oldham and Crewe. The Oldham game, played on October 2nd 1961, attracted 4,396 to Peel Park, an indication that the town had not completely abandoned its club, but attendances generally reflected results. The defeat of Crewe on October 14th, in front of 2,713, turned out to be Stanley's last League victory.

By the end of the year, regular attendees at Peel Park had shrunk to a core of around 1,500. For these loyal supporters, it was heartbreaking to see their club in such a sorry state. Most blamed the board for mismanaging the club's finances, and events in November served to further inflame a tense situation between boardroom and terrace.

In the face of widespread disillusionment in the town over the decline of Stanley, the diehards in the Supporters'

Club found fundraising increasingly difficult, but still generated around £200 per week for the club through various fundraising schemes. They had put to the board the proposition that they use £100 of this weekly income to service a loan of £5,000, which they would give to the manager to recruit a couple of much-needed players.

A meeting was scheduled for a Thursday night, November 16th 1961, to discuss this. Even club president Sir William Cocker, in Accrington and witness to a 4-0 humiliation at the hands of Workington the previous Saturday, said he would stay in the town to attend. It was supposed to be a constructive event ending with a convivial potato pie supper, but the evening turned nasty. The fans rounded on the board, accusing them of not taking the Supporters' Club seriously or treating them with any consideration. It descended at times into a slanging match.

An exasperated Jimmy Harrower looked on. "If this is your idea of a social evening," declared the manager, "I have another name for it." Both the board and Harrower were sceptical of the loan idea, arguing that they needed more than one player to solve the team's problems. The board wanted to continue receiving the full £200 each week. They pointed out that with two League fixtures and a cup tie to follow away from home, Stanley faced virtually a whole month without the income of a home gate, and needed to find £1,250 to cover costs.

The fans, far more sensitive to the mood of the town, urged the board to make a statement of intent with a couple of imaginative signings – anything to spark some interest in the club. One letter in the *Accrington Observer* demanded that the board "give us action or resign." Another argued with absolute prescience that the sale of three forwards, Swindells, Jimmy Anders and George Hudson, had brought in just £5,000, a paltry amount that would cost Accrington Stanley their Football League place.

The division between the boardroom and the fans, played out as it was in the pages of the local paper, undermined terribly the efforts of the club to tempt back to Peel Park the many thousands who had stopped attending. But, incredibly, it was about to get perceptibly worse.

Stanley had battled to an unlikely 1-0 win at Stockport in the first round of the FA Cup, their last victory in any competition. But in the aftermath of the second round tie on November 25th, a 2-1 defeat at Hartlepools, it emerged that the players and 200 Stanley supporters had journeyed to the north-east alone, with not one board member accompanying the team or even sending the traditional "good luck" telegram. Chairman Edwin Slinger told the *Accrington Observer* that the board members had all had other club commitments, but this did not placate the supporters or even the loyal town paper itself, which commented: "The club is now fighting for its very existence, and a strong lead is needed from the top down." One of the fans who had gone to Hartlepool offered a more emphatic analysis:

"Now that Stanley are out of the Cup, who is going to give a lead to lift the club from the canvas before the count is taken? The weeks and months have passed by while paralysis has crept on and, as far as the public know, nothing but a disastrous inertia in the boardroom at Peel Park."

This correspondent finished by asking whether Accrington's Mayor could not organise something, a knowing request, since the Mayor, Wilf Wallwork, was a long-standing Stanley fan.

On the evening of Wednesday December 6th, Wallwork chaired an emergency meeting at the Town Hall, called by the Supporters' Club. The aim was to find new fundraising initiatives to generate money towards the purchase of new players.

In his opening address, Wallwork made the obvious point that past mistakes could not be unmade, and begged those present that they focus on what was important – and everyone present agreed what this was – that the very survival of Accrington Stanley was at stake. Despite this common understanding, there was once again an incendiary atmosphere, with the supporters unable to contain their anger at the board.

In spite of the flying accusations, Wallwork successfully launched the 'Mayor's Appeal Fund' as part of a 'Save Stanley' campaign. Thanks to various suggestions from Supporters' Club mainstays, people like Dick Briggs, Bert Gresham and Tom Langton, a number of other initiatives were also agreed, but some of them – such as whist drives and dances – had the whiff of the shillings-and-pence mentality: well-meaning, but hardly appropriate given the gravity of the situation.

Another Supporters' Club member, Cliff Birch, courageously defended the directors, arguing that they generally co-operated with the Supporters' Club, and were putting their own money into Stanley to keep the club going. One board member would later recall that eight directors each put in £40 a week, but with a weekly wage bill of £650 and gate receipts of £250 a game, it was not enough to stop the debts mounting. Birch's interjection was a rare gesture of conciliation, and one can in hindsight see his point, but the evening ended with yet another disagreement about taking a collection on the door. The alienation of director from supporter could hardly have seemed greater.

Another misfortune quickly followed with the resignation of manager Jimmy Harrower the following Thursday, December 14th. Any sense of renewed purpose in the aftermath of the meeting was extinguished by the manner of Harrower's departure, which brought yet more accusations of boardroom incompetence. Harrower had retired from playing at the end of the previous season despite taking the job on a player-manager basis.

The board had not been happy to lose Harrower's defensive services, and, four months into the season, gave Harrower an ultimatum that he regain match fitness and play as soon as possible. Harrower reluctantly agreed, but was dismayed when the board went to the press and announced his imminent return. Harrower, adamant that he needed more time to train, found the board equally determined that he should play. There was little option for Harrower but to resign.

It was a shabby way to treat a man who had managed the club conscientiously in the harshest of climates. He departed with a cutting comment that "anyone who knows anything at all about football" would have appreciated the impossibility of reaching match fitness in a week, and pointed out, quite fairly, that it was not the defence but the attack that needed reinforcements.

The club never appointed a replacement for Harrower, although ex-England international Frank Soo applied, as did ex-Blackburn player Tommy Briggs, who as both a striker and player-manager seemed to fit the bill. The board maintained that no suitable candidates had come forward. Harry Hubbick and player-coach Bill Smith took over the position on a caretaker basis, but there was little that the respected trainer Hubbick could do. By this time, Stanley had become, effectively, a part-time team, with the best of the young, local amateurs drafted in from the reserves in the hope that they might make an impression.

A 4-0 home defeat at the hands of Colchester on January 13th 1962 was an especially grim way to welcome in the New Year. Only 1,430 were there to witness it, one of the lowest recorded post-war gates at Peel Park, and the result sent Stanley to the bottom of the Fourth Division. The amateurs drafted into the team battled mightily to help their club, and, to be fair to these lads and to the pros that remained, Stanley were never thumped during this time. But they struggled terribly to finish the chances they created. When someone did find their range, the rest of the team competed well.

On February 9th, for instance, Stanley travelled to promotion-chasing Aldershot and came away with a 2-2 draw. This kind of result suggested how likely it was that Harrower's team would have survived had the board not been forced to sell Hudson. But without the big striker, goals were all too rare an occurrence; indeed, Jim Milner's brace at Aldershot that Friday evening ended a run of five matches without a goal and, finally, Hudson's reign as leading goalscorer, four months after his departure. The following Friday night, February 16th, just 1,760 turned up at Peel Park to see Stanley lose 2-1 at home to Stockport, but from this point on, the football was to take a supporting role to a bigger drama.

The resignation of chairman Slinger on February 12th was the precursor to the crisis that was about to engulf the club. That week, Stanley were reported to the Football League for the non-payment of transfer fees, and the League placed an immediate embargo on the club, refusing to accept any more player registrations from Peel Park. The board, now reduced to just six, called in the most experienced and influential hands they could think of, club president Sir William Cocker and vice-president Sam Pilkington.

Cocker, Pilkington and Mayor Wallwork went to the *Accrington Observer*, which splashed an appeal across its pages. The Saturday edition of February 17th could not have been clearer: the very existence of Accrington Stanley as a League club was in the gravest peril, and the town needed to rally round as a matter of urgency.

Pilkington said: "It's gone beyond anything the directors can do. Only the public can now save this old and famous club." Director George Clarkson, asked whether the board was scraping the barrel, replied: "I think we have nearly scraped the bottom out of it. We are determined to do our best to keep the club alive as long as we possibly can – but, of course, there's a limit to everything." Wallwork called Stanley's levels of support deplorable, and revealed that only £100 of the £450 in his appeal fund was derived from public donations. "I have never known a time in Stanley's long history," he lamented, "when there has been so little interest in the club."

The *Accrington Observer* urged its readers to respond, but also noted that: "...a full and frank admission of the situation at least six months ago might have brought the matter to the public's attention before it was too late."

On the following Monday, February 19th, a letter arrived,

dated February 18th, from the Football League, asking for a detailed report on Stanley's financial position and future prospects. The club had failed to produce accounts for the 1960–61 season, and now, in an embarrassing indictment of the club's leadership, they were being forced to open their books to the authorities.

Suspicions about the motivation and timing of the letter were fuelled when Sam Pilkington revealed he had been sounding out an old football friend over the weekend who had agreed to help Stanley out. It turned out to be none other than Burnley chairman Bob Lord, who also happened to be a big cheese on the management committee of the Football League.

Lord's involvement in the final days of Accrington Stanley remains, to this day, a matter of bitterness and regret among the Peel Park faithful. The precise role that the Burnley chairman envisioned for himself was unclear. He kept his options open, telling the press that he was helping Sam Pilkington merely as a personal friend and that he would do what he could to help. He also mused on the possibility of buying shares and joining the board.

Lord made his move two days later, on Wednesday February 21st, when he announced that the price of his involvement would be the resignation of the six remaining Stanley directors, who, he declared, were "not capable of running a football club". If he was to become involved at Peel Park, he would buy enough shares for a place on the board, and would run the club in conjunction with Sam Pilkington. Lord envisaged Pilkington reprising his role as chairman.

The six directors named by Lord – Slinger, Clarkson, Walton, Armitage, Eddleston and Daniels – were hardly in a position to argue. Slinger and Walton resigned with immediate effect, and the other four agreed to resign if Lord made his proposed investment. But for Stanley fans well aware of his unstinting and often-stated devotion to do what was best at all times for Burnley Football Club, the sight and sound of Bob Lord playing the potential saviour of Accrington Stanley was deeply unsettling. "I shall try to keep them in the League, of course," said Lord, before adding, "But I cannot guarantee that that will be done."

Pilkington, who was reluctant to return to the chair, spent the Friday of that week in Lytham with Football League secretary Alan Hardaker, assuring him that Stanley would be able to continue. He returned to Peel Park that evening for a board meeting, the outcome of which was the announcement of a creditors' meeting at Accrington Library on the evening of March 6th.

It was just Stanley's luck that all this publicity preceded a home game that clashed with a Blackburn v. Burnley 'derby'. An only marginally improved gate of 2,650 turned up at Peel Park for the game with Rochdale, and they witnessed a familiar plot unfold, with Stanley falling behind to an early goal and struggling to make headway before conceding a late second. Three days later, Stanley had better luck at Doncaster, where inside-forward Mike Ferguson scored his first Stanley goal to earn a point. The gate at Doncaster of just 1,981 was proof that Stanley were not the only ones struggling to survive on insufficient support.

As for Ferguson, any pleasure derived from his first Football League goal was tempered by a row behind the scenes, of which he was the focal point. Stanley had received a bid of £3,000 for Ferguson from Workington Town, then also a Fourth Division club.

Stanley gratefully accepted the offer, but Ferguson was far less impressed with the prospect. He refused to move, denying Stanley cash for which they could hardly have been more desperate. It was a tough situation for a teenager to handle, but Ferguson, a confident young man who had been transfer-listed at his own request, was convinced that he was destined for far better things than Workington. He resisted all attempts at persuasion.

With the club's accounts almost ready, the creditors' meeting loomed, but before this there was an away fixture at Crewe on Friday evening, March 2nd. In wintry conditions, Stanley turned in one of their poorest performances of the season and were soundly beaten 4-0. It was the prelude to a devastating Monday night in the library.

At the creditors' meeting, the club's accountants revealed the extent of Stanley's debt, which, all things considered, totalled £62,000. Some sources of the debt were commonplace in football, such as the bank overdraft of £9,000 and the £3,000 owing in transfer fees, and only around £4,000 was required in the short term. Required immediately was £400 to meet final demands from the public utilities.

However, other elements of the debt were intolerable. In front of Norman Thomas, a Football League accountant who was there as an observer, it was revealed that Stanley had neglected to pay National Insurance contributions for its players all season. This was an illegal practice usually associated with disreputable employers. Club solicitor Harry Disley concluded that the club was bust and would have to go into liquidation.

As the administrators finished their grim analysis, the meeting turned to the question of what happened next. It was at this moment that Bob Lord made his intervention. He stood up, and declared: "Well, you won't be the last ones to go under. That comic in London's doing it."

Lord's diagnosis was clear. In a game where players could now demand £100 per week (first granted to Johnny Haynes by Fulham chairman – and comedian – Tommy Trinder), small clubs like Accrington Stanley could no longer survive. As far as Lord was concerned, the financial pressures of post-maximum wage football had claimed its first victim.

Lord's intervention was important, for he was by far the most prestigious and famous face at the meeting, and as such his opinions carried the most weight. His statement was bound to affect the direction of the meeting, and before there had been any chance of a discussion getting underway, Lord had put his oar in and advised the directors that resignation from the Football League was the only option. Crucially, Sam Pilkington took Lord's lead, agreeing that the scale of the club's debts made Stanley a hopeless case. Pilkington, along with Lord, withdrew his offer of help.

The manner in which Bob Lord imposed his opinion on the meeting that night is the most compelling evidence for those who remain convinced to this day that his intention was to see Stanley go under. But just as damaging was the reaction of Sam Pilkington. No one could accuse Sam of not having the best interests of the club at heart.

In the face of this collective opinion, the remaining four directors, George Clarkson, Stan Armitage, Lawrence Eddleston and Jack Daniels, decided that there was nothing for it but to resign. The news was released to the waiting press, and the letter – a few short, terminal sentences – was drafted that night and sent to the Football League the following morning.

Any other decision would have gone against the grain of all the advice the four directors had received, but questions remained. Why the haste to resign? Few creditors were pressing for immediate payment. So many clubs before Stanley had been in this hopeless position that the survival strategy was well-established. Clubs in this position made noise, appealed for the town to rally round, approached local government for help, refinanced debts, accepted any shilling on offer – but the one thing they did not do was resign their precious membership of the closed and elite society that was the Football League.

Then again, had Accrington Stanley not tried to rally its people before? The headlines in the most recent editions of the *Accrington Observer* had made it quite clear that the club was on the point of receiving the last rites, but still the crowds had not returned to lend support. Less than 3,000 at Peel Park and over 33,000 at Ewood Park for the local 'derby' summed it up neatly. What, therefore, would be the point of yet another appeal?

Given the statements of Pilkington, Lord and the opinion of the club's solicitors, the morning press announced the passing of Accrington Stanley. The midweek edition of the *Accrington Observer* mourned, "STANLEY – THE END".

There was a terrible irony in the reaction to the news. The town exploded with indignation, and offers of financial help started to pour in. Within a few hours of the news breaking, the club had the money to pay the public utilities. This was critical, since two home games loomed, one an attractive Lancashire Senior Cup tie against Burnley which had the potential to generate a decent crowd. But the gas company had already sent someone to turn off the club's supplies. An exasperated board could have been forgiven for wondering where this heartfelt support had been all those months when they had been scratching around for every penny. There was nothing for it but to postpone the tie with Burnley.

As the players turned up for training on Tuesday morning, club secretary Jack Wigglesworth informed them that the club had resigned from the Football League. As they milled around, coming to terms with the news, a photo opportunity of rare poignancy was captured and relayed around the world. But some of the players expressed relief that the struggle was over, as well as surprise that no directors had turned up at the ground to let the players know officially that it was all over. Trainer Harry Hubbick was left to muse on what might have been:

"Something could have been done with this side if only a little money had been spent on forwards. Instead, it's been all selling and no buying. You work your heart out night and day for a club, then this happens, and no one bothers to come to the ground and tell you about it."

Reactions to Stanley's demise in the national press ranged from unsympathetic to patronising. Most were of the opinion that Stanley were only the first of many smaller clubs that would find it impossible to continue in an environment of declining gates and higher wages. It was a familiar sentiment that illustrated the social mood of the time. The early 1960s was a period of 'brave new world' thinking. The emergence of global air travel, coupled with advances in fields such as satellite technology and medicine, transformed the notion of 'global football' from a fanciful concept to a real possibility.

Many commentators on the game reasoned that market forces would inexorably lead football in this direction, with the inevitable victim being the small, community club. A club, in fact, just like Accrington Stanley. This way of thinking led even thoughtful and respected football journalists to make some observations that, in hindsight, sound horrendously callous.

David Miller, of *The Daily Telegraph*, spoke for many when he argued that the bigger clubs were unable to fulfil their potential because they had to subsidise the likes of Accrington Stanley:

> "It is ridiculous that our international club and national fortunes should be jeopardised by the deadweight of a domestic league loaded with near bankrupts."

The tabloids were just as unforgiving. In *The Daily Herald*, under the headline "Don't Weep for Accrington", Steve Richards wrote:

> "Accrington failed to escape the fallout of football's Atomic Age. I interpret this as an indication that the Football League is about to acquire a healthier look. Accrington's sad ending should be the start of a new era, the era of reassessment. The bottom-of-the-form boys should ask themselves: Is it worth the financial struggle? Are we helping football or hindering it?"

Desmond Hackett, of the *Daily Express*, tried to sound a more sympathetic note, but his arrival at the same conclusion made for an unbearably condescending tone:

> "For too many seasons, League football has been geared to the Accrington Stanleys and, bless their honest Lancashire hearts, Accrington did their best. But they were the brake on any surging forward to a plan of super leagues, European leagues and, in this pet age, even a world league."

Almost exactly the same line was peddled by John Macadam, writing in *Charles Buchan's Football Monthly*.

> "Worldwide soccer has left far behind the tram tracks of Accrington to move off to the jet age in which a World Football League is not so far away. So, with the deepest regret, Accrington Stanley must go and must be followed by all the other lagging clubs."

All of these words illustrate just how pervasive was the sense that football, and wider society, was moving into a sleek, modern age in which the likes of Stanley had no place. But they betray the haste with which they were written. Even if football was some kind of Darwinist struggle, as they implied, it did not follow that the demise of one club would precipitate a wave of lemming-like resignations from others. Neither did the First Division consist solely of big city clubs, all geared up for a global future. On the contrary, it was the innovative smaller clubs who often led the way, such as Burnley with their unrivalled youth system, or the pioneering 4-4-2 formation introduced by Ipswich Town which brought them the League Championship in 1962, just weeks after Stanley's resignation had supposedly heralded the end of such possibilities.

A handful of journalists, at least, resisted the half-baked commercial logic of their colleagues. Esther Rose, writing in the *Daily Express*, had a greater sensibility to what had happened:

> "Accrington lost more than a football team. It lost its identity. Everyone knew Stanley. It sounded human and quite unlike all the other 91 teams in the League. It wasn't fierce like Hotspur, or flip like Chelsea. He sounded dependable, Stanley did. Now Accrington is on its own, and it faces a kind of odd oblivion. What has Accrington got, now that Stanley's gone? A disturbing sense of shame, too late, and of regret. Accrington, they sense, feels gritty on the tongue without Stanley."

But even as these words passed through the hot metal of the presses, Accrington itself started to find its voice.

Given what had gone before in the pages of the local press, it hardly seems credible to suppose that the public were in the dark about the club's plight. The warning signs had been there for months and numerous appeals for more support had failed.

Nonetheless, the uproar with which the news was greeted was significant, even if long overdue, indicating perhaps that people had assumed that the latest crisis at the club would somehow be negotiated just as all the others had been previously. But with Stanley's letter of resignation now on the desk of the Football League secretary, Alan Hardaker, those who wanted the club to survive had no option but to get involved and do what they could.

Club president Sir William Cocker led the campaign to withdraw Stanley's resignation. To questions about his apparent inactivity before the resignation, Cocker insisted that he would have called a creditors' meeting and thrashed out a deal much earlier if he had known the true extent of the club's problems. This sounded disingenuous to those who had been there that November night when Cocker had witnessed for himself the bitter hostilities between the board and the fans. Even so, Cocker was a knight of the realm, something that still carried a little weight, and there's no doubt that he succeeded in quickly raising enough cash to see the club through to the end of the month.

The most astonishing story of this frenetic period is that on the Thursday, March 9th, a man walked into Peel Park with £10,000 in cash and offered it to the club as an interest-free loan. If this remarkable act of generosity did actually happen, the club itself did not let on, though an ebullient Cocker certainly told the press of "fantastic" pledges of money.

On the same day at the Football League, Alan Hardaker indicated that he had received Accrington Stanley's resignation and that the League Management Committee would meet on the Sunday to discuss it. This in effect put Stanley's resignation on the back burner until the weekend, but Hardaker crucially ruled that Stanley's scheduled home game against Exeter at Peel Park on the Saturday could not go ahead.

William Cocker desperately tried to convince Hardaker to let Stanley host the Exeter game. Both Burnley and Blackburn faced away ties in the FA Cup, and the publicity generated by the week's events would have ensured a bumper crowd at Peel Park. Cocker pointed out that the League had not yet accepted the club's resignation, and as both Stanley and Exeter were willing to play, there was no reason why the game could not go ahead. Hardaker refused, and an incensed Cocker went to the press and declared that Stanley would fight for its Football League life, slamming Hardaker's "dictatorial" attitude in the process.

A meeting of directors and legal advisors, chaired by Cocker, met on the Thursday evening. Stanley sent a second letter to the Football League, asking that the original letter of resignation be withdrawn and that the club be given three weeks to finalise a rescue plan. The Football League issued a statement merely confirming that they would meet on Sunday to consider the facts.

On Friday, George Clarkson, assuming the role of club chairman, admitted to the *Lancashire Evening Telegraph* that events had moved too quickly after the creditors' meeting four days earlier:

"Why should Stanley die when there are a lot of clubs so badly off? We obviously have the sympathy of our creditors since none has made the necessary move to put us into bankruptcy. We have the wages for this week and the next. We think we can increase very substantially the money from the pools. We honestly think we have a chance of making a go of it provided we get the opportunity from the Football League."

Stanley remained in the press spotlight through the weekend. William Cocker used the opportunity to emphasise that Stanley were now in a position to continue at least until the end of the season. The club president had, at least, secured a promise from the League that Stanley would be allowed to argue their corner in front of the League Management Committee on the Sunday.

Chairman George Clarkson and club solicitor Harry Disley presented Stanley's case. It did not help matters that Disley had been the official who, in front of Bob Lord, had declared Stanley bankrupt at the meeting of creditors. The Burnley chairman, as a member of the League Management Committee, now had to be convinced by Disley that Stanley were solvent.

Clarkson and Disley said their piece, and the whole of Accrington held its breath. As secretary of the Football League, it was in Alan Hardaker's remit to call an Emergency General Meeting of the 92 League clubs and put to them whether Stanley should be allowed to continue. Instead, Hardaker and the League Management Committee decided to accept Stanley's resignation, and on Monday afternoon, March 12th, the decision was relayed to the club. Hardaker argued that the resignation had come into operation as soon as the League had received the letter, leaving them with little choice in the matter.

According to the strict letter of the law, Hardaker was right, but there was leeway there for him to put the judgment into the hands of the League clubs. And what about Bob Lord? In the light of the new money at the club, could he not have used his influence to exercise this option for Stanley, the club he had been offering to help out just the previous week?

Hardaker had little sympathy. Stanley's plight had left his blueprint for a 100-strong Football League dead in the water. In spite of Hardaker's wish to actually expand the League, he saw no conflict in declaring to the press that, "Once a club can no longer pay its way, it clearly cannot expect to remain a member."

This conveniently ignored a fact that Hardaker knew all too well: that most clubs for most of their existence had not been paying their way. The vast majority of Stanley's Fourth Division contemporaries were in debt, as were other much bigger clubs. That most of them survived was testament to the understanding that a town's football club is not just any old business but a living thing that embodies the identity of the community, a sentiment that Hardaker was willing to employ only when it suited his purposes.

There was little that Stanley could do; they had tendered their resignation, after all. The reaction of William Cocker highlighted the club's weak position. He thought that Stanley should get another chance because of their role in pioneering the game. The board met the day after the decision, Tuesday 13th, and decided to pursue legal action against the League.

When, on the following day, the League's Norman Thomas showed up at Peel Park with money to pay the players, he was turned away, with Stanley insisting that since the issue of their League membership was still ongoing, they would continue to pay their players. But Hardaker had already circulated a memorandum around the clubs inviting offers for Stanley's players. As far as he was concerned, the Football League now held their registrations, not Accrington Stanley.

And what of the players? They all continued to train, and some, like captain Bob Wilson, declared spirits to be good. But others were not prepared to hang around to see what transpired. Mike Ferguson had started training with Burnley reserves, and, on the day of Hardaker's memo, was tracked down by Blackburn Rovers' manager Jack Marshall, and a deal was quickly concluded.

Harry Disley was not impressed with Hardaker's hard line. On passing Ferguson's FA transfer papers to Ewood Park, he said: "We are only doing it because Mr Marshall has been extremely frank and kind, and because we did not wish to do anything to the detriment of Ferguson, or stand in his way of fixing up with another club."

Others around Peel Park for longer than Disley were more sceptical of Rovers' intentions, with many suspecting that the First Division club had refrained from making an offer for Ferguson on the presumption that Stanley would soon go bust. Director Stan Armitage hinted as much when he told the *Accrington Observer*: "If the clubs who are so interested in the players had been as interested a month or two ago, the club would not be where it is today."

This sense of injustice was further heightened when Stanley's most prized asset, goalkeeper Alex Smith, was sold for the pitiably low fee of £750 to Bolton, another First Division club well capable of paying the market value for the player.

Also showing a distinct lack of charity were the non-League clubs who jostled to take Stanley's place. Morecambe, Chelmsford, Nelson, Cambridge City and North Shields all contacted the League about taking over Stanley's place immediately, fulfilling the remaining fixtures. Stanley received more consideration from some of their fellow League clubs. Wrexham offered to play a fundraising friendly, and both Stockport and Rochdale donated £100 to Stanley's funds.

By the end of the week, it was difficult to see how Stanley could force the issue further. On Friday 16th, Cocker told the press that he felt personally affronted at the lack of consideration shown to his club, and defiantly signalled the board's intention to go ahead with legal action, declaring with inappropriate boldness that "the gloves were off".

Hardaker responded by placing all remaining Accrington Stanley players on free transfers, and this quickly led to the departure of Alex Hamilton, signed by York City, and Willie Devine. A shareholders' meeting on Monday 19th backed the board in its intention to launch legal action, but Stanley had by now missed two League fixtures and had no registered players. The game was clearly up, and some prominent figures in the town urged the board to accept the inevitable. One such voice was ex-chairman George Pratt, who argued that any remaining money be put towards a Lancashire Combination side in the hope that something better might result in the years to come.

It was a suggestion that came to be adopted as the most sensible course of action. Thus it was that Accrington

Stanley (1921), a founder member of the Football League Third Division, both regional and national, lost its Football League status.

Stanley's experience was an unfortunate consequence of changing social attitudes, lack of leadership and too many strategic mistakes. As much as one can point to individual events, such as the unfortunate termination of the lottery money or the disastrous resolve of the board to bring the Aldershot stand to Peel Park, the full picture of Stanley's demise needs to be viewed against a wider backdrop of social change. For Britain in the early 1960s was a rapidly changing place.

Though Harold Macmillan was still Prime Minister, his Eton tones had started to grate with a society losing its appetite for deference and learning instead to question authority. As Stanley struggled for survival at the foot of the Fourth Division, the AEU union brought out on strike all 8,000 workers in the engineering factories of the district, demanding equal pay for the female workers and better pay for everyone. It was an impressive display of solidarity.

Bubbling under a tranquil social surface was an irresistible urge to throw off the austerity of the 1950s. Television, identified by many as the scourge behind falling attendances and all other manner of social ills, began to take its cue from British 'new wave' cinema, producing plays that highlighted the realities of working class life. This echoed with a nation more mindful than ever of the North–South divide, particularly in terms of economic opportunity.

The most ambitious youngsters in Accrington took advantage of the grammar school system and advanced to university, but even they were learning to question the conventional wisdom of those around them. This was witnessed in 1962, the year of the Cuban Missile Crisis, when a group of Accrington Grammar School boys were disciplined for demonstrating against the US embargo on Cuba, with the headmaster charging that their actions were bringing the good name of the school into disrepute.

Even the youngsters who stayed at home found their horizons broadening. Improved public transport systems and wider car ownership brought the bright lights and the cosmopolitan social life of the city within easy reach. When Harry Hynd, Accrington's veteran Labour MP, enthused about a Boys' Brigade march in the town because it had contained no "long-haired freaks", he also unwittingly mirrored the widening gap between the generations.

In the midst of these changes, austerity gradually lifted. The disposable income of young working people rose just as their leisure options expanded. No longer was Saturday afternoon football the only show in town.

It was in this context, of a society breaking free of the stifling cocoon of scarcity and asceticism, that football clubs found life increasingly difficult. Even Blackburn Rovers and Burnley, though they could offer First Division football, found their gates declining throughout the 1960s. Quite simply, people found other things to do with their time. The sudden broadening of horizons had snapped like a sun-dried elastic band the attachments to community upon which the smaller clubs like Accrington Stanley relied.

This did not make their demise inevitable. Those suffering alongside Stanley in 1962, clubs like Hartlepools, Stockport, Darlington and Rochdale, remain to this day perennial strugglers. But they have survived, proving wrong those false prophets of global football who shrugged indifferently when Stanley succumbed. What has survived with them is a lesson in civic pride and responsibility.

Although individuals can 'own' football clubs in the sense of possessing a majority shareholding, the moral ownership of a club always rests with the supporters, for without them there is no football club. But with this moral ownership also comes a heavy responsibility – that the well-being of your club lies in your collective hands, regardless of what's going on in the boardroom.

In these liberal times, it is not always easy to see things in collective ways, but events at Peel Park showed that even in the 1960s, communal bonds could simply wither and break if ignored for too long. For all the abject mistakes and incompetence of those in 'legal' charge of Accrington Stanley in 1962, we cannot ignore the uncomfortable truth that the moral owners of the club, the people of Accrington, did not take that very real responsibility seriously enough, and that something cherished was lost forever as a result.

A few years after Stanley's resignation, Alan Benson, then the mayor of Accrington, was interviewed in the *Football League Review*, and his comments are tinged with a bitter regret:

"People do not realise just how important a League club is to a town's status and prestige until it is too late. Accrington was known nationally by reason of its soccer team. When you travelled to another part of the country and mentioned where you were from, people immediately linked Accrington to its football club. Now they say, 'Ah, the town which couldn't keep its football team'. Accrington Stanley could have survived with the proper backing."

Proper backing is, of course, the prerequisite for the survival of any football club. In Accrington Stanley's case, it came too late. As the club scrambled to withdraw its resignation in the light of numerous offers of financial support, a writer in *The Guardian* of March 8th 1962 observed with agonising accuracy:

"So many people loved Accrington Stanley in life too little; it appears they love them in death too well."

A few people in the town wanted to right that wrong. Only due to their actions has Accrington, forty-four years later, been handed an unexpected opportunity to make amends. This is the story of those people and how their club, Accrington Stanley 1968, created from memory and born of hope, fought its way back to the Football League, to the place that history and instinct told them was home.

Chapter Two

1962–70
Hope's Harvest

THOUGH ACCRINGTON STANLEY had resigned from the Football League, none of the creditors had yet taken the steps to put the club into liquidation. Most of the people to whom Stanley owed money were supporters, ex-directors and local businessmen, groups understandably reticent about demanding money that everyone knew the club did not have. The sale of Mike Ferguson and Alex Smith had realised the scandalously low sum of £2,750, and though the Football League had the right to keep the transfer money, it was used instead to pay the wages owed to the two players and overdue transfer payments to Darlington, Preston and Burnley.

With no creditors yet pressing the club for payment, chairman George Clarkson received permission from the receivers to continue using Peel Park, and Stanley successfully applied to the Lancashire Combination for the first team and the West Lancashire League for the reserves. Stanley offered the manager's position to Bill Eckersley, formerly of Blackburn Rovers and England. Eckersley's initial reaction was promising, but he eventually turned down the opportunity; instead, it was announced at the end of July that Harold Mather, the ex-Burnley full-back, had got the job.

Stanley appealed in the local media for players, and more than seventy wrote to the club asking for a trial. A series of practice games commenced. Of the early signings, the best known was Jackie Boyes, a full-back who had played with Blackburn Rovers, though the club quickly signed a number of local youngsters on amateur forms, who were able to compete in the FA Youth Cup as well as play in the reserve side.

By mid-August, Mather had most of his first team squad in place, though he continued to make additions through September. To add to the players with Football League experience, Mather signed right-winger Tommy Henderson from Burnley and inside-left Des Lancaster, who had League experience at Darlington and Tranmere Rovers. Striker Bill Dodd had also been on Burnley's books; full-back Jack Leaver likewise at Watford. Most players, though, came in from nearby amateur clubs like Haslingden, Great Harwood, Padiham and Bacup Borough, the latter being where Jimmy Hinksman, Ronnie Kershaw and goalkeeper Harold Greenwood had been playing. Alan Leighton was signed from Chorley.

The wage bill must have been quite considerable, around £75 per week, a lot for the second tier of the Lancashire Combination, but crowds were initially encouraging, with around 1,000 turning up for Stanley's opening fixture at home to Rolls-Royce. With admission costing 1s 6d, such a gate brought in around £75, and if maintained might have provided a base sufficient for Stanley to make a future bid for the Northern Premier League.

As it was, crowds started to dwindle as the winter months progressed, even though Mather's team was playing well and challenging for promotion. At the beginning of October, 'Old Red' wrote in the *Accrington Observer*:

> "The quality of play so far has surprised those supporters whose hearts have not been broken by the League exit disaster and can still find pleasure in watching their own lads, however modest the competition."

Indeed, the interest shown by League clubs in some of Stanley's players – such as David Shuttleworth, Russell Cuddihey, Don Bramley, Harold Greenwood and Dave Baron, all of whom were being checked out by League scouts, illustrates that just the name of Accrington Stanley had been sufficient to attract some real talent to the club. In November, Dave Baron was signed as a full-time professional by Blackburn Rovers, and David Shuttleworth, an ex-Accrington Schoolboys player, went to Hibernian and Liverpool for trials.

Stanley entered the Christmas period in fourth place and looked well set to push on for one of the two promotion positions, but the winter was particularly severe and the club were out of action for some eight weeks between Boxing Day and mid-February. Whether the team was playing or not, running costs of £60 per week were inevitable, and this caused the directors some real problems given that the club's fundraising pools scheme did not cover these costs. Average gates, too, through the autumn and early winter months had disappointingly slipped to below 500.

The lay-off did not seem to immediately affect the players. On the resumption, Stanley embarked on an unbeaten run through to April, and looked as if they had as much chance of promotion as any of the other challenging teams. However, the winter freeze left the team with chronic fixture congestion through April and May, which meant they had to play their final seven matches in fourteen days. Injuries and fatigue saw Stanley run out of steam, and after occupying a top-four position all season, they eventually finished in eighth.

It had been a season of contrasts, with the encouraging emergence of a number of good local players being offset by the disappointing fall in support on the terraces. The long-term viability of the debt-laden club remained questionable. In June 1963, the Inland Revenue once more began making noises about winding up the club, and Clarkson had no option other than to release all 40 players on the books, including eight on semi-pro contracts and manager Mather, so as to avoid paying summer wages.

Events elsewhere served to reinforce the sense of outrage and injustice over the fate of the club. In April 1963, Peterborough sold ex-Stanley striker George Hudson to Coventry for £20,000. The sale of Hudson to Peterborough in November 1961 had realised just £3,500 and the loss of their star striker had effectively sealed Stanley's fate. How galling it must have been to see four ex-Stanley players – Ian Gibson, Mike Ferguson, Alex Smith and George Hudson – now established Football League professionals collectively valued in excess of £80,000, with Stanley having collected barely £5,000 for the lot of them.

There was some cause for hope, though. In March 1963, the Hardaker plan for 100 League clubs and regional Fourth Divisions had been revived, with talk of the new structure being in place in time for the start of the 1964–65 season. Clarkson reckoned that Stanley would be in line for a Fourth Division (North) berth if they could apply as a Lancashire Combination First Division club. With the ground at Peel Park remaining virtually as it was, with a capacity of 25,000 and nearly 3,000 seats, their application would not, at least, be hindered by a lack of facilities.

With Harold Mather deciding not to continue at Peel Park, midfielder Jimmy Hinksman was given the task of constructing a team for the new 1963–64 season, a team that would inevitably be virtually all-amateur. Hinksman persuaded the core of local players from the previous season to sign again and the team started well, but the off-field events of the previous year were about to catch up with the club.

Indeed, the financial situation at Peel Park was never far from the surface as an issue that might disrupt the smooth running of the team. In August 1962, Stanley had received a cheque from the Football League for £2,106. It was money accrued from the transfers of some players who had been part of the 1961–62 squad, as well as Stanley's share of prize money from that season's FA Cup and League Cup competitions. The club had no choice but to use the cash to pay off some creditors, and primary consideration went to the Inland Revenue, who received £500. The club also had to pay the National Insurance contributions that they had reneged upon, as well as £50 to the Ministry of Pensions.

One Stanley creditor objected strongly to this, resulting

in a creditors' meeting in the public library. The club argued that the Inland Revenue had to be prioritised as they were the organisation who would most readily move to have the club wound up if no money was forthcoming. Clarkson asked the creditors for a two-year 'moratorium' to enable the club to straighten out its affairs, on the grounds that the club could run its Combination side on less than £100 per week provided they had the holiday from debt repayments.

The twenty creditors present agreed to a one-year moratorium, but just a few months later, in November 1962, Clarkson and club solicitor Harry Disley were summoned to London for a meeting with the Inland Revenue. The tax office agreed to a 15-year repayment schedule of £5 per week, provided Stanley could pay off £300 of the debt right away.

The directors agreed. Clarkson claimed that the club was now running on a balanced budget, but the action of the Inland Revenue in June 1963, sending a final demand for £750, indicates that the club had not kept to the deal.

In November 1963, as Hinksman's team challenged at the top of the Combination Second Division, a group of creditors finally took action to seek compensation for their losses. The group in question were the holders of Accrington Stanley debentures, who appointed a receiver to realise the assets at Peel Park in their name. They were entirely within their rights to do so. Stanley debentures had been offered by George Pratt as early as April 1953, at the very outset of his chairmanship, and had raised £7,500 by the time they had all been sold four years later. Holders expected an annual 5% dividend, but they had received nothing since 1961, and were owed nearly £8,500 collectively.

The action of the debenture holders elicited an avalanche of claims from the other creditors. The Inland Revenue, owed more than £3,500, moved a winding-up order in the Chancery Division of the High Court on December 2nd 1963. It was the end of Accrington Stanley (1921) Ltd.

Just days later, on Boxing Day 1963, it was announced that Fred Carr had passed away aged 93. Fred had been the last surviving member of the first Accrington Stanley side to play competitively, on September 1st 1894. His death, alongside that of the club started by his friends in the Stanley Street area of the town, held an eloquent symmetry.

Two of the remaining directors, George Clarkson and Stan Armitage, oversaw the preparation of the club's final financial statement. The only assets remaining at the club were the actual materials that constituted the ground and the land that the stadium occupied. The board tried one last throw of the dice with an appeal to Accrington Council to buy Peel Park from the club and lease it back at a peppercorn rent. At precisely the same time, this exact arrangement was being finalised between Stockport Corporation and Stockport County FC, a move that would save the Edgeley Park club from a winding-up order. Accrington Council refused.

On January 22nd 1964, Accrington Stanley's final statement of affairs was published, and the club was wound up, owing £63,688. In order to avoid any responsibility for these liabilities, the club was forced to drop its famous name and play simply as Accrington FC. George Clarkson did at least receive a guarantee that the club could play out their remaining fixtures at Peel Park.

In the circumstances, one could have forgiven the team for packing it all in as a hopeless case, but, remarkably, the exact opposite happened. In the face of all this turmoil and uncertainty, Hinksman's Accrington side stormed to the 1964 Lancashire Combination Second Division title, winning 23 of their 34 games and succeeding in bringing back some of the crowds to Peel Park. With a squad consisting almost entirely of amateur players and a wage bill of around £25 per week, it was some achievement.

With the title came promotion to the Lancashire Combination First Division, the competition Stanley had left in 1921 to enter the Football League. This was a far more formidable challenge than the lower tier, for it contained some of the teams destined to become founder members of the Northern Premier League just a few seasons later.

Hinksman remembers approaching the new season with confidence, thinking his team sufficiently skilled to cope with the higher standard of football, but he found his position undermined by a dispute with chairman Clarkson. The chairman wanted Hinksman to concentrate on managing the team. Hinksman refused. At just 32 years of age he was not yet ready to retire, and he argued that his young side needed the hard-edged experience that he brought to the midfield. As far as Hinksman was concerned, it was a blatant attempt by Clarkson to interfere in team affairs.

Tensions between the two started to simmer after Accrington's fixture at Fleetwood on September 8th 1964. Hinksman had picked himself ahead of a younger midfielder, Ronnie Schofield. After the game, Schofield confronted Hinksman about being left out of the team. When, later in the week, Clarkson again suggested to Hinksman that he was picking himself ahead of better players, it seemed to the Accrington manager that his chairman's actions had gone beyond mere interference and were now undermining his authority among the players.

Hinksman tendered his resignation, and Clarkson accepted. The chairman told the *Accrington Observer* that it had been a mutual decision, adding:

"There is no ill-feeling in any way. Jimmy did a splendid job last season in helping us to win promotion to the First Division, which was his goal from the time he took over, and we are very grateful for his efforts."

Goalkeeper Terry Neville agreed to manage the team, but he inherited an inconsistent young side, albeit one containing some good players. Neville struggled from the outset to improve matters in what was already a difficult situation. As the team started to fall towards the relegation places, he stood down from the manager's position just three months into his tenure and with the team having collected just one point from eight games.

Reserve team boss Ian Brydon, who had played for Stanley in the Football League, moved up to take over the first team, and he recruited an old team-mate in Norrie McCreadie to bring some guidance to the youngsters in the team. Results did stabilise a little, but an 11-0 defeat at Chorley in January 1965 underlined the limitations within Accrington's amateur ranks.

A 2-0 defeat of Prescot Town at Peel Park on April 7th 1965 was the team's first victory in 14 games, and though it kept them in with a shout of safety, they were eventually relegated back to the Combination Second Division before the season's end.

With Accrington back in the second tier of the Lancashire Combination and the title-winning side of 1964 now broken up completely, Accrington's town team was in a critical state, and things were not helped by the sale of Peel Park in February 1965. The new owner was Sydney Littler, a scrap metal dealer from Wigan, who paid just £8,000 for the stadium, a price which Accrington Council had not been prepared to pay.

With Peel Park in private hands, the club could have been evicted overnight from their historic home. Small wonder, then, that chairman George Clarkson praised Littler effusively in the press when he settled for a peppercorn rent and guaranteed that the ground could be used by the Accrington club for as long as they continued to operate. Littler also offered to sell the ground back for the price he had paid, but he must have known how unlikely that eventuality was.

With their tenure ostensibly secure, Clarkson and manager Brydon resolved to continue, albeit with an all-amateur team. The opening game of the 1965-66 campaign, against Blackpool Mechanics, attracted 300 spectators, and in mid-September the club advertised for a player-manager, offering a semi-professional contract to the successful applicant. A spokesman for the committee that now helped to run the club – a body that included some names who would go on to form the new club, such as John Duckworth, Tom McColm and Tom Lee – told the local press that it was something they would have liked to have done from the start of the season, but only now did they have the money to finance the position.

The man chosen by the committee was inside-right Peter Dewhurst, with Ian Rawstron and Ian Brydon acting as coaches. By this time, though, Accrington were struggling terribly, firmly rooted to the bottom of the Combination Second Division with just one point from their first five games. Dewhurst lasted barely three weeks. An exasperated Clarkson accused him of simply "chucking the sponge in", but Dewhurst alluded to boardroom interference in team selection and thought that without semi-pro reinforcements, neither he nor anyone else would be able to rescue the situation. Ex-Great Harwood and Padiham veteran Danny Parker became Stanley's third manager of the season, though he was signed as an amateur.

In November 1965, it was announced that the ownership of Peel Park would soon pass into the hands of Lancashire County Council, and though the council would not confirm precisely what they intended to do with the ground, a well-sourced rumour was that it was to be used as a playing field for the adjacent school, which was to be extended. Over the Christmas period, it was confirmed that Peel Park, once one of the finest stadiums in the Third Division with the capacity to accommodate 25,000 spectators, was indeed to become a school playing field.

The county council's decision was the *coup de grâce* for Accrington FC, and given the degree of suffering at Peel Park since the turn of the decade, most thought it was a merciful ending. Interest had declined to the point where one public meeting for those interested in helping the club attracted exactly no one. The weekly cost of running the club was around £30, but barely £50 had been taken through the gate during the entire season. By now playing in front of just a few dozen people, and propping up the table having not won a fixture in 16 attempts, Accrington FC announced that their game at home to Glossop on January 8th 1966 would be their last. They had become the second Accrington town team in less than three years to resign mid-season.

The team rallied to end on a high note, defeating their opponents 3-2, but Garth Dawson's famous and deeply evocative photograph showed the reality of the situation at Peel Park: in its day such an important hub of life and leisure in Accrington, the once vibrant Football League ground was slowly crumbling in front of the town, hosting amateur football with little more than 50 people present. As the country made its final preparations to host that summer's World Cup, football could hardly have been at a lower ebb in the town. Football-mad youngsters looking for a team to support had no option but to trek to either Burnley or Blackburn, and some of Stanley's younger fans, not yet so dyed-in-the-wool, transferred their allegiance and made their way to either Turf Moor or Ewood Park.

But the same cannot be said for the older generation of Stanley followers. Some of them had watched Stanley at Moorhead Park before the 1914–18 war, and for these loyal supporters there could be no such re-alignment. Many would never set foot inside a football ground again. Some would even refuse to venture into Burnley, such was their conviction that Bob Lord had deliberately seen the club to its grave. And though the sadness and anger at events continued to smoulder underneath the surface, it seemed unlikely that these folk would find within them the energy and wherewithal to re-ignite an Accrington town team.

But history would prove to count for something. Accrington and neighbouring villages like Church had been football pioneers in the district, boasting strong teams with the odd semi-professional long before the bigger industrial towns had muscled in. And the most senior club of them all, Accrington FC, had been founder members of the Football League, one of just twelve clubs who, one Saturday afternoon in September 1888, kicked off a competition that colonised the world. With that proud pedigree, could Accrington really tolerate for any length of time its absence from the football world?

Hindsight may lend a degree of inevitability to the rebirth of Accrington Stanley, but the reality was far removed from any such notion of destiny. It would prove to be far from an easy path. Though Peel Park in its ever more decrepit state served as a nagging reminder that Accrington was lacking a part of its historic identity, the very earliest efforts to relaunch a town team quickly floundered. A couple of fundraising initiatives were started in 1967, but without any kind of 'official' endorsement, they failed to attract much interest.

But at least the conditions for a new football team were slowly ripening once more. In the country at large, football was once again in vogue thanks to England's World Cup win, though the clubs in the old industrial towns were finding things harder. Blackburn Rovers suffered an emphatic relegation from the First Division in May 1966, their season disrupted by a polio outbreak in the town that saw a raft of fixtures postponed. Bob Lord's Burnley, though still in the top flight, found their attendances declining and the club slowly sinking from the heights of the early 1960s.

But for all these wider social trends, observed throughout the north of England, it was a resolutely local affair that saw the competitive hackles rising in Accrington: the unlikely ascent of tiny Great Harwood FC. Located between Accrington and Blackburn, Great Harwood had spent most of its post-war football life in the Lancashire Combination Second Division. But in 1963, businessman Derrick Keighley took the chair, and he implemented a programme of serious investment in the club. Starting with promotion from the Combination Second Division (alongside Stanley) in May 1964, Great Harwood rapidly ascended the non-league ladder and timed their rise perfectly to coincide with the creation of the Northern Premier League (NPL). Season 1968–69 saw a well-funded and high-profile drive for the NPL, with Keighley assembling a strong squad, including some ex-Football League stars.

Everyone recognised that Harwood were punching above their weight only because of Keighley's largesse – indeed, he had publicly expressed disappointment that Harwood averaged just a few hundred for home games.

But all the same, to those remaining faithful to Accrington Stanley – or at least to the idea of Accrington Stanley – the question was unavoidable. If Great Harwood could aspire to the NPL, surely Accrington could? As parochial as this seems, there was no question of Stanley fans throwing their lot in with Great Harwood. It was Stanley or nothing.

It was in this context that a series of letters in the *Accrington Observer* sparked the idea of Accrington Stanley back into life. In the midst of the summer lull, the paper had asked its readers what they thought Accrington was famous for, and alongside the usual suggestions – textiles, snooker tables, bricks – inevitably came a story from an Accringtonian who, far away from home, had mentioned the town's name, and had been met with the reply of "Accrington Stanley!"

The letter, published in June 1968, was from the pen of George Goodwin, not just an Accrington citizen but also an avid Stanley fan who had been involved in the old Supporters' Club. Goodwin's letter encompassed not just a nostalgic reminiscence, but a call to arms:

"It was the name of Accrington Stanley which really put us on the map. We were one of the originals, and Accrington Stanley was a household name throughout this island of ours. Are we ashamed to mention the name of Accrington Stanley? Let us remember that the younger generation of Accrington have never thrilled to a goal scored by Stanley. To them it is only history. Before we pride ourselves on what we are famous for, let us try to get back in some form into the football world again."

From the tone of Goodwin's letter, it seems clear that the social network of old Stanley loyalists in the town had started serious discussions about relaunching their club. But now, instead of isolated attempts by a few enthusiasts, they put in place a more co-ordinated strategy involving the town's dignitaries and some of the club's most well-known supporters. One of the instigators, and the figurehead, was

Bill Parkinson, both a town councillor and renowned Stanley fan. Bill secured a headline in the *Accrington Observer* of July 6th 1968 with the news that a public meeting was imminent to discuss the possibility of forming a town football club for the 1969–70 season. Parkinson reckoned that interest in the idea was gaining ground in the town:

"I am convinced that the people of Accrington want a football team. People have stopped me in the street to ask if there is anything I can do about it. Because of this undoubted interest, I have made tentative inquiries and the prospects of once again having a team to represent the town look quite good. A public meeting would, I feel, confirm my opinion."

The meeting was held ten days later on July 15th, a Monday night, at Bold Street WMC. The organisers would have been unsure of the response, but they were probably a little disappointed that only around 50 people turned up, even though the time and place of the meeting had not been well publicised. But progress was made, with around fifteen of those present agreeing to administer the formation and operation of a Supporters' Club.

Another attendee that night was Great Harwood's Derrick Keighley, who suggested that the new Accrington team could start with a friendly against his club. The meeting agreed, and the fixture was quickly arranged for Saturday August 10th. This might have seemed a good way to generate interest in the nascent Accrington team, and it may have offered the prospect of raising some funds if a good crowd could be tempted to the game. In hindsight, it was an unwise move. The game clashed with the opening day of the Football League season, and though Accrington could call on some familiar names from the 1963–66 Combination days, they were a scratch team compared to a Harwood side gearing up for the Lancashire Combination title win that would secure a successful application to the NPL.

Tom Lee was put in charge of the Accrington team, and he caused a rumpus by announcing a side that included two ex-Stanley players on Great Harwood's books, Don Bramley and Bryan Pemberton. Harwood manager John Bray was in no mood to compromise, and in the event he named a full-strength team and ruled out the participation of Bramley and Pemberton. Stanley's squad was: Terry Neville, Ian Rawstron, Charlie Wade, Jimmy Hinksman, Frank Mitchell, Jackie Boyes, Ray Pearson, Michael Lee, Fred Bartram, Ted Squires, Ronnie Kershaw and Alan Braithwaite.

The Accrington team battled as gamely as one would expect, but they ran out of steam against superior opposition and lost 9-0. Given the result, it was probably a blessing that only around 75 supporters turned up. It was a rude awakening for anyone who thought that the process would be relatively straightforward. Instead, it was clear that a long and hard road lay in front of the Accrington organisers, and the idea of further fundraising games was quickly dropped.

Those who had volunteered for Supporters' Club duties at the Bold St meeting gathered at the Grafton Club on the Monday after the Harwood defeat, August 12th. There the Supporters' Club committee was formally elected. George Goodwin took the chair. Dick Briggs became vice-chairman and Michael Kneafsey the secretary. Others on the committee included Tom McColm, George Buller, Dennis Yardley, John Duckworth and Tom Lee.

Given the events on the Saturday, the meeting was a muted affair, but those around the new organisation were determined that the club should be formed and start playing as soon as possible. It was following this meeting that the activists announced their intention to call the new football club, not yet formed, Accrington Stanley 1968.

Monday night meetings for the Supporters' Club committee became a routine, and George Goodwin continued to appeal to the public for support through the pages of the *Accrington Observer*. A very useful ally emerged in the shape of Councillor Robert Rigg, chair of the council's Parks Committee, who offered two potential grounds, both of which were quickly inspected. The council did, however, make it clear that Peel Park, now owned and administered by them, was out of the question. The issue of Peel Park, for many Stanley fans the spiritual home of the club, would rumble on well into the 1970s, despite this early line in the sand.

With the new Supporters' Club well into its fundraising stride, Bill Parkinson laid out the blueprint to the local paper. It was the aim that a new Accrington Stanley would be competing in the Lancashire Combination in August 1969. There was an ominous footnote, however:

"We still have our sights set firmly on the Lancashire
Combination, but if our application is not granted
we would join some other league."

The thought of watching Accrington Stanley playing in parks football was hardly designed to stir the blood, and so the next step was quickly announced – there was to be a public meeting the following month, chaired by the mayor, to formally institute a new football club and elect a club committee. This public meeting was delayed until early October, but September 1968 did see the committee members apply to use the Livingstone Road site that would become Accrington Stanley's new home.

The public meeting to officially form Accrington Stanley 1968 finally took place in Accrington Library on the evening of Monday October 7th 1968. By this time, the Supporters' Club had succeeded in recruiting around 200 members, but less than half of these turned out. Jack Barrett remembers counting 25 in the room, though press reports at the time suggest an attendance of around 70. Gerald Berry recalls that the collection that night raised just 13s 4d, and that the meeting room certainly was not full.

What did emerge was the uncertainty that continued to surround the viability of a new Accrington Stanley. The mayor, Jim Madden, chaired the meeting as he had pledged to do, but wasted little time in subjecting the plans of the Supporters' Club to some harsh scrutiny. Jack Barrett recalls:

"The first question that he asked was: 'Was there any need for a football team in Accrington?' given the sparse attendance. The mayor was a grand bloke, but he started to make things difficult at the meeting. He kept saying that he couldn't see it happening, and gave the impression that he wanted the meeting over and done with. He gave us a bit of a lacing, really. He said, 'You've got no ground, no money, nothing. How are you going to achieve this?' This was the mayor of Accrington at the time!"

In the face of the mayor's scepticism, Barrett pointed out that although they wanted to see the club start in August 1969, there was not such a strict time limit on their efforts. Whether it took twelve months or more to raise the necessary cash, they would at some point have enough to enter the new Accrington Stanley into the Lancashire Combination provided they were prepared to persist in their fundraising efforts.

Jack Barrett's intervention helped to turn the mood of the meeting away from the gloomy prognosis of the mayor. A club committee was successfully elected, with Bill Parkinson becoming the first chairman of Accrington Stanley 1968. Dick Briggs, who was elected secretary, invited Barrett onto the first club committee, and he was joined by Gerald Berry and William Thompson. It had been a difficult gestation, but as a result of the meeting in the library, the embryonic outline of Accrington Stanley 1968 could now be seen. There was a club committee to oversee the administrative tasks of registering Accrington Stanley 1968 with the football authorities and of meeting the various regulations required of the Lancashire Combination.

Key to the whole enterprise, however, remained the question of whether the club could raise the required capital in the ten months before the scheduled August 1969 kick-off. With a club committee now in place, fundraising became the *raison d'être* of the Supporters' Club. Those in the library that Monday evening had overcome the pessimism of the mayor, but he was not the only one to question the feasibility of the enterprise. *Accrington Observer* journalist David Allin had done some calculations of his own, and they made a sobering read. Allin pointed out that it took £130 a year to run a mere Accrington Combination team. A basic Lancashire Combination set-up would need £1,500 a year, rising to £4,000 annually if the team was to challenge for honours. Allin concluded that Accrington Stanley would need to find £3,000 a year to be a going concern. At the time, just a matter of months before applications opened for new clubs to join the Combination, Stanley had little more than £100 in the bank.

The experience of Great Harwood gave more pause for thought. Chairman Keighley had sunk £20,000 into the club, including £4,000 on floodlights, £6,000 in the social facilities, which included a nightclub, and a considerable investment in the playing staff. In Bryan Douglas, John Connelly and Adam Blacklaw, Great Harwood had three ex-internationals in their side, but players of that calibre were not cheap to employ. Harwood were top of the Lancashire Combination and heading for the bright lights of the NPL, but their average gate was still only 700. An exasperated Keighley warned that the added costs of NPL football would mean a break-even gate of 2,000 if Harwood did secure their place in the higher league.

At least Stanley were spared those concerns, but it was not as if Accrington was giving its new town club unconditional support. As Great Harwood clinched the Lancashire Combination title at a canter, winning 33 of their 42 games, Accrington Stanley's committee had to admit defeat in their efforts to bring football to the town in time for the 1969–70 season. The financial targets had proved too great. While Great Harwood, a town of little more than 10,000 people, celebrated their admission to the NPL and prepared to lock horns with the giants of Northern non-league, Stanley faced another year of fundraising and preparation.

There was at least one concrete result of the time and effort put in so far, and that was Stanley's residence at the Livingstone Road ground, behind the Crown Inn. The council had bought the ground for £200, and the lease to Stanley was signed in January 1969. Stanley stalwart Wilf Wallwork pulled a few council strings behind the scenes and procured the site for a nominal fee of £3 per year, and the local authority also purchased the wooden pavilion, the only construction on the land, the use of which was included in the peppercorn rent. With an actual base, the club could point to material progress, though the surroundings were anything but salubrious. The regulations of the Lancashire Combination were hardly demanding, but then again, few clubs had to deal with a ground in the condition of the Crown (as it became known) when Stanley moved in.

The field had always been a works sports ground, and had been used most recently by the Ewbank firm, but it had fallen into a state of disrepair. The committee and a team of helpers had to put in long and hard hours at the Crown whenever they could. As such, practical skills were of the most use around the club at this time. The wooden pavilion, perched adjacent to the halfway line, would provide changing facilities, but it was regularly broken into by local youths, and the committee moved quickly to secure the building. Other than the pavilion, there was no other cover at the ground.

The pitch was another huge problem. It had no drainage system, and the neighbouring brickworks said everything about the physical geography of the area. The pitch was laid on top of a bed of clay. When the Stanley committee moved in, they found a stagnant pool of water in one corner big enough to have enticed the local children to build a raft! The man credited with making the pitch at all playable was Dick Briggs, who invested many hours on the playing surface, installing a drain that ran the length of the pitch and at least partly levelling what was at first merely an undulating stretch of meadow grass. Although the council provided some help, Briggs tackled most of the work himself without any mechanised assistance. It was an arduous task for a pensioner to undertake.

The committee used every business contact they possessed to cast around for materials and resources. The yard of the Nori factory was swept for discarded bricks, and eventually enough were gathered to build a communal bath in the pavilion, with cement being used as rendering. Second-hand timber was scrounged from various sources.

One example illustrates the typical scenario. The committee discovered that a job lot of old railway sleepers was available for nothing from the sidings at Rosegrove, a station on the outskirts of Burnley, but it needed a lorry to bring them to Accrington. Local haulage contractor Richard Heap, who emerged as a valuable supporter in the early days of the club, stepped in and lent the club a lorry and a driver. With the help of a group of supporters, Heap delivered the sleepers free of charge to the Crown Ground, where they were used to bank up a small section of terracing next to the pavilion.

Without this and many other acts of similar generosity, Accrington Stanley may never have made it back into the football world. The extreme frugality of the likes of Dick Briggs, who was even seen extracting nails from bits of old timber and straightening them for use elsewhere, made sense in the light of Stanley's precarious finances. The club had no assets upon which they could borrow money to invest in the ground, and they could not be certain of the levels of support they would receive from the town if and when Stanley started playing again. In any case, most on the committee were determined to avoid debt. Jack Barrett, for example, had agreed to take over as club secretary in January 1969 on the proviso that the club would not buy anything on credit, and his attitude was representative of most of the committee.

Their extreme sensitivity to money reflects not just their experience as fans of the old Accrington Stanley, but also of the problems faced by its successor, for effective fundraising proved to be a struggle. The Supporters' Club had launched a prize draw, but ticket-sellers reported great difficulties in convincing their workmates and neighbours that the new club was worth a flutter. Determined to overcome the doubts of the community, secretary Barrett announced that he would undertake a sponsored walk to Liverpool in the summer of 1969. As a postman, Jack was used to pounding the streets, but what made a difference here was that the ambition of his aim attracted significant publicity. Barrett was given a civic send-off and even attracted sponsorship and some coverage from the *Daily Mirror*. The Supporters' Club assiduously made the most of it, collecting pledges from hundreds of townsfolk.

The initiative was to provide a useful shot in the arm for the fledgling Stanley. Barrett's efforts raised a considerable sum, and Accrington Council also weighed in with a grant of £1,000 to enable the club to fit a main drain down the length of the pitch. With the development of the Crown Ground ongoing, the town finally began to take seriously the endeavours of the couple of dozen people who had involved themselves in committee work. By May 1970, the new club was at last in a position to show the town that the new Accrington Stanley was a going concern. In a short space of time, the committee both applied for membership to the Lancashire Combination and appointed a team manager.

It was decided that Jimmy Hinksman was the man to manage the new team. Dick Briggs went to his place of work to ask him if he would be interested in the position. At the time, Hinksman was assistant manager at Bacup Borough, but his connections with Stanley went back to the 1950s, and he needed little further encouragement to join the new venture, even though he knew that he would have to recruit a playing squad from scratch and run the team on the tightest of budgets.

The following month, the Lancashire Combination gave Stanley a hearing about their application. Chairman Bill Parkinson and committee member Gerald Berry represented the club, and they faced two separate grillings, one in front of the Executive Committee in the afternoon, and one in front of the other clubs in the evening.

Berry remembers a nerve-wracking barrage of questions about Stanley's ground, financial status and reasons for applying to the Lancashire Combination. The evening session culminated in a vote, for Stanley faced competition from Kirkby Town Reserves for the single Combination vacancy; the ballot went Stanley's way by the decisive margin of 11 to 2.

With that overwhelming endorsement, Accrington Stanley were back in the Lancashire Combination, a competition they had first graced in 1901, and which they had departed twenty years later to become founder members of the Football League Third Division (North). In 1970, the very thought of finding a way from the Lancashire Combination to the Football League was little more than a fantasy for Bill Parkinson and his committee, but that mattered little to the Stanley chairman and the people who had laboured for two years for this moment. With a broad grin, 'Bill Parky' took his seat at the table as the chairman of Accrington Stanley 1968, the latest recruits to the Lancashire Combination with a fixture list to fulfil – a real club at last. The only thing missing was an actual team!

What remained was a hectic eight-week period for both the committee and the manager. The supporters had to complete the improvements to the Crown demanded by the Lancashire Combination, while Jimmy Hinksman scoured the local amateur clubs looking for the best young players to bring into the Stanley fold.

This was not as desperate an idea as it sounds. After the demise of football at Peel Park in 1966, the *Accrington Observer* had little option but to turn to the local Combination for its football coverage. Team photographs were a regular feature, and the top fixtures of the day were the subject of detailed match reports. Perhaps as a result of this, the Accrington Combination grew to become one of the strongest amateur competitions in Lancashire, consisting of 70 teams and attracting some 3,000 spectators between them on a Saturday afternoon. The top clubs, such as Altham and

Whinney Hill, were well-organised outfits who ran reserve teams and nurtured some of the best youngsters in the area. Little wonder, then, that Hinksman viewed these teams as useful nurseries for future Stanley players.

The manager organised open trials in an Accrington public park and invited all comers:

"Those who feel they are good enough to make the grade will have every chance to prove themselves. There are certainly some players in and around the Accrington Combination who would do well. But there could be others – those who play in poor sides and subsequently do not show up so well – and they will be very welcome too."

Hinksman was as good as his word. By the time of Stanley's AGM at the end of June, he had signed 15 amateurs to form the core of Stanley's reserve team, which had been entered into the West Lancashire League, a grade of football slightly higher than the local leagues and therefore a good indicator of how players might cope in the Lancashire Combination. An enthusiastic Hinksman told the assembled committee members and supporters that he had earmarked the semi-professionals he wanted to sign and was confident of a top-four finish.

The AGM, on June 29th 1970, combined anticipation and optimism with a sense of loss. Accrington Stanley had been reborn in the face of widespread doubt and apathy, and everyone was now itching to see their new team in action. But the meeting was deeply saddened by the passing away of Sam Pilkington. By a poignant coincidence, the man who had done more than anyone to revive Accrington Stanley in 1919 after the deep trauma of the war had died just as a new Accrington Stanley celebrated its imminent arrival into the football world. Glasses were raised in memory of the man known as 'Mr Accrington Stanley', a tribute made in the knowledge that Sam would have approved of their efforts and all they represented.

Two weeks later, on Saturday July 11th, the *Accrington Observer* noted with alarm that Hinksman had not yet signed any players on semi-professional terms, but the manager was more sanguine, pointing out that some players were on holiday and others were considering offers from several clubs. The paper had also reckoned without the persistence and ingenuity of Hinksman when it came to tracking down the highly promising youngsters that would form the core of his Stanley teams for a few years to come. He recalled:

"We had three or four players good enough for the Football League – John Nuttall, Ian McCrae, Alan Davies and Dave McDowell. John Nuttall had played for Manchester University, and I spotted Alan playing for Clitheroe Grammar School. Dave McDowell had played for Ireland schoolboys. I had a lot of contacts around Blackburn and Clitheroe, and a few around Bacup and Burnley. I used to ring the PE teachers at different schools and find out about any good lads leaving school and ready to come through the ranks, and that's how I got a lot of the younger players in."

The following few weeks saw Hinksman finalise his line-up. Terry Tighe, who had made 117 League appearances for Stanley between 1957 and 1960, combined a playing role with that of assistant manager. Those players on contracts included goalkeeper David Bywater, midfielder Mel Widdup (who had played for Stanley in their mid-60s Combination days), and forwards Stuart Illingworth and Benny Newell.

A pre-season friendly against Great Harwood resulted in a narrow 2-1 defeat for Stanley, an encouraging sign that they would be able to compete once the Lancashire Combination got underway on August 15th. Stanley had been given an opening day fixture at home to Formby Town, and the last few days saw the finishing touches put to the Crown Ground in order to ensure that it met Lancashire Combination requirements. Thankfully, the Combination was not too fussy about these domestic arrangements. A narrow wooden fence enclosed the playing area, and two small dugouts squatted on the side of the pitch. This, it seemed, would do for the time being.

With the chimneys of the brick factory looming over the far side of the ground, it hardly made for a picturesque setting, and for many years hence the Crown Ground would reflect its makeshift origins. It was a home-grown shanty town of a football ground, knocked together from bits of second-hand wood and rusty nails. But it was home to a club that represented a kind of redemption for those who had struggled to bring it to life. They had proved a point to a sceptical public, and now they challenged the community of which they were a part to join them on an unlikely adventure. For some diehards, Accrington Stanley meant Peel Park and the Football League, and they would decline the invitation to the Crown. But for a few hundred others, the argument that the new Stanley was but a pale imitation of the old one merely stated the obvious and missed the point. The community once more had a team that it could call its own. For them, that simple fact alone was enough. It was a matter of pride and hope, not status and silverware.

On the eve of Stanley's return, George Goodwin, the man whose letter had started the ball rolling in the early summer months of 1968, once more put pen to paper, and his words remain as fitting today as they were when he wrote them 36 years ago in August 1970:

"A few hours after your readers read this letter, Accrington Stanley will step back into the football world again and before the season has come to an end we shall know for sure whether the public of Accrington want a town team again. There has been a lot of hard and heart-breaking work put into this to make it possible. Let us hope that all this has not been in vain. It is going to be a long, hard road before we return to our former glory, but with the backing of the public, and patience, it can be done. Let us not forget that in the boardrooms of most of the big clubs the names of the twelve originals are on the wall, and Accrington is one of them. We belong in the football world."

Chapter Three

1970–75
Muck and Brass

AFTER THE TROJAN industry of those who had set out to bring Accrington Stanley back to competitive life, the very least they deserved was a home fixture to start off the season and a sunny day to entice the fans, and they had their wish on both counts. With no sheltered accommodation at the Crown, the 620 paying spectators had little option but to soak up the summer sun, though manager Hinksman had a far less relaxing time of it. Though he had signed around five or six players on contracts, he still faced the usual non-league problems of players being away on holiday or at work.

For the opening game, at home to Formby, striker Stuart Illingworth had agreed to drive back on the morning of the game from a holiday in Colwyn Bay. To Hinksman's relief, his No.9 made it back without any problems. Illingworth was the man Hinksman was relying on to score the goals, and his absence would have caused some disruption to the team.

At 3pm, to a great roar, Accrington Stanley kicked off and in doing so picked up the baton, dropped in 1962, and once more began to play football for the pride and honour of the town. The occasion demanded a Stanley win, but Formby immediately pushed their hosts back and after just five minutes had the ball in the back of the net. To everyone's relief, the scorer was ruled offside, but shortly afterwards Stanley had their 'keeper David Bywater to thank as he superbly blocked a short-range Formby effort.

It had been a hesitant start, but with Jimmy Hinksman

urging his men forward, Stanley started to gain more ground. Hinksman by instinct set his teams up to attack, and in the 35th minute, Stanley's adventure paid off. Stuart Illingworth hoisted a high ball into the area, and after a part-clearance had been returned into the box, John Nuttall pounced from a few yards out to score Stanley's first competitive goal at the Crown Ground.

The game developed into an exciting encounter, and though Nuttall had another goal ruled out, Formby deserved their equaliser, which arrived just after the hour. Stanley, however, were not to be denied, and attacking midfielder Alan Davies clinched the victory, running onto a long ball and neatly rounding the 'keeper before finishing. It was a day that everyone present would recall with fondness. After so much uncertainty, everything had gone right. Future chairman John Prescott had gone along simply as an interested football fan, and remembers John Nuttall's opening goal reducing an elderly gent to tears. The old boy explained that he never thought he'd live to see Stanley score another goal. For Prescott it was a formative moment. He only then realised quite how much it meant to some people that Accrington Stanley were once more around. He would soon volunteer for the committee.

Though the opening day had gone as well as anyone could have hoped, problems remained. The pitch was poor, and the lack of any covered accommodation for the spectators was clearly something that had to be addressed before the winter months. Shortly after the Formby game, the club applied for planning permission to build a small shelter along the side of the pitch, and chairman Bill Parkinson put out a public request for anyone with tools to turn up at the Crown and help out.

Stanley continued to impress in the early weeks of the season, remaining unbeaten through August. Games came thick and fast. The Combination League Cup operated on a round-robin group basis, and Stanley played three of these ties in the first fortnight, claiming draws at Clitheroe and Nelson, and defeating Nelson in the return at the Crown.

And when, on August 29th, Stanley knocked a rated Radcliffe Borough side out of the Combination Cup, even the cautious *Accrington Observer* reckoned that Stanley could challenge for honours. Attendances too were edging up to the symbolic 1,000 mark. The visit of Bacup Borough on Monday September 7th attracted 840 to the Crown, and the following Saturday saw a bigger crowd still, with 891 attending the League Cup tie against Clitheroe.

These gates were exceptional at the time for the Lancashire Combination, but just a couple of miles down the road, Great Harwood were doing their utmost to attract greater numbers too. Managed by Tommy Cummings, for many years Burnley's defensive hard man, Harwood continued to bank on the star attraction of the ex-international, and had reunited the famous Blackburn Rovers duo of Bryan Douglas and Ronnie Clayton, as well as signing the Welsh international Roy Vernon. A bright start to their NPL campaign saw gates of 1,500 at the Showground.

It was an incongruous situation that these tiny neighbouring non-league clubs should be attracting such healthy gates in competition with each other, and predictably something had to 'give'. In this instance, it was Accrington Stanley who suffered a downturn in fortunes after the adrenalin rush of the first few games. First Clitheroe exposed Stanley's inexperience with a 6-4 victory at the Crown, and then the team suddenly found goals difficult to come by.

But as the warmth of the late summer gave way to the chillier autumn months, perhaps the biggest disappointment was the decline of the crowds at the Crown. The construction of the small stand had begun, but, as was the way in those days, the club had to scratch around for the materials needed. Richard Heap again proved a valuable ally as he passed on to the club the unwanted timber that came his way as part of his haulage business, but as the winter climate took hold, there was still no shelter for the spectators at the Crown.

Hinksman's answer to Stanley's loss of form up front

was to sign Don Bramley, a long-standing friend and ally of the manager who had been part of Stanley's 1964 title-winning side. Bramley was an experienced campaigner, and he also took on the additional role of assisting Hinksman. Boxing Day 1971 saw just 220 brave the elements for Stanley's clash with Clitheroe, and the team itself was on a poor run, with the local media musing on an apparent inferiority complex at the club.

The New Year did not start auspiciously either when a mix-up over fixtures led to some unfortunate press coverage. Stanley had been due to play at Leyland Motors on December 28th, but the game had been postponed and rearranged for January 2nd. However, Leyland had arranged to play Darwen on that day instead, and the Stanley officials discovered the mistake too late to stop some supporters and the match reporter from the *Accrington Observer* making the trip.

Understandably, the supporters voiced their anger to the journalist, and the row became front page headlines. Bill Parkinson assured the supporters that Stanley had been the victims, and went so far as to publish the letters that had been exchanged between the two clubs making the ill-fated arrangements.

The row quickly died down, and as the team prepared for their remaining fixtures, Hinksman employed centre-half Jim Howley as a target man up front, and the tactic worked. With the additional presence of Howley in the attack, Stanley embarked on an impressive run that took them to within touching distance of the Combination leadership.

A 'four-pointer' at Clitheroe on February 5th saw a magnificent performance from Alan Davies, who scored all the Stanley goals in a resounding 4-1 victory, a result followed by another two points at home to Nelson in front of an improved crowd of 627. Another away success at Ashton United made it nine straight wins, leading the *Accrington Observer* to tip Stanley for the Combination title in their debut season. However, it was too much to expect

Hinksman's men to win every game, and in the crunch fixture at home to leaders St Helens Town, Stanley ran out of steam and were narrowly defeated 2-1.

Stanley completed their first season back in a creditable sixth position, but their achievements were soon cast into a less than flattering perspective by a debate about the merits of the Lancashire Combination itself. This was a debate that rumbled on without resolution for a number of years, but Stanley had not finished their debut season before yet another tranche of clubs took the decision to leave Lancashire's oldest League competition. Prestwich Heys, Radcliffe Borough and Formby indicated that they would seek membership of the Cheshire League for the following season.

These moves merely reflected the drastic implications that the formation of the NPL in 1968 had had on the Lancashire Combination. Though initially the NPL had accepted applications from Combination clubs, by the early 1970s the Cheshire League became the competition to which the NPL looked for new recruits in the event of a vacancy. The Cheshire League thus became the only serious option for upwardly mobile clubs in the north-west. The Lancashire Combination offered no scope for a club to make headway, other than to prove itself worthy of a higher league. The *Accrington Observer*'s Richard Crossley noted:

> "Other clubs will be replacing those who leave, but as the cream is skimmed off the top of the Combination, Stanley must beware of finding themselves surrounded by nothing but sour milk."

Chairman Bill Parkinson staunchly defended the Combination in the face of this analysis. When, that very April, Rossendale United clinched the Cheshire League championship straight after moving from the Combination, where they had not been title contenders, he suggested, perhaps with tongue slightly in cheek, that this proved the Cheshire League to be an inferior competition.

One can empathise with Bill Parkinson's loyalty to the grand old Lancashire Combination, fondly recalling as he no doubt was the days under Galbraith when Stanley Reserves were a Combination force, but his argument was barely credible. The truth was that Stanley too would have jumped at the chance of NPL or Cheshire League football had the facilities at the Crown allowed it. But Stanley's ground was nowhere near the standard required. Only the Lancashire Combination would take Stanley and their rustic, home-made surroundings.

The Stanley chairman's comments provoked a reply from representatives of Cheshire League sides Rossendale and Horwich, who accused Parkinson of being "way off beam", but their indignation was a little misplaced. The Cheshire League had bigger clubs, better grounds and higher attendances, and everyone knew it. During the harshest winter months of 1970 and 1971, Stanley's gate had dropped at times to around 200, but their average of 400 over the season made them easily the best supported team in the Combination.

For all of Bill Parkinson's denials, Stanley had to soldier on in a league that was rapidly filling up with village teams and the odd reserve side. Not until the Crown had developed as a place to watch football could the club hope to advance, but they could not develop the ground without cash that a league like the Combination could not hope to generate. Stanley were in a poverty trap. Though the Supporters' Club presented the committee with a cheque for £300 in March, it paled beside the thousands sunk into Great Harwood by Derrick Keighley. Without a benefactor on that scale, Stanley faced a long and piecemeal haul back to respectability.

For all the enforced limits on the progress of the new club, Stanley's first season back in 1971–72 had at least confirmed that the town could again maintain a team through a full campaign. The guidance of Jimmy Hinksman had proved, too, that there were enough decent players in the area for

Stanley to challenge for Combination honours. There was nonetheless the sense that the club could only truly mark their existence by winning the right to inscribe their name forever on a piece of silverware, and it was as the 1971–72 season drew to a close that Accrington Stanley 1968 made their first mark on the football world. But it was not easy.

Stanley had fought their way to the final of the Lancashire Combination Challenge Cup, where they faced Nelson in a two-legged final. Stanley had roared into pole position with a 3-1 first-leg win at Nelson, but any idea that the return at the Crown would be a procession was soon quashed, and Stanley proceeded to put every one of their 600 supporters through agony during an evening of wildly swinging fortunes.

Nelson were no pushovers at Combination level, and had a skilful side that did its best to play football. At the Crown, they quickly pulled a goal back, and though Alan Davies soon restored Stanley's two-goal advantage, Nelson were the team playing with confidence and fluency. The visitors converted a penalty just before the break to narrow the aggregate to 4-3.

Then, after an end-to-end second half, Nelson were awarded an 88th-minute penalty and the opportunity to take the tie into extra time. But Nelson's spot-kick specialist McHugh had converted their first penalty only after a retake, and, no doubt feeling the pressure of the situation, he proceeded to place a weak spot kick straight at Trevor Morris in the Stanley goal.

A mightily relieved Stanley surged forward and won a free kick outside the box. Stuart Illingworth's effort hit the bar, but captain Mel Widdup was there to smash home the rebound and seal the tie. The party could begin! The final whistle brought scenes of jubilation as the Stanley fans ran onto the pitch to celebrate with the players. After so many years of sadness and regret, this represented a minor but defiant triumph. The Lancashire Combination Challenge Cup might have been small beer for some, but it mattered little for those loyal fans when the magnificent silver trophy arrived at the Crown, newly engraved with the famous name of Accrington Stanley.

But the real value of that first cup win was that it showed the people of Accrington that their fledgling club could bring honour to the town, for the 1971–72 season had not been without its disappointments and periods of crisis. Stanley's first venture in the FA Cup, eagerly awaited since they had not been eligible the previous year, was an anti-climax. They were easily dispatched from the competition by NPL side Morecambe in the opening qualifying round, a defeat that dashed hopes of an income-generating run.

Stanley gave a better account of themselves in the Lancashire Junior Cup, where they drew Cheshire League high-flyers Rossendale United at Dark Lane. The tie, played in January, turned into quite a tussle. With the scores locked at 1-1 and Stanley more than a match for their opponents, the tie turned on a nasty incident in which Rossendale 'keeper John Wood put Stanley striker Colin Smith out of the game with a broken arm. A weakened Stanley succumbed 3-1 and were left to muse about what might have been.

Another concern was the poor level of support coming through the gate. Early season crowds struggled to go much beyond 200, a situation that deeply worried some people around the Crown. *Accrington Observer* journalist Richard Crossley was especially pessimistic when he wrote this in September 1971:

> "It's a fundamental fact of life that you can't force an unwanted article on people. In this case, the unwanted article appears to be Accrington Stanley. However much the officials at the club feel the public ought to come and support the team, it's pretty obvious that the public of Accrington don't feel the same way. It's a great pity when one considers the effort and enthusiasm which has been put into the club by the small band of dedicated officials, but it's the grim truth."

Quite simply, Accrington Stanley were not immune to the whims of the fickle spectator. Although the Crown could now provide rudimentary shelter, other facilities, such as the provision of food and drink, were non-existent. A winning team ought to have persuaded some fans to overlook these shortcomings, and the turn of the year saw Stanley challenging again for the title, and, moreover, playing a brand of football whose quality had the *Accrington Observer*'s David Allin going so far as to suggest that a League and Cup double was not beyond the team. The paper's Mervyn Kay agreed that Stanley would easily hold their own in the Cheshire League, and manager Hinksman was given due credit:

> "No-one under-estimated the job that Mr Hinksman took on when he agreed to manage the club, and he has had to put up with a certain amount of criticism from both the local press and an impatient public, but he stuck to his guns and now the results of his labour are beginning to blossom. Stanley have been moulded into a most attractive team to watch."

A run of six straight wins through late December and January did not, however, stop the club experimenting with Sunday football in an attempt to increase support. The local paper thought it a shame that Stanley had to resort to this, asking rhetorically whether Accrington deserved a town team.

It was in this context – of a club doing its utmost on a shoestring to attract support – that Stanley's Challenge Cup triumph against Nelson mattered. The sense that there was no longer much competition for these trophies did not matter. What was important was that the townsfolk could feel proud of their club and its achievements, and could see a day when it would count for something a bit higher up in the world of football.

Though Stanley's league challenge had ultimately fallen short, that was less of a disappointment in the light of the Challenge Cup win. Furthermore, the team went to Ashton Town a few days after the defeat of Nelson and won another piece of silverware, this time the Combination League Cup. There were once again pots in the historically dusty trophy cabinet of Accrington Stanley, and in putting them there, Jimmy Hinksman and his team had started the process of reconnecting the umbilical cord between town and club. The club could now say to the town: look what we can achieve when we have just a few hundred on board. What might we do with more of you?

As if to emphasise the point, Accrington Council displayed the trophies in the Town Hall throughout the following twelve months, but 1972–73 was to contain all the troubles of the previous season, and with far fewer happy endings.

Jimmy Hinksman retained his squad, and the club began the new season enjoying the hospitality of the Isle of Man, whose authorities invited the club over for a friendly played at the Douglas Bowl. Stanley graciously allowed their hosts a 5-2 victory.

Back home, signs that things were as precarious as ever came at the club's AGM, held on the eve of the season's opening. Here it was revealed that the club owed its solvency to the tireless work of the Supporters' Club, which raised £1,720 over the course of the year to meet expenses that were inevitably higher. One highly regrettable drain on resources that the club could have well done without was the £1,000 bill to repair various acts of vandalism to the ground.

Gates had been disappointingly lower, with the 600 attendance at the Challenge Cup final the best of the season. The committee that ran the club had clearly shouldered a heavy financial and administrative burden and the workload had by this time reduced their number to six, one of the casualties being Bill Parkinson himself, who resigned from the chair, arguing that it was time for someone else to take the reins for a while. Others at the AGM, club stalwarts like Derek Proctor, Gerald Berry and John Duckworth, all appealed for more help from the public, whether from those wanting to get involved, or those prepared merely to buy raffle tickets.

Alan Cotton became Stanley's second club chairman. He was a Rishton-based businessman with a chain of local shops that sold and repaired televisions. At 32 years of age, he was considerably younger than his predecessor, though energy alone could make little headway against the problems he inherited.

Gates remained modest through the 1972–73 season. Though the Lancashire Combination tried to raise interest by expanding from 15 to 19 clubs, most of the newcomers – such as the Ford Motors works team and Skelmersdale United Reserves – were hardly likely to bring the crowds flocking. The one new team with potential pulling power as far as Stanley were concerned was Great Harwood Reserves, but those hopes proved unfounded when the 'derby' brought gate receipts of just £20, leaving both sides with £5 after expenses.

Early season form was good, including a run to the first round proper of the FA Trophy, a competition Stanley had never before entered. They advanced at the expense of some unfamiliar opponents in Boldon Colliery Welfare and Blaenau Ffestiniog, before Southern Premier League side Grantham won 2-0 at the Crown. The FA Cup also saw senior opposition arrive in Accrington in the shape of NPL outfit Runcorn, and Stanley forced a 1-1 draw before narrowly losing the replay 2-1.

In the Lancashire Combination, Stanley occupied their usual position at the top end of the table, but as Christmas approached, the Crown Ground pitch became unplayable. It had never been anything less than a problematic surface, but this time the retention of water and the cloying mud were so bad that it was feared that the main drain, re-installed by Dick Briggs during the summer, had either collapsed or become blocked. However, tests depressingly proved this to be unfounded. It was quite simply the physical geography of the site. Bill Parkinson's sentiments the previous year, published in the *Evening Telegraph* as part of a profile of the then Stanley chairman, had summed it up for everyone at the club:

"I often think how nice it would be for the lads if they had a good pitch. They'd be twice the team. But when you're next to a brickworks, you are on heavy clay and the water lies. I don't think we'll ever manage to have an ideal playing surface here."

As the postponements, and games in hand, piled up, Stanley secretary Jack Barrett wrote to the local Education Authority seeking permission for Stanley to use Peel Park, by now established as a playing field for the adjoining school. Stanley were given the go-ahead, apparently at the nod of the headmaster of Peel Park school, who was given the right of veto. Joy at the news was tempered by the caution of the authorities, who warned Stanley that it could not be a permanent arrangement and ought to be treated as a one-off.

All the same, the news that Accrington Stanley were once more going to run out at their traditional home was greeted with great excitement, and the date was fixed for the afternoon of Sunday March 4th, with mid-table Nelson the visitors. With none of the terrace covering remaining at the old ground, the last thing Stanley needed was a wet homecoming, but that's precisely what the weather had in store for them as it proceeded to pour down all afternoon.

Witnesses outside the ground estimated that at least 200 people turned up at the ground but decided against the idea when they were told there was no cover. Despite the conditions, a larger-than-average crowd of around 700 braved the elements till the end, though Stanley themselves struggled in the rain, the result being a disappointing 2-2 draw that did nothing for Stanley's title hopes.

The improved turn-out at Peel Park convinced the club that a permanent return to the ground, still possessed of its changing rooms and terracing, represented the only feasible option if Stanley were to quickly make strides up the non-league ladder. The experience had been richly nostalgic for the ex-Peel Parkers in the crowd, so much so that it was strongly rumoured that after the Nelson game the club had lobbied the authorities strongly for a permanent return to the ground. An accompanying petition had also been launched by some Stanley fans to convince the authorities to allow Stanley back.

The campaign did not attract the support of everyone. The headmaster of Peel Park School was not impressed by the state of the pitch after the game, and matters were worsened when a cold snap immediately afterwards had frozen the rutted surface before it could be rolled, making it temporarily too dangerous for the schoolchildren to use.

Accrington Observer reporter David Allin also rounded with scorn on those who were arguing that Peel Park represented a chance for Stanley to move quickly into the Northern Premier League.

He headed his article with a statement from Gordon Lee, future manager of Everton, who was quoted as saying: "I would never live in a town that did not have a League club because there would be no interest there. I went to Accrington recently and with all respect to them, it seems that the town has died since League football stopped."

Allin himself crudely dismissed the idea that Peel Park could set Stanley on their way back to the Football League, and proposed instead that the solution to what Gordon Lee had claimed to observe was a joint Harwood/Stanley team:

"The clubs could pool their resources and the area would get one decent football team. And no longer would we have ridiculous statements about Accrington Stanley returning to its former greatness. That's the biggest load of ballyhoo that I have heard in years. The plain fact is that top class football in Accrington is finished forever and no amount of planning and dreaming will bring it back."

At least in putting Stanley on a par with NPL Great Harwood, Allin was paying a compliment, albeit a back-handed one, to the standard of football Stanley were producing.

But it was an unnecessarily harsh indictment of those

who had suffered greatly when their team had gone under
– through no fault of their own – in 1962. The editorial was
more sympathetic to the Stanley stalwarts, but essentially
agreed with Allin:

"Peel Park is but an empty shell. The stands have
gone, and with them the ghosts. Could anyone
truthfully say that he stood on Peel Park on
Sunday afternoon and for a moment, just a fleeting
moment, ran over in his mind an action replay of
a long-savoured goal? I think not. The occasion for
many was one of infinite sadness and depression.
For the sake of the 'old faithfuls', Sunday's match
should never have been played at the old ground.
Peel Park died at 4.40pm on Saturday, January 8th,
1966. Perhaps now the ghost can rest in peace."

Another *Accrington Observer* writer, Alan Simpson, at
least offered a more practical suggestion. Since the council
owned the Crown and Stanley was not incorporated as a
limited company, Simpson argued that the club could be
eligible for a council grant in much the same way that any
other community organisation was. At the time, Stanley
were aiming to raise £2,000 to build new changing rooms
with showers, facilities that would be needed if the Crown
was to be acceptable to the NPL.

In an example of how hard the club was working to
raise the money, the Supporters' Club had already banked
just under £1,000 when Simpson floated the idea of a grant.
They had been helped greatly by Bolton Wanderers, who
had invited Stanley to join in their 'Grand National Draw',
which had a first prize of £1,000, well above anything that
Stanley could offer at the time. The draw proved to be a
real success, with Stanley banking £300 as their share of
the profits.

On the field too, despite the Crown's appalling surface,
Hinksman's team continued to battle away, and when, on
March 15th, Stanley routed Prescot Town 5-0, they moved
to the top of the Lancashire Combination. The issue of the
council grant ticked away quietly in the background as the

committee liaised with the appropriate people, but the race for the Combination was quickly coming to its conclusion.

A Combination title was something that Hinksman most coveted. He had won the competition as a player in Accrington Stanley's all-conquering reserve team of 1955, and now he saw the chance of completing an unusual double. The club, too, saw the Combination championship as a possible passport to a higher league. Unfortunately, the backlog of fixtures caused by the Crown pitch, combined with injuries, saw Stanley's form dip in the course of a hectic run-in, and the team had to settle for third place.

They continued their unbeatable form in the Combination Challenge Cup, however. After seeing off the challenge of St Helens Town in the semi-final, 4-2, Stanley faced Skelmersdale United Reserves in the two-legged final. A 2-1 win at Skelmersdale put Stanley in charge of the tie, and though the 1-1 draw in the return at the Crown saw Stanley some way off their best form, it was enough for the club to successfully defend the Challenge Cup.

For manager Hinksman and his players, therefore, the season's toils were not without reward. The top-three finish and their successful defence of the Challenge Cup made for another satisfactory campaign. But they had fallen short again in the quest for the Combination championship, and the likelihood of the club finding a solution to the playing surface at the Crown seemed more remote than ever, despite the sterling efforts of Dick Briggs.

These somewhat mixed feelings made themselves heard in an interview given by the manager to the *Lancashire Evening Telegraph* after the completion of the club's fixtures. Said Hinksman:

"I don't know why it is, but we never seem to get the credit that the lads feel they deserve. We have the most faithful fans in the Combination, the only trouble being that we could do with more of them. The enthusiasm, the team spirit, is everything. Often some of the lads have finished a shift and then high-tailed it straight to the match and played their hearts out for the full ninety minutes. This sort of thing is what football is really all about. You've got to love playing for its own sake otherwise it's no use, especially at this level, where the financial rewards are very little. Our players even have to buy their own boots!

"What the lads are really aiming for is the Combination championship and after that a possible move to a higher grade of football in the Northern Premier League. I am optimistic about the future. Basically, we want to put Accrington Stanley on the map again: the players and the staff feel they are doing their bit. We would like the public of the town to give us that little extra support which would make such a difference. There is no doubt in my mind that with a little more financial support we could be one of the leading clubs in the Northern Premier League."

Stanley returned to the Isle of Man in July for another friendly in the Douglas Bowl, this time defeating the Manxmen 4-2. Jimmy Hinksman made an important addition to the squad in the formidable shape of centre-half John Hubberstey, yet another talent spotted and lifted from local amateur football by Hinksman and trainer Peter Dunn. Dunn, although not as well known a name as Hinksman and Don Bramley, had nonetheless been involved at Stanley since the 1950s, where he played in the same Stanley reserve side as Hinksman, as well as the Combination title-winning side of 1964. Now Dunn served Stanley as a trainer, and his contacts in the Blackburn area served the club well – he spotted Hubberstey playing for Blackburn Combination side Cob Wall. John Nuttall, one of Hinksman's original signings, rejoined the club.

Stanley took on and defeated Clitheroe 2-0 in the opening fixture of 1973–74, but just 184 spectators turned out to see them. A little financial compensation arrived with a cheque for £154, Stanley's prize money for the previous season's FA Trophy in which they had gone through three qualifying rounds to reach the First Round proper, but the prelude to the club's annual meeting was a disappointing 3-1 league defeat at Bacup. At the AGM, chairman Alan Cotton announced he was standing down after just one year in the position, citing a lack of time due to his business commitments. Jack Hudson stepped in to become Stanley's third chairman.

While Stanley had to some extent acclimatised to the poor playing conditions at the Crown, Hinksman's men relished a decent surface on which they could really play, as they showed in September when they went to Holker Street and thrashed NPL Barrow 4-0 in an FA Cup qualifying game. This was an outstanding result for a Lancashire Combination side against a team voted out of the Football League only a couple of years before.

The quality of Hinksman's squad was underlined by the interest of Bury, who approached Stanley for the services of Ian McCrae, Glyn Burr and John Nuttall. Of the trio, perhaps Burr was the most exciting prospect, shining in Stanley's midfield while still a pupil at the town's Hollins School. Hinksman was having none of it, however, turning away the Fourth Division club empty-handed. The manager told Bury that Stanley had too many forthcoming fixtures for him to lose three core members of his squad, and he was not being disingenuous. Although their FA Cup run had come to a disappointing end when Stanley had missed a late penalty in losing 2-1 at NPL side Netherfield, the team had their revenge by knocking the same club out of the FA Trophy, 4-2 at the Crown.

Yet, despite the team's spectacular successes against higher opposition, the attitude of the Accrington public remained indifferent, with just 203 turning out for the Netherfield tie. A frustrated Jimmy Hinksman vented his feelings in the pages of the *Accrington Observer*. While praising the committee and the council for their hard work and help, the manager had this to say to the town:

"Myself, my players and my committee are disgusted by the mild response shown by the public of Accrington to the success of our team. If Accrington people expect the side to improve and move into a better standard of football, the next step must be made by them. We have proved we are a good side, but if they are not prepared to support the club, how do they expect us to do well in a better league? To play in the Northern Premier League with gates of only 200 would be a waste of time."

Stanley drew a plum local derby tie in the First Round of the FA Trophy, being paired with Cheshire League side Rossendale United, and hopes were high for a much-improved gate. The club were a little unlucky, however, in that the tie clashed with the visit to Burnley of First Division leaders Leeds United, who drew a gate in excess of 30,000 to Turf Moor. Nonetheless, Stanley once again rose to the occasion, defeating their higher-status opponents 2-1, and gaining ample revenge for that controversial 3-1 defeat two seasons before.

It all served to reinforce Hinksman's point, but it was difficult to see quite how such stinging rebukes would improve matters. One wonders also what the committee members thought about being quoted in such a manner, for at this time they were putting the finishing touches to an agreement with Accrington Council. As had been suggested by Alan Simpson in the *Accrington Observer*, it proved to be the case that since the council owned the Crown, it was permissible for them to invest in developing the facility as something that would benefit the wider community. The council could not use ratepayers' money to pay the players, but they could invest in bricks and mortar on what was their land.

In November, work started on a new block of changing rooms to replace the rather basic communal set-up that was housed in the old pavilion. Accrington Council had given a £2,500 grant towards the project, leaving Stanley with just £500 to find for the remaining costs. Stanley chairman Jack Hudson, a builder by trade, led the construction work. Since it was widely assumed that it was partly the state of the Crown that kept people away, any signs of progress on that front could only benefit the club.

But even as the new building in the corner of the ground slowly took shape, the problems with the Crown pitch remained, and things were not helped by the three-day working week, imposed because of widespread industrial action and fuel shortages. With Stanley still involved in three cup competitions, the fixture backlog was fearsome, but the team hit a vein of form that carried them through the heavy demands of the final two months of the season.

Signs that Hinksman's side was at last starting to turn heads came with the interest shown in a Lancashire Junior Cup quarter-final tie against NPL neighbours Great Harwood at the Crown. The game, long scheduled but a frequent victim of the Stanley pitch, finally took place in March and drew a much-improved crowd of 714 to the Crown in a Sunday afternoon kick-off. Stanley triumphed 2-0 on a pitch covered with 60 tons of sand in an effort to soak up the surface water.

Stanley's defeat of their neighbours so rattled a group of Harwood businessmen and club chairman Derrick Keighley, that they put up £200 prize money for a one-off, winner-take-all game to be played at Great Harwood, where the playing surface was better. Their manager, Roy Cheetham, argued that his team would win were the game to be played on grass rather than mud and sand.

It sounded a resentful gesture, but the achievements of Accrington Stanley were now a real cause for concern at Great Harwood. Though a Northern Premier League club, they were one of the League's smaller outfits, and survival at this decent level of non-league, against clubs like Boston United and Wigan Athletic, was never less than a struggle. The last thing Harwood needed was a resurgent Stanley, and their defeat at the Crown that Sunday in front of over 700 locals was in danger of being seen as a decisive shift in the balance of power between the two clubs. Harwood had the status, but Stanley had the weight of history behind them and, it appeared, momentum on the field. The £200 was a crude way of luring Stanley to the Showground to put them in their place.

Not that the prospect worried the ever-combative Jimmy Hinksman, who positively thrived on such challenges: "There's no danger of us losing – we'll murder 'em!" enthused Jimmy. "Harwood can make whatever excuses they want. The best side won and won easily." Stanley secretary Jack Barrett was a little less up-for-it, but he still could not resist a playful dig, suggesting that "The idea could backfire on Harwood, because our lads will be raring to go."

In the end, Stanley won the war of words with the much more calculated argument that they could not fit in the challenge game since they were still engaged in so many competitions. In a final flourish, Hinksman said he would consider it as a pre-season friendly. Much chastened, Harwood did not raise the matter again and the '£200 challenge' never happened.

Stanley did indeed have other things occupying their minds as the season's finale approached. The problems with postponements during the winter months had left the team with just six weeks to play half their Combination fixtures, this on top of their remaining interest in the Combination Challenge Cup and the Lancashire Junior Cup. It was a daunting schedule, but Hinksman's Stanley proved equal to the task. Their Junior Cup semi-final, against Wigan Athletic, was played at their opponents' Springfield Park ground on March 17th, with Stanley losing 2-0 in front of 825 spectators, but it was a rare reverse. Between March 23rd and the end of April, Stanley remained undefeated in the 17 games they played, a run which included a club record eleven consecutive clean sheets.

On the brink of the title, a crowd of 657, the best league gate of the season, turned up at the Crown to see if Stanley could clinch it with a defeat of Skelmersdale Reserves. As so often happens in such situations, Stanley played over-cautiously and were held to a 1-1 draw. With Bacup still in a position to overhaul Stanley, the next game at Wren Rovers on the Tuesday was another tense, goalless affair for an hour, but then left-winger Dave McDowell scored one of Stanley's goals of the season with a run and emphatic, top-corner finish. It settled Stanley's nerves, and urged on by 200 travelling supporters, they scored again four minutes later through Stuart Illingworth. The 2-0 victory was enough to bring the Lancashire Combination title to the club for the first time since 1955.

Postponements were a way of life at the Crown, but this time it was a celebration rather than a game that had to wait, for just two days later Stanley faced another important tie. After defeats of Ellesmere Port Town, Kirkby Town, Clitheroe and Great Harwood Reserves, Stanley had reached their third consecutive Combination Challenge Cup final, and the first leg at the Crown, against St Helens Town, was played on the Thursday.

No doubt feeling the pace by now, Stanley struggled to force a 2-2 draw, but the second leg on the Monday night was settled by a single goal, and it came from Stanley striker John Nuttall. Jimmy Hinksman and his indomitable squad of players had emerged triumphant from one of the most testing periods in the short history of the club. Faced with a punishing itinerary, including four matches in six days at one point, Accrington Stanley had beaten all comers and achieved the Lancashire Combination League and Cup double.

Jimmy Hinksman was the subject of a heart-warming feature in the local press, in which he made clear his feelings about his team and their achievements:

> "These lads are like golden apples. There's not just the odd one; it's the whole lot. They're so willing, so keen to win, I think they'd play barefoot on a pitch full of broken glass – it couldn't be any worse than kicking through some of the awful, muddy, corrugated pitches they've had to play on during the season. I'm so proud of them. Sometimes I

wonder just how good some of them could be if they were in full-time training. They play their hearts out every home game in front of crowds of only 500 people or so. They know that there's no money in the till and financial support has virtually to be cadged. But it doesn't stop them playing football until they drop. They play the game for its own sake and they play it damned well! I think we deserve better recognition. Lads who try as hard as these and get results like they have done, deserve to get a lift."

On May 4th, the club announced further plans for expansion and development, including the start of an Accrington Stanley Youth team. More importantly, the club seemed to have earned the respect – if not yet the regular support – of the town. Things appeared set to move on. The feeling was that Stanley, as Lancashire Combination champions, had shown to the rest of northern non-league football that they were ready to progress, to challenge themselves with a higher grade of football. And with no automatic promotion from the Combination, Stanley could at least apply to join a higher League once they had put the Crown in order.

The question was whether they could do so in time to take advantage of the squad that Hinksman had assembled, whose average age was just 24, but only five of whom had a part-time contract with the club. Team spirit clearly counted for a lot, but no matter how enjoyable the pursuit, there was only so much you could expect from amateur players on just £2 expenses a game.

Stories abounded of players on shift work putting in 90 minutes after a day's work, with no time to eat a meal beforehand, or going on shift immediately after a game. These were common enough routines in the purely amateur game, but Stanley had set their sights on semi-professional non-league.

Some clubs in the Northern Premier were strong candidates for elevation to the Fourth Division. Stanley could not expect their players to perform at that level without more support.

If Stanley were serious about playing in the Northern Premier League, as some on the committee insisted, then significant investment had to come from somewhere so that the pitch and surroundings matched the quality that the managerial team of Hinksman, Bramley and Dunn had brought to the field of play. The committee had tried to attract investment and sponsorship from local businesses, but very little had been forthcoming.

John Prescott, a future chairman of the club and on the committee for most of the 1970s, sees it as a simple case of financial policy mirroring a generational attitude to money:

"There was very little money coming into the club at the time, there was a raffle on the match days and programme sales, but financially we weren't very astute. There was no sponsorship, no boards around the ground. They'd had to build the ground from nothing, and so this affected the make-up of the people involved; there were a lot with practical skills, but no real experience of commercial sales. And a lot of them, even in those days, were in their 50s and 60s, so they were naturally slowing down a bit. They were an older generation brought up on the principle that you didn't spend before you had it. This was well before the days of credit cards. It reflected the reality of those times. If you saw a coat and it was ten quid, if you didn't have the ten quid you didn't have the coat; it was as simple as that."

During the summer of 1974, the debate continued at the club about how Accrington Stanley might forge ahead more quickly. The majority on the committee could see no feasible alternative to the policy of gradual and piecemeal investment by developing the ground as and when the money was raised. The figures released in August's AGM suggested that no matter how much success was achieved on the field, the club could only hope to break even, and even this was reliant on donations and fundraising.

Chairman Jack Hudson announced that Stanley had made a profit of £70 on the year, with wages and expenses totalling £2,099 against gate receipts of just £1,177, the difference being largely met by the £878 raised through the '200 Club' lottery scheme. The club had just £280 in the bank.

The AGM also saw the resignation of Hudson, the second chairman in as many years to last just the one season at the helm of the committee. The issue of money had been the cause of some stress when the project to construct the new changing rooms had gone £500 over budget. The new facilities had been built free of charge by the chairman using labour and machinery from his building firm. He decided that his company could absorb most of the additional cost, but he asked six committee members to put in £25. It was the first time the committee had been asked to put their own money in, and not many could afford it. It understandably caused tensions.

Bill Parkinson took over for his second stint in the chair. Jimmy Hinksman was having a trying time of it as well, for he had scarcely had time to organise his pre-season schedule before he was hit with the loss of four key players. At the AGM, he played down expectations:

> "This coming season will be a very difficult job for me as manager because we have lost four of our players – Colin Smith, Ian McCrae, Jim Howley and Kenny Millar. It will be a difficult task to replace them. The club has no money to get players who are of the same standard as those who have left. We will just have to carry on and find players who will more or less play for nothing."

The point about money was salient, for Hinksman was convinced that his players had been 'tapped up' and offered far better terms by more affluent clubs. Colin Smith and Ian McCrae were two of Stanley's most successful strikers. McCrae signed for Nelson, although the Pendle club claimed that he had signed as an amateur and would only receive expenses. Smith was the subject of an approach from Bacup Borough. Bacup claimed to have gone about everything in the right way, but the Stanley manager was having none of it. He revealed to the press that virtually every member of his Combination League and Cup winning side had been approached by other clubs, for the most part illegally:

"You do so well and then this happens. You find the players, bring them along, and then other clubs come along. It's all wrong. This is the price you pay for success. It's not just Bacup but other clubs as well. Some were even approached before the season ended, and Ian McCrae was offered more money by another club. I'm going to bring it up with the Lancashire FA. It is time something was done."

The loss of such an accomplished finisher as Smith, the scorer of 15 goals the previous season, could have been mistaken for a minor disaster, but one of Stanley's strengths at this time, born of necessity, was their ability to spot raw talent in the local amateur leagues. It was this self-reliance that saw Stanley unearth a rare gem from the humble environs of the Accrington Combination – a striker called David Hargreaves.

Affectionately known by all at the Crown as 'Haggis', Hargreaves made his debut on August 10th 1974 in a pre-season friendly against Radcliffe Borough. His league debut came shortly afterwards against Dukinfield Town, and he duly scored in a 3-0 victory. Jimmy Hinksman innocently told the press: "I'm sure we're going to see many more goals from Dave Hargreaves." No one could have guessed what an understatement that would prove to be.

With Haggis in harness, the question of who was going to put away the chances was never an issue. Hargreaves was brave, had an excellent turn of pace, good control, and could time his advances in the face of an offside trap. But what really marked him out was an almost zen-like calmness in front of goal. Haggis could keep his head when most at that level lost it. Whether slipping the ball under an advancing 'keeper, passing it in through a defensive gap or simply cracking it home from distance, Hargreaves was a phenomenal goalscorer. On one occasion, he received the ball from the kick-off and sent a measured 55-yard effort over the 'keeper and straight in without a bounce. That extraordinary goal even had an old grumbler next to me waving his walking stick in delight. Quite simply, Hargreaves was, and remains, the most natural finisher the town has ever produced.

Though Stanley's goalscoring worries were solved with the discovery of Hargreaves, there was no such resolution to the ever-problematic playing surface at the Crown. A photo in the *Accrington Observer* of that season's FA Cup tie against Bacup shows the players ankle-deep in mud, and it was only September 2nd. The following week's game against St Helens Town was subsequently called off with the pitch waterlogged.

The club had also become embroiled in a row with nearby residents who had objected to Stanley's plans to build a shelter along the side of the pitch between the Crown pub entrance and the pavilion. They saw it as a threat to the value of their houses. The shelter was just part of a set of proposals announced at the AGM, the cost of which, it was reported, had been met by an anonymous donor. With the new dressing rooms complete and operational, the committee also planned to turn the pavilion into a clubhouse, complete with bar and lounge. Most non-league clubs relied on a good social set-up to raise money, but this was something that Stanley had been entirely without.

Chairman Bill Parkinson contended that the club had to develop the ground as quickly as possible due to two things – not only was the team achieving and the committee active, but the non-league world was also awash with rumours at this time about the creation of a nationwide competition immediately below the Football League, with automatic promotion to the Fourth Division for the winners. Stanley had to be in the running, and that meant a lot more work on the Crown:

"One never knows what the future will hold for smaller clubs like Stanley. The time is ripe for improvements, and we must take this opportunity to push on with our plans. It would be a pity if this wave of enthusiasm were not to carry a lot of improvements which would amount to a big step on our long journey back..."

Parkinson's reply, though absolutely honest, did nothing to soothe the concerns of the residents, one of which was the suspicion that the stand would only be the first of many new constructions at the Crown as the club sought to move up the football ladder. In reply to this, the Stanley chairman made the familiar case that success for the town's football club could only be good for the town as a whole. True enough, but appeals to the common good, then, as now, often fell on the stony ground of self-interest.

The objections of the residents would eventually be over-ruled and the primitive wooden stand given the go-ahead, but problems with the pitch remained. Home postponements caused by the waterlogged pitch created financial pressures. Gate money, though still modest, did contribute significantly to the club meeting its wages and running costs. Perhaps with this in mind, manager Hinksman mused openly on the necessity of a Cup run and urged the town to support the club in greater numbers.

On September 18th, Great Harwood Reserves ended Stanley's 30-match unbeaten run in the Combination, an early sign of the dip in league form that was to come, but Hinksman got the Cup run he was hoping for, and it was achieved mostly against opponents from higher leagues. After the defeat of Bacup, they knocked out a handy Cheshire League side in the shape of Chorley, who were defeated 2-1.

And when, on October 19th, Stanley went to then Cheshire League leaders Horwich RMI and won 2-0 in the third qualifying round, it left the club with just one more hurdle to clear for a return to the FA Cup first round proper, last graced by Stanley in 1961.

They were slightly unlucky in drawing the toughest tie of the lot, away at Altrincham, then a real non-league power. Stanley competed well for the first half hour, but an aerial clash put Stanley's John Hubberstey out of the game with a head injury, and Stanley missed the big centre-half thereafter. Altrincham went on to win 3-0 and, bizarrely, complained after the game about Stanley's ferocious tackling, this from a non-league side renowned for their physical approach to the game. Clearly, Hinksman's Stanley boys could look after themselves.

But the high of the FA Cup run led to a Combination hangover, and Stanley failed to win a league fixture in November, leaving them mid-table and some distance from a successful defence of their title. They were also disappointingly knocked out of the FA Trophy by Liverpool Combination side Earle FC.

But even this paled next to the other unintended consequence of Stanley's Cup form, for their run to the brink of the first round ignited another contentious issue that rumbled on for the whole season. With Stanley in the draw for the fourth and final FA Cup qualifying round, they had to plan for the eventuality of drawing a League club at the Crown if they were to win through to the First Round. In the process of doing so, it emerged that Stanley would not be allowed to play a home first round FA Cup tie; the facilities were deemed simply not up to standard for such an occasion.

Had Stanley got through and received a dream tie like Blackburn Rovers or Preston (both of whom were then in the Third Division), they would no doubt have switched the game anyway in the interests of finance. But the thought that Stanley would never be allowed to host a big cup-tie as long as the Crown remained as devoid of facilities as it was struck some fans as both unjust and intolerable. A small group of them, led by Harry Hall and Ted Hillman, started yet another campaign through the pages of the *Accrington Observer* to relocate the new Accrington Stanley to Peel Park, and urged the council to consider the idea.

Chairman Bill Parkinson and the Stanley committee

enthusiastically endorsed the campaign, which was presented in the media as the first move in a determined attempt to claim back Stanley's place in the Football League. This certainly was not the first time that a return to Peel Park had been suggested, but a steadfast opponent emerged in the headmaster of Peel Park School, who said:

"As far as I am concerned, Peel Park is a school playing field. The field was bought and it belongs to the purchasers. They are entitled to do what they want with it and I can't see any point in people trying to get them to part."

It was the occasion of one of the chairman's more combative public statements:

"I would like to answer the headmaster who opposes us. I would like to tell him that the ratepayers, who pay so heavily towards education, are the rightful owners of Peel Park. It does not belong to any committee because committees only represent ratepayers. I contend that if the ratepayers wish that Peel Park should become available to Stanley, then it should be made available."

The campaign was given added momentum by the continuing rumours of a nationwide non-league 'premier' division with automatic promotion into the Football League. Bill Parkinson reiterated again the likelihood of this reform and its implications for Accrington Stanley:

"If Stanley can be in the premier league...the way is open to the club to get itself promoted back to Division Four. But to achieve this we must have ground facilities and we hope the whole of Accrington and district will support us. The town knows what a wrench it was when it lost Stanley's League status, and the town would never let the club down again. It's up to us all to get moving on what is going to be a very hard slog."

Anyone visiting the Crown at this point in time could not, with the best of intentions, envisage League football being played there in the near future. The swift return of

Accrington Stanley to the Football League, however fanciful or unlikely the thought, rested on an equally swift return to Peel Park. The danger was that if this latest campaign floundered, then Stanley would be locked out of Peel Park for good, leaving them with no option but to embark on the much more daunting task of developing the Crown. But it was undoubtedly worth a go. Even then, the terracing and changing rooms remained at Peel Park, and, crucially, the playing surface was far superior to that at the Crown.

That clay bed at the Crown kept Stanley out of action for six weeks between December 1974 and January 1975, with the team agreeing to play some of their scheduled home games at the grounds of their opponents. On January 18th, the referee called a game off at the Crown just an hour before kick-off, with fans already starting to turn up. The committee worried that such a long gap between home games would lose the club the patronage of some of their regulars. The team also faced another backlog of fixtures and the prospect again of three games a week throughout April.

A similar thing happened as late as March 16th 1975, when a game was postponed just 40 minutes before kick-off, this after the ground had been sanded. The club's sand bill had reached £200 for the season, but Bill Parkinson thought the referees were not being fair, as he made clear in this priceless comment to a journalist:

"Unfortunately our ground has got a very bad reputation and referees are pre-judging it without giving us a fair chance. There are some bad patches around the centre circle which are underwater, but the rest of the ground, where most of the action takes place, is perfectly fit for play."

One cannot help but smile at Parkinson's insistence that an "underwater" patch in the middle was acceptable because the rest of the pitch was playable, but it does crystallise the problems that Stanley faced.

On April 4th, the future of the Lancashire Combination once more emerged as an issue when four clubs announced their intention to leave the Combination for the Cheshire

League. The four included Darwen and St Helens Town, two of the division's strongest teams. Only one Lancashire club, Colne Dynamoes, had applied to join the Combination in their place. The exit of Darwen and St Helens Town left Stanley as the only team in the Combination to have won the competition since the formation of the NPL in 1968. With the state of the Crown thwarting Stanley's own upwardly-mobile intentions, the committee resorted to asking the Lancashire FA to ban any further Lancashire clubs from moving to the Cheshire League, and to put pressure on Lancashire clubs to return to the Combination.

It was a fanciful demand that merely underlined the weakness of Stanley's position, and, according to Jimmy Hinksman, it was about to worsen. The status of the amateur – the player who did not receive a match fee – was to be abolished at the end of the season. This meant that any player could be approached and signed on a contract for a guaranteed weekly 'wage', regardless of the arrangement with his current club. In effect, the market for players was to be completely opened up. Hinksman had lobbied the Stanley committee for an increased wage budget in the light of these changes, warning them that half the squad would be offered better terms elsewhere, but he had been rebuffed.

Hinksman thought it unrealistic that Stanley could progress if they insisted on maintaining a team consisting largely of amateurs. The prevailing trend in the competitions to which Stanley aspired, the Cheshire League and the NPL, was for players to be paid a weekly wage on top of their expenses. As the season drew to a close, it became clear that there was to be no repeat of the previous season's heroics. Instead, an inconsistent Stanley were heading for a mid-table finish, their most modest return since reforming.

With no progress in the efforts to return Stanley to Peel Park, and sensing there was not much more that he could do at the club, Hinksman tendered his resignation, which was accepted by the committee. Though the manager had been an increasingly agitated figure during the last few months of the season, his decision to leave Accrington

Stanley still came as a shock to supporters. Hinksman told the press:

"I think I have gone as far as I can go as manager with Stanley. One reason for leaving is the lack of club funds. I wanted to get better players and improve the team, but the future is not very good. If the club does not get the money, the better amateurs will just go elsewhere – money talks wherever you are. Next season they could have only half the players, and I'm not prepared to start all over again, scratching for money to build a team.

"It's not much of an achievement to win the Lancashire Combination now. The standard is going down all the time. I wanted to be going places, and make the side a first class one. But to do that you need good players, and you can't get them for nothing. Until there is a reorganisation in the club, and there is more financial backing, I am afraid that Stanley will be at a standstill. I can see all we worked for just fading away, and Stanley becoming just an average Combination side, and I don't want to be a part of that. What we have done in five years has been great, but I wanted to go further. I wanted to prove to those who doubted when we re-formed that Stanley could go places again."

Hinksman's comments about a reorganisation at the club hint at disharmony behind the scenes which is confirmed by others on the committee and around the club at the time. It seems that the division was a fundamental one about how the club ought to be run. One long-standing committee member recalled:

"Jimmy couldn't get two pennies off the committee. They used to say: 'We haven't enough yet, Jimmy.' He worked for nothing. He just got his telephone bill paid for. And they said: 'How much have we to allow him for his telephone bill?' And there was silence, because they protected the money they had, and then someone suggested three quid! For

someone who was never off the phone! It went up
to £5, and that was all Jimmy ever got here, and he
was out recruiting players, taking trials, all sorts.
Only three of the players got paid, no-one got much
more than a fiver, and the non-contract players got
a bit of petrol money because they used their own
cars to get to matches."

One of the newer members of the committee was
John Alty, who had joined in January 1975 and had been
immediately voted in as club treasurer on the grounds
that he was a chartered accountant. Alty would quit in
frustration at the committee's financial caution a few years
later, so it would not be a surprise if he was one of the
committee members in favour of more investment in the
team, but as a newer member he perhaps did not have the
authority then to push through such decisions.

This certainly was not the case when Alty returned as
chairman in 1981, but the majority view of the committee in
May 1975 was that Accrington Stanley (1968) would not go
the way of her predecessor. As such, the financial policy at
the club remained one of strict prudence. If the committee
voted for a new ground facility, then the money had to be
found first.

Expenditure was balanced carefully against income,
which was always estimated on the conservative side.
Stanley would typically make a small profit on the year,
once fundraising and donations had been included. When
Stanley secretary Jack Barrett announced at the AGM of
August 1973 that:

"I cannot end on a happier note than to tell you that
Accrington Stanley, for the third successive season,
have no debts," he neatly summed up the dominant outlook of the committee.

In some respects, this was entirely the right way to go
about things. Who could argue that the club had to watch
the pennies when annual expenses of over £2,000 were met
by gate receipts of around £1,200? Most of those on the
committee and in the Supporters' Club had been dedicated

Peel Parkers in 1962. They needed no lessons on the need for financial probity.

But there were those on the committee who could see things from the manager's point of view. On a very limited budget, Hinksman had put together a squad easily good enough to play at a higher level and had forged among them a strong sense of loyalty and togetherness. After five years of achievement, was he not entitled to a greater financial commitment from the club, an investment that could see them quickly into a better league with the hope of further advancement to come? There was some force in the argument that the very last thing that Stanley needed was to stagnate in the Lancashire Combination.

These opposing views both had merit and the intentions behind each were entirely honourable, but it was a fundamental divide. Even when Hinksman, having had a short time to consider his position, offered to withdraw his resignation, the committee decided to stick to their original decision. They thought that it was time for a change, and some of them had tired of the constant requests for more money that the club did not have and could not raise. It was an indication of how divisive the issue was that it had eventually alienated the committee from their club manager, a man whose devotion to Accrington Stanley was acknowledged by all.

For Hinksman, his departure from Accrington Stanley was tinged with regret and an undoubted sense of unfinished business, but that ought not to detract from what he achieved. For it is difficult to envisage any other non-league manager embarking on the task in hand with such a combination of energy, know-how, dedication and optimism. He created from nothing a title-winning team, and motivated them to play above themselves and for each other.

Hinksman was also tenaciously competitive and expected the same will-to-win from his players. It was asking a lot, and it speaks volumes that so many of Hinksman's players stuck with him for the full duration, some accumulating more than 200 appearances for the club.

Although prepared to wield the whip privately, Hinksman always defended his players in public against any criticism and was prepared to treat them as individuals. Hinksman reflected later:

"There's an art in managing. You can be one of the lads sometimes, but you have to clamp down whenever the situation calls for it. One lad was a beggar for going out for a drink on Friday night, and I had warned him a couple of times. Anyway he turned up one Saturday and I thought he wasn't fit, but he said he was and I played him. I had to pull him off at half-time, and I suspended him for a fortnight without pay. He was only a young lad, but he had to learn and he didn't do it again. It was the same in training. I was a training instructor, so I knew when someone was going through the motions. I fined and dropped a first-team regular once for missing training without reason. So the players knew that they wouldn't be able to get away with it.

"After Monday training in the gym, I'd go round to each of them and say how they'd played, where I thought they'd gone wrong, and how they could put it right. And I made it clear that I wasn't going to do this behind anyone's back, so that everybody knows where we're going right and where we're going wrong and what we wanted as a team. And I think they understood and respected that. You had to know what each individual would respond to. I'd blast people who you could blast, but others needed an arm round them. Stuart Illingworth needed reassurance, so we'd talk quietly about his form and I'd tell him to get his head up and show the others what he could do, and that worked for him.

"And I'd always back my players against people who were having a go at them, including committee members at times. I remember when we went up to Barrow and beat them in the FA Cup. Mel

Widdup had been booked because he'd committed a professional foul. He'd brought down a player on the edge of the box, just as he was going through on goal. The committee wanted Mel to pay the fine for his booking, and I went berserk at them for that. I had to explain to them that there was a difference between a dirty foul that set out to break a leg and a professional foul. Mel had committed a professional foul, and very important it was, too, because it was 0-0 and if they had scored it would have been a very different game. We went on to win 4-0. But that got me the respect of the players as well."

Inevitably, there were some who found Hinksman's methods not to their taste, but not until the era of John Coleman was Hinksman's five years at the helm surpassed in terms of either longevity or success.

Like Coleman, Hinksman placed the greatest emphasis on team spirit and endeavour, and his Accrington Stanley sides were typified by both. Bryan Pemberton, a member of the first Hinksman squad of 1970, recalled:

"The one thing I do remember about those early days was the spirit of the players, they were there for Accrington Stanley; they played their socks off every game. Other teams were far more established, their players better paid and with better facilities, but it didn't matter. On match days the spirit was tremendous and only a win was satisfactory. This, from a bunch of quasi-amateurs playing against established semi-professionals, was a memory to treasure."

Hinksman proved to be the right man at the right time for Accrington Stanley. He ensured that Stanley's return to the football fold was a matter not merely of subsistence but also of success, and once more gave the town reason to be proud of its football club. You'll still see Jimmy Hinksman every now and again at the Crown, and he's thrilled that his club is back in the Football League. You might remind him, if you see him, that Stanley wouldn't be there without him and his determined team of Accrington lads.

Chapter Four

1975–82
Moving On

IN THE WAKE of Jimmy Hinksman's departure, the committee moved quickly to promote Hinksman's assistant, Don Bramley, to the manager's position. Dave Baron, a senior player at the club, became Bramley's assistant. As Hinksman's deputy, Bramley had become accustomed to playing the pacifier, smoothing over the disputes that occasionally arose between Hinksman and the committee. But the new manager had to forge his own style now, and Bramley had barely settled into his new role when he found the club in the middle of a difficult debate that threatened to change everything.

The first week of July 1975 brought great excitement in the non-league world when the Football League approved the idea of what was then referred to as the 'Football Alliance', today known as the Conference. The principle was the same: one nationwide non-league competition immediately below the Football League, with automatic promotion and relegation between it and the Fourth Division.

The idea, long talked about, would eventually materialise in the 1979–80 season as the Alliance Premier League, and non-league clubs would have to wait a further six years before securing automatic promotion to the Football League. But the agreement of the League to sanction the formation of the Alliance represented a victory of sorts, and most of the credit for this major development for non-league went to a man uncomfortably close to home for Accrington Stanley fans – none other than Great Harwood chairman Derrick Keighley.

Though a minnow in the company of clubs like Boston United, Macclesfield, Wigan Athletic and Altrincham, Great Harwood were managing to survive in the NPL, and Keighley had risen to become the chairman of the NPL itself. Along with Alan Cherry, chairman of the Southern League, Keighley had carefully brokered the deal with the football authorities. The approval of none other than Alan Hardaker, secretary of the Football League, was the culmination of his efforts and represented a real advance for non-league clubs in their fight to secure a meritocratic relationship with Hardaker's organisation.

The week before the decision was announced, Hardaker had spoken at a Great Harwood sportsman's dinner, no doubt a reflection of the friendly relationship that Keighley had cultivated. One cannot help wondering, though, what reception Hardaker would have received at a similar event in Accrington, given he was the individual who had refused to hand Accrington Stanley a lifeline in 1962.

Hardaker's decision to give the go-ahead to Keighley's 'Football Alliance' proposal had immediate repercussions for the new Accrington Stanley. Keighley went to the press with his plans for a merger of Accrington Stanley and Great Harwood under the name Hyndburn Borough FC, excitedly claiming that League football could return to the area within five years. Put somewhat on the spot, Bill Parkinson used his years of council experience to send a solid return serve to Keighley, diplomatically expressing an interest in the idea but emphatic that the name of Accrington Stanley would not be lost to the town again.

Parkinson was right to tread carefully, for this was a delicate issue that opened up all sorts of questions about the area's future identity. Just a few months previously, Accrington and its surrounding towns had merged to become the Borough of Hyndburn, with the various district councils forming the new Hyndburn Borough Council. The merger had been bitterly fought by those who opposed the abolition of the district councils, but now that it had been implemented, what better way could there be to cement the arrangement than to create a single football club for the new borough?

Keighley remained vague with the precise details, but he insisted that the new club should play at the Showground, the home of Great Harwood and a venue into which he had sunk many thousands of pounds. This was another worry for the Stanley committee, because no one could deny that Harwood's facilities were vastly superior to those at the Crown, or that the Showground was the only stadium in the area with the potential to host a Football League club.

To make matters worse, Keighley had clearly done some lobbying beforehand, and had won the support of the mayor, Donald McNeil, and the *Accrington Observer*. When the Stanley committee rejected the idea outright, they were the subject of both criticism and scorn. The local paper wrote:

"The Accrington Stanley committee are living in dreams, and it's time they woke up. That's if they ever want the one dream that matters to come true – to have a team in the Football League. Stanley will never get the support because they'll never progress, and they'll never get top players without money."

It was a harsh statement, but one which at least partly mirrored the analysis of Jimmy Hinksman as he had left the club. As long as Stanley continued to merely break even and survive on subsistence gates, it was difficult to see a future for them beyond local non-league.

Some fans rallied behind the club. One wrote to the *Observer* accusing the council of being consistently anti-Stanley, and an incident in May, just after Hinksman's resignation, certainly seemed to give this impression.

It revolved around the club's doomed attempts to provide a working drainage system for the pitch. With all their own efforts having largely failed, the committee invited the opinion of some experienced professionals. John Prescott remembers their advice well:

"The regular routine was to put 10 tons of sand on the top every Saturday morning. The problem was that there was no proper drainage system, so when it got wet, instead of draining and then drying on top, it just held the water. A lot of people were telling us to roll it to get rid of the footmarks, but that just spread the water. We asked in some turf specialists from Bingley who were well known for dealing with playing surfaces. They basically said: 'Spend £20,000 and it'll still be poor; spend £40,000 and it won't be too bad but it'll take a lot of work to maintain; spend £80,000 and it'll be okay, but ideally find somewhere else to play.' In other words, don't really try to make this a proper footballing surface as it'll never be like that."

If this verdict was right, then the committee reasoned that either Stanley spent some serious money on the pitch or they might as well not bother about it at all. In the light of this, one of the club's staunchest supporters on the council, Wilf Wallwork, appealed to Hyndburn Council's Performance Review committee for substantial financial assistance so that the club could sort out the pitch once and for all.

The committee refused point-blank to consider such a costly scheme, and in what seemed a calculated snub, even turned down Stanley's request for £150 to reseed the pitch.

But though most fans backed the club in its wrangles with the council and in its efforts to stave off the advances of Derrick Keighley, another letter in the local press struck a particularly unsettling note, coming as it did from a disillusioned Crown regular:

"I remember the first league game that Stanley played at the Crown in August 1970. Optimism was overflowing that day, but where is the optimism now? It has been shattered. What does the future hold for Stanley playing on a terrible pitch in a league that deteriorates season by season?"

None of these questions could be dismissed merely as the usual carping from a Stanley grumbler, for all the points were relevant. The Lancashire Combination was a dead-end league. The area's best clubs had undeniably gone to seek broader horizons and better standards elsewhere. And for all the effort invested in the Crown Ground pitch, Stanley still could not provide their team with a decent playing surface.

The background to the 1975–76 campaign was thus one of gloomy reflection and uncertainty. The AGM announced that the club had made a small surplus of £116, lifted into profitability by fundraising efforts that had raised £2,219. The highest gate of the season was put at around 700, the lowest around 200.

At least manager Don Bramley could see cause for optimism, pointing out in his address to the meeting that the average age of the team was just 21, and that in Dave Hargreaves, Glyn Burr and John Hosty the club had three quality youngsters, all of whom were being monitored by Football League scouts. The AGM also saw the end of Bill Parkinson's formal involvement with the club as he announced his retirement from the chair. John Prescott, one of the youngest committee members, whose family owned a baking business, stepped in to become Stanley's fourth chairman in five years.

Bramley's managerial style was somewhat more relaxed than Hinksman's, but he continued his predecessor's policy of attacking football. To this end, Bramley dipped once more into the familiar environs of the Accrington Combination to recruit striker Jack Brydon from Altham. Jack was the son of Ian Brydon, who had served Stanley both as player and manager in the 1950s and 1960s. Bramley also succeeded in persuading goalkeeper Dick Ellis to stay at the club. Ellis had become disillusioned with the set-up at the club, but he was rated as one of the best goalkeepers in Northern non-league and Stanley could ill afford to lose him.

Bramley's Stanley started with two league wins, including a 1-0 defeat of Kirkby, who were bound to be title rivals. But then the season's endeavours were thrown into doubt with four consecutive defeats, including elimination from three cups. First Lytham, hardly a Combination force, denied

Stanley in the Combination Cup with a 2-1 win. The following week, Cheshire League side Hyde United progressed in the FA Cup with a 3-2 win at the Crown, before Midland Premier League side Bridlington Trinity completed a miserable hat-trick for Stanley with a 2-0 win at their east coast home in the FA Trophy first qualifying round.

Stanley did make progress in the Combination's Bridge Shield, and in the league itself proved to be by far the most prolific team. With two attacking wingers supplying Hargreaves and Brydon in the middle, and Alan Davies scoring regularly from midfield, Stanley scored 104 goals in 34 league games, and 128 goals in total. Hargreaves topped the scoring charts again with a club record 55 goals, Brydon notched 35, and Davies managed 14 goals in his attacking midfield role. The form of Brydon led to his selection for the Lancashire FA side, and an approach from Great Harwood that annoyed Bramley, who first heard of it in the papers.

The season also saw the first move made for Dave Hargreaves by Blackburn Rovers, who approached Stanley with a loan proposal. Both Prescott and Bramley thought this unfair, and told Blackburn to either make an offer or leave their man alone.

In spite of Stanley's feats in front of goal, this was ultimately to be a frustrating season. The Combination had now deteriorated to the point where only three teams – Bootle, Kirkby Town and Stanley – could win it, and this small elite would invariably defeat all comers, with the games between them being the decisive clashes. Stanley lost just four league games all season, but with two of them rare home defeats at the hands of also-rans in the shape of Clitheroe and Wren Rovers, the lost points condemned them to the runners-up position.

A shock defeat in the final of the Bridge Shield at the hands of mid-table Nelson meant that the season would be without silverware. Having won the away leg 3-1, Stanley perhaps approached the home leg in an overly casual manner, and found themselves 3-0 down after an hour.

With just two minutes remaining, Hargreaves converted a penalty to level the overall score, but then Dick Ellis mishandled a last-minute free kick and gifted the winner to Nelson, who took the Shield 5-4 on aggregate.

The season also saw the end of all the manoeuvring to merge Stanley with Great Harwood, who were continuing to struggle on in the NPL in front of gates of a few hundred. Despite the Stanley committee remaining solidly against the proposal, Stanley chairman John Prescott agreed to meet the Harwood board and hear them out, if only to put an end to all the rumours. The meeting was held in the first week of October 1975, and Prescott remembers that the offer made by Harwood was more like a takeover than a merger:

"What Derrick Keighley basically offered us was two seats on the board. The team would play at Harwood and he'd hope that the crowds that were going to Stanley would go to Harwood instead. At the meeting, he was trying to put pressure on me by saying, 'You're the chairman, make the decision.' I said, 'I'm the chairman of a committee. If I turn up on Tuesday and say anything wrong I can be sacked like that. I chair by consent, not like you as a shareholder.' We discussed it at Stanley, but no one was interested."

In what was unquestionably the right reading of the situation, Prescott also pointed out that even if the present committee agreed to what Harwood wanted, which they had no intention of doing, there would be another Accrington Stanley the following season playing at the Crown. The diehard Stanley fans would simply set up another club – the ground would be available and the council would let them have it.

There was simply no will on the part of Stanley – either the club or its supporters – to merge with Great Harwood. The commercial logic of the deal was no match for the heritage that it sought to deny. For Stanley fans, it was the very presence of their club that mattered, not its status. Prescott remembers being consoled by John Duckworth during a particularly trying period of his chairmanship a few years later. Duckworth told him:

"John, the only thing that matters is that Accrington Stanley have a team that play football. If it's in the third division of the Combination, if that's the best we can do, then so be it."

For that generation of supporters who had lived through the death of their beloved club and laboured so hard to see a new one born, the thought of throwing their lot in with another town just to climb a couple of leagues was both disloyal and distasteful. Whether in the Football League or in parks football, it was Accrington Stanley or nothing.

Prescott's firm resistance to the Harwood board essentially put an end to the idea, and though the chairman remained diplomatic with his public pronouncements, the same could not be said for Gordon Clark, chairman of Stanley's Development Association. Clark voiced what were obviously the very real perceptions of some Stanley fans that the club was being coerced into a move that it did not want. In a letter to the *Accrington Observer* of October 11th 1975, he charged:

"Once again, Mr Keighley has put forward his scheme for Hyndburn United FC, and once again Hyndburn Council, or should I say the usual members of Hyndburn Council have refused to improve the Crown Ground. Of course, it may only be my imagination but the timing of these pronouncements seems to be becoming more and more coincidental. To the worthy members of Hyndburn Council I say thank you, but the implications contained in your statement that financial support could be more forthcoming to one team representing the whole borough are too distasteful to consider."

In November, Keighley announced (falsely as it turned out) that Great Harwood would start the following 1976–77 season as Hyndburn FC. It would be his last throw of the dice in this particular game; Stanley had no intentions of taking the bait. Club secretary Jack Barrett, newly elected onto the management committee of the Lancashire Combination, announced that Keighley's move was nothing to do with Stanley, who were not interested in moving to a higher league:

"You only have to look at Harwood's position at the moment to see what a better league of football would do for us. At the moment we have a clear balance sheet, but Harwood are in debt, and if that is any indication of a higher standard of football then we don't want to know. It's no good thinking that we might get more support and be better off financially if we move to a higher league. We must have the support before we move up."

As the 1975–76 season drew to a close, Keighley resigned as the chairman of Great Harwood, and though he continued to be a guarantor at the bank, it was the beginning of the end for Harwood's unlikely adventures in the NPL.

Embarking on the second season under Don Bramley, the team started to evolve from being a continuation of the mid-70s side to one more definitely of his own making. Though some of Jimmy Hinksman's key players remained, other familiar faces, such as Mel Widdup and Dave McDowell, moved on, and Bramley introduced some of his own preferences, including Ronnie Haworth and Tony Monks. Stanley continued to profit from the health of the Accrington Combination, with proven performers like Dave Parr, Keith Walkden and Dave Hindle all signed from local amateur sides around this time. Bramley was, however, expected to continue with a largely amateur side; just three first team players, Jack Brydon, Alan Davies and John Hubberstey, were given contracts.

The season was very much a continuation of the previous campaign. Stanley were almost invincible in the Lancashire Combination, but struggled to make an impression on

This mid-1990s photo might suggest a poor Crown Ground surface, but it was a manifest improvement on the Lancashire Combination days. In the background can be seen the Jack Hudson Lounge and the John Duckworth stand, both built in the late 1980s. (Roy Gabryszak)

6th May 2000 – Russell Payne (no. 10) and John Coleman congratulate Jonathan Smith, who has just opened the scoring against Farsley Celtic to send Stanley on their way to a 3-0 victory and the NPL First Division title in front of 2,468 at the Crown. (Roy Gabryszak)

May 2003 – Stanley celebrate their retention of the Unibond Challenge Shield. This team also won the Northern Premier League, gaining promotion to the Conference. Back row from left: Jimmy Bell, John Coleman, Mark Brennan, Paul Mullin, Jamie Speare, Paul Howarth, Steve Hollis, Robbie Williams, Steve Flitcroft, Andy Proctor, David Pierce, Brian Welch, Steve Halford. Front: Andy Gouck, Peter Cavanagh, Jonathan Smith, Lutel James, Russell Payne. Not pictured are Mike Marsh, Simon Carden, Dean Calcutt and Rory Prendergast. (Roy Gabryszak.)

Andy Todd turns in celebration after scoring a last-minute winner against Scarborough, April 17th 2006, two days after the win at Woking had secured promotion to the Football League. (www.kipax.com)

The 2005-06 squad with the Conference trophy at a civic reception in Accrington Town Hall, Sunday 23rd April 2006. On the far left of the front row is player-coach Paul Cook, whose experience was invaluable in the club's transition to a full-time operation. Second right on the front row is Ian Craney, whose performances earned him the Conference Player of the Year award. (www.kipax.com)

John Coleman, just moments after the final whistle at Woking, 15th April 2006.
(www.kipax.com)

Chairman Eric Whalley and granddaughter, Claudia, with the Conference trophy.
www.kipax.com

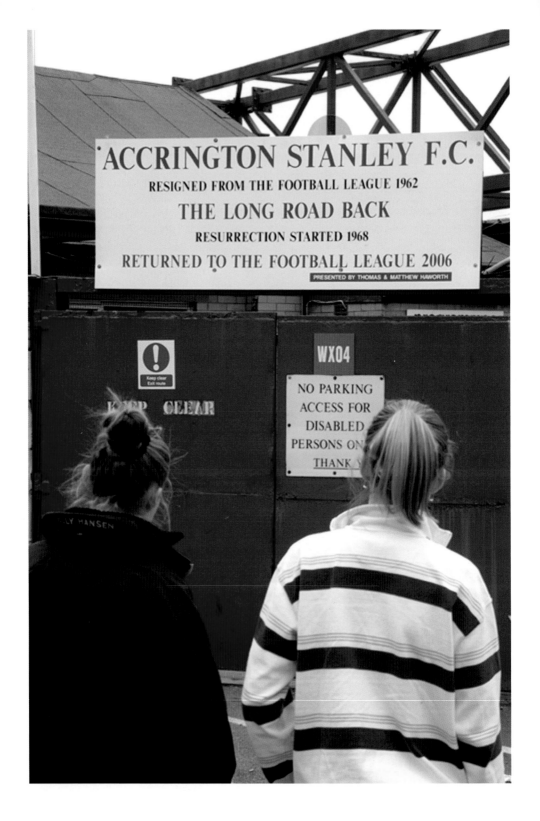

The sign at the Crown says it all. (Garth Dawson)

either of the wider Cup competitions. Whitby Town, a strong Northern League side, eliminated Stanley from the FA Trophy in a replay at the Crown, 4-2. Stanley's interest in the FA Cup was ended disappointingly at the hands of Formby, who came to the Crown and won 3-0 in the second qualifying round. Stanley had beaten Formby when they had clashed in the Lancashire Combination in that memorable opening game in August 1970, but Formby had left the Combination at the end of that season. Their elevation to the Cheshire League had clearly made them a stronger outfit in the intervening years, and it was more grist to the mill of those who thought that Stanley had to get out of the Combination to prosper.

One development off the field was the incorporation of Accrington Stanley as a limited company. Completed in November 1976, this move was largely at the behest of treasurer John Alty, who, as a chartered accountant, had the know-how to make the most of the legal provisions that allowed growth-minded small companies to minimise their costs. But it gave notice to Stanley's committee system. They would soon have to reorganise themselves as a board with a chairman, company secretary and directors. In particular, the role of company secretary was a very different one to that demanded of the committee secretary, and Jack Barrett decided that it was not for him. John Alty combined the duties of treasurer and company secretary, and Jack, along with Bill Parkinson, was given a life vice-presidency for his services to the club.

Stanley did not suffer a Combination defeat until their 29th game of the season, when Wren Rovers defeated them 1-0 at the Crown on April 27th. It ended a run of 44 Combination games unbeaten that went back 15 months to January 25th 1976. The following week, Stanley slipped to another defeat at Bootle, only their second of the season but enough to confine them once more to the also-rans. The two defeats came in the midst of typical fixture congestion that saw the club squeeze 18 games into the last 48 days of the season.

There was at least some consolation in the form of the Combination Cup, for not only did Stanley lift this fine trophy for the fourth time in six years, but they did so the hard way by eliminating both Bootle and Kirkby Town, the only teams to finish above them in the League. Stanley faced Wigan Athletic Reserves in the two-legged final, and were given a jolt when a combative Wigan side took the first leg 2-1. But Stanley fought back three days later in the return at the Crown. Two goals from Dave Hargreaves and one each from the evergreen Alan Davies and defender John Hubberstey secured a 4-1 win, and a 5-3 aggregate victory.

Hargreaves ended the season with 45 goals from 44 appearances. These goalscoring exploits alone were enough to make 'Haggis' a folk hero at the Crown, but in February he further endeared himself to the Stanley faithful by turning down an offer of full-time football from Crewe Alexandra, telling the *Accrington Observer* that "The offer will have to be the right one to make me move from Stanley."

But the season was to see the end for some notable Crown players, such as goalkeeper Dick Ellis and defensive midfielder Dave Baron. Ellis broke his leg in the 2-1 defeat of Bootle on April 20th, and though Mick Finn was signed only as temporary cover for as long as it took Ellis to recover, the big 'keeper left the club without making another appearance, with rumours suggesting that there had been a dispute about money. Finn would eventually agree to sign permanently. As for Dave Baron, he remained at the Crown in his capacity as Bramley's assistant, but his decision to retire was categorical.

As Stanley prepared for 1977–78, another season of Lancashire Combination football, manager Don Bramley was bullish about his expectations:

"I take the view that the Lancashire Combination Championship must be won just as it was in 1973–74 in order to prove what I firmly believe – that

Stanley are the best team in the League. With our present squad we are good enough to win the championship, but there are so many inferior teams in the League that to do so we must aim to drop no more than 8 points in 34 games if we are to have serious hopes of bringing home the trophy."

Bramley's outspoken reference to "so many inferior teams" indicated his frustration with the Combination. In his two seasons in charge, Bramley's Stanley side had lost just four Combination games out of 70, and yet had failed to win the title. With no promotion available, there was nothing to be gained for a hard-fought runners-up position. Little wonder, then, that the intermittent debate about the future of the Combination re-ignited during the close season when the Cheshire League announced that it was forming a second tier, with automatic promotion to their well-regarded First Division.

The Cheshire League First Division did not then offer automatic promotion to the NPL. Instead, clubs applied for consideration when a vacancy arose. By this time, the NPL had grown from its original 20 teams to the maximum 24, but the demands of the league had seen casualties at a fairly regular rate. In the first eight seasons of the NPL, up to and including 1975–76, eleven of its clubs had either left or folded. Not that this was a problem – there were many others waiting and eager to fill the vacancies – but by the late 1970s, there was only one option for a Lancashire club aiming to reach the NPL, and that was the Cheshire League First Division. It was the only feasible route, and with the creation of a Cheshire League Second Division, Stanley could at last see their way to a higher grade of football.

For the Lancashire Combination, however, it was a disaster in waiting. Its secretary, Ken Dean, wrote to the Combination clubs, assuring them that plans were afoot to regenerate the league:

"... as far as today's Lancashire Combination officials are concerned, we shall carry on, sparing no effort to ensure a bright future for Lancashire's premier

County League. Mark my words, the Combination powers-that-be mean business. We are building a League fit for ambitious and go-ahead clubs who won't need to look elsewhere for a competitive and rewarding game of football."

Fighting talk, but it was difficult to see quite how Dean could conjure up this exciting new competition with the materials he had at his disposal. The Stanley board debated the issue at length, for they were divided as to the way ahead. Some board members felt that a move to the Cheshire League was risky and a betrayal of the Combination, a competition that had long provided a home for Accrington Stanley. Those who thought it was time for Stanley to move on argued that the Combination was a comfort zone that failed to challenge the club or the players, and gave no incentive to improve.

The debate continued in the months that followed, and by the time the Cheshire League invited applications for the new Second Division, the board had come to a settled majority view: Accrington Stanley would apply for membership. The club were represented at a meeting in Crewe in late November, where they formally expressed their intention to apply to the new league.

Some individuals in and around the club, including a couple of seminal figures from 1968, argued passionately for Stanley's continuing membership of the Lancashire Combination, but they were in the minority. The most compelling argument to move was based on the intentions of the other teams at Stanley's level. From his discussions with other Combination chairmen, John Prescott was convinced that around eight of the Combination's biggest clubs were set to leave the competition. If this proved to be the case, Stanley would be left in the company of little more than village and park team opposition.

More food for thought arrived in December 1977 with the news that Hyndburn Council were to put the rent for the Crown Ground up to £240 from £25, a huge 860% increase. Councillor Bill Parkinson objected in the strongest terms at the following council meeting, pointing out that the club was struggling to make ends meet as it was. He conceded, though, that the £25 was a nominal sum, and suggested £120 would be a fairer price.

Other councillors were not so charitable to the borough's premier club, arguing that the club had received a pretty good deal down the years. Councillor Winifred Frankland noted that when Accrington Council rented the ground to Lancashire County Council in the mid-1960s, they had received £160 per year.

In spite of Parkinson's entreaties, the club had no option but to swallow the rent hike, which if anything must have strengthened the hand of those arguing that the club had to step up to a higher standard of football. The club confirmed that they were leaving the Lancashire Combination just before Christmas 1977, and the news was greeted with both astonishment and applause. A couple of long-standing fans wrote to the *Accrington Observer* demanding that the club's supporters be given a vote on the matter, and sounded confident that the majority would not be in favour of the move:

"It would seem that the committee of Accrington Stanley FC have no consideration for their faithful supporters. Surely the gentlemanly thing to do is to find out the feelings of REAL supporters and also the feelings of the dedicated lads who provide us with entertainment with which we are completely satisfied. They hint about promotion and a gateway to the Football League. What sort of dreamers are they? We haven't a cat in hell's chance, and anyway, I am sure that most of us are just not interested in the Football League."

Another letter questioned whether the club could say that standards would be higher before it was known which clubs would be applying. Prescott defended the move on the grounds that it was the only way for Stanley to reach the Cheshire League First Division, which was their real aim, and a realistic one. Don Bramley, who fully supported the club's application, pointed out that the standards of the new league could hardly be lower than those of the Lancashire Combination.

As if to prove the manager's point, Stanley were in the middle of yet another campaign in which they routinely trounced half of the teams in their division. In two games just days apart, Stanley put 11 goals past Clitheroe, including a 7-1 victory at Shawbridge. Progress in the wider Cup competitions remained elusive, though. In the FA Cup, Burscough prevailed 1-0 at the Crown after Stanley had forced a 2-2 draw at the Cheshire League club, and for the second consecutive season, a Northern League side knocked them out of the FA Trophy, in this case Durham City, who forced a 0-0 draw at the Crown before defeating Stanley 1-0 in the replay.

By mid-October, there was nothing for Stanley to prove except that they could maintain their league form through the season and clinch the Combination title. By the turn of the year, Stanley had won 14 of their 18 league games and had lost just the one, at Leyland Motors, but a dropped point in the 2-2 draw at Ford Motors on New Year's Eve was enough to knock Stanley from the top of the Combination.

Even the *Accrington Observer*'s Bill Palmer, never one to undersell the Stanley cause, sounded concerned when he wrote, in January 1978:

"What's been most worrying has been the sagging of team spirit with notable exceptions. The Reds must snap out of the doldrums, roll up their sleeves and again turn on the championship style which is their true worth."

Losing the leadership of the Combination hardly constituted a crisis, and on January 14th 1978, nearly 1,000 spectators watched Stanley score twice in the last six minutes to force a thrilling 2-2 draw at Colne Dynamoes, with the point sending Stanley back to the top of the Combination. Though there did appear to be some concerns about form, few supporters would have guessed what was about to transpire. On January 23rd, it was announced that the club had parted company with manager Don Bramley. Both parties were vague as to why Bramley had been sacked. It hardly seemed fair to have based the decision on a minor blip in form, and some suggestions did emerge that there had been differences over the running of the team, particularly the feeling that Bramley had allowed the separation between manager and players to erode excessively.

Bramley himself sounded completely bewildered at the decision, but did indicate that the release of two players, Dick Ellis and Tony Monks, had been the cause of some disquiet in the boardroom, with the directors feeling there had been a lack of communication about the moves.

But as Bramley pointed out to the local press: "Who is more qualified to run and pick the team than the manager?"

One could not help but agree with Bramley's assertion that after seven years' service at the Crown he had been treated poorly by the board.

They had taken the decision to sack Bramley without the manager even being aware that his managership was under serious review, and he claimed never to have been given concrete reasons for the decision. Members of the board went to speak to the players on the day of the announcement, and it seems that some of the players were as mystified as Don Bramley himself, and none too impressed by his treatment.

Within a couple of days, Bramley's assistant and Stanley reserve team manager Dave Baron had been promoted to first team manager. Baron told the press: "Though disappointed at the manner Don finished, the players accept the fact that there is a job to do. The main thing is to pick up morale, and the best tribute we can pay to Don is for us to go on and win the league, a job he has three-quarters completed."

As was usual during the winter months, the state of the Crown pitch meant that Stanley only rarely completed a home fixture, leaving the team with the annual backlog of fixtures that invariably saw them playing at least twice a week through April and May. In the four months between December and March, Stanley played just seven times at the Crown. A fixture that did go ahead, however, was one of the most eagerly awaited for many a year, for Stanley had drawn neighbours Great Harwood in the quarter-finals of the Lancashire Junior Cup.

A large crowd of around 800 gathered at the Showground for the tie, and NPL side Harwood unsurprisingly were the main attacking force in the game. Stanley defended tenaciously but looked to be going out of the competition when Harwood took the lead and held it until late in the game. Then, with no more than a couple of minutes remaining, Stanley's right-back Ian Wilcox popped up in the area to scramble the ball home from close range and earn Stanley a replay. The return was played the following Saturday, March 4th, in front of 770 spectators, easily the largest gate of the season at the Crown. Goals from John Lamb and Alan Davies saw Stanley through to the semi-finals, 2-0.

Not part of the team at this point was Dave Hargreaves. Having scored another 24 goals in the 20 games he played up to early December, making it 141 goals in 132 games for Stanley, Hargreaves was finally made an offer he was unable to refuse when Second Division Blackburn Rovers offered him a month's contract. He decided to try his luck, and departed the Crown with the best wishes of the Stanley faithful. Don Bramley said:

"If he gets down to it and with the sharpening of a month's full-time training, he WILL make it. In my experience, including a spell at Burnley, the only player I saw sharper in the box was Jimmy Greaves. Some supporters will be up in arms, but David has to think of himself."

Blackburn eventually extended Hargreaves' contract till the end of the season and paid Stanley £1,000 for his services, with more due if they signed him permanently. It was the first transfer fee Stanley had received for a player since their rebirth, and the deal also included a friendly between the two clubs to be played at the end of the season.

Although the absence of Hargreaves was bound to be felt, Stanley progressed serenely to the Lancashire Combination title, winning 11 of the remaining 14 games under Dave Baron. Two ex-Stanley forwards, Dave Parr and Ian McCrae, returned to the Crown and played a full role in the second half of the season. Stanley clinched the title with three games to spare and ended some five points clear. For once Dave Hargreaves was not the leading scorer. Jack Brydon, quite a talent in his own right, was the top marksman with 29 goals, with Alan Davies contributing 17.

After two seasons in which the club had frustratingly fallen just short of the title, here at last was some reward for those efforts. The only figure who had cause for some bitterness was Don Bramley.

That Stanley's Combination triumph had been achieved with few changes to the team he put together was of only minor consolation. He could now argue with some conviction, but with little redress, that the board had panicked in the midst of a minor wobble.

For the players, the only lingering regret was the outcome of the Lancashire Junior Cup semi-final. Stanley had gone to NPL side Wigan Athletic and for an hour had outplayed their hosts and built a 3-1 lead, only to go down 4-3 with the home side netting the winner in the dying moments. It was a hugely frustrating end to what had been a highly eventful Cup run.

Those two tussles with Great Harwood gained added significance when, just weeks later, Harwood's owner, Derrick Keighley, finally drew a line under his efforts to make his club solvent. Though occupying a mid-table position in the NPL, Great Harwood had failed to attract the gates to break even, and without any further subsidy, the club withdrew from the NPL at the end of the season and was wound up. Headed in the other direction were Stanley's semi-final conquerors Wigan Athletic, who, twelve months later, were celebrating their election to the Football League.

Though this promised land was still some distance away for Stanley, they would at least leave the Lancashire Combination as reigning champions, for in March it had been confirmed that Accrington Stanley had been accepted as a founder member of the Cheshire League Second Division. Perhaps as a goodwill gesture, Stanley applied for their reserve team to take their Combination place, but this was rejected.

The confirmation of Stanley's move brought concerns from the Stanley faithful that some clubs would be too distant for them to travel. Director Roy Tomlinson assured them through the pages of the *Accrington Observer* that there was little more travelling than before. Of the clubs in the new division, only two were from Cheshire; most were located within the Greater Manchester area, although two – Glossop and Eastwood Hanley – did involve longer-than-usual journeys. Stanley journalist Bill Palmer thought that the club had done the right thing:

"It's an historic move in Accrington's chequered soccer story and, on the principle that, if a club tries to stand still they will only slip backwards, it could prove a profitable one."

From the look of the new Cheshire League second tier, it was clear that Stanley had indeed made a judicious move. Seven other Combination teams, including recent champions Bootle and Kirkby Town, had also transferred their allegiance, and the club's pre-season handbook made no apologies for the decision:

"...the inclusion in the new division of the majority of the Combination's leading clubs shows that progress at the Crown can only come via the Cheshire League. It will be no easy task to win promotion in our debut season. This, however, must be the immediate and principal target, for all our supporters have become accustomed to watching a team that is expected to win and chase hard for honours. There is nothing in football for unsuccessful clubs and our new life in another league must continue to bring its rewards."

On the playing side, there were some changes for 1978–79. Wide midfielder Alan Davies left the club after eight seasons during which he had made over 300 appearances and scored more than 140 goals.

Davies had played in Stanley's first game against Formby in August 1970 and in the intervening years had been a remarkably consistent presence in the team. He was one of Jimmy Hinksman's very best signings for the club. Also on the way out was centre-half Jim Hubberstey, who was forced into semi-retirement with injuries to both knees although Stanley retained his registration.

A significant boost to Stanley's promotion hopes came in September when a familiar figure reappeared. Dave Hargreaves' efforts at Blackburn Rovers had been marred through injury and clashes with management. Despite receiving offers from other Football League clubs, he decided to return to the Crown. Quite simply, 'Haggis' was happiest knocking them in for Stanley, and after recovering from ankle injuries, he made his comeback and was soon back in his familiar, prolific groove. Sadly, manager Baron's hopes of re-establishing the highly effective striking partnership of Hargreaves and Brydon were foiled when the latter was forced to have a knee operation just as the former returned to the club.

Faced with the uncertainties of a new league and some unfamiliar opposition, Stanley struggled to find consistent form in the opening weeks of the season. There was an embarrassing postponement on the August Bank Holiday Monday, Stanley's first home league fixture, when the referee ruled the pitch unplayable after a tractor mowing the pitch on the morning of the game had left ruts in each goalmouth. The Stanley board argued furiously with the referee and were adamant that the problem could soon be rectified, but the infamous Crown Ground pitch would be the subject of more criticism before the season's end. By the last week in February, Stanley had managed to play just seven of their 17 home league fixtures, an average of one a month, though some cup games had been possible in the interim.

Able only to fulfil their away fixtures, Stanley struggled to lift themselves from mid-table, but an unbeaten run of 14 league games between mid-November and mid-April saw the team make a late surge for promotion. This run included six consecutive away games, five of which were won, and two home games played on the adjacent pitch of Accrington Amateurs, both of which were also won. Stanley finally returned to the Crown on April 23rd, with a 3-0 defeat of bottom side Ashton Town, and when, two days later, they travelled to promotion rivals Prescot Town and came away with a hard-fought 1-0 win, Stanley looked set to achieve their goal.

They had five home games remaining, and seven points would have seen them up. It was the least convenient moment to lose form, but hit by injuries caused in part by the unrelenting demands of the fixture backlog, Stanley managed just a solitary win in those remaining home games. They limped home in fifth position, completing their programme on May 17th with a 1-1 stalemate against champions Bootle.

That their ex-Lancashire Combination rivals Bootle had taken the title could have been interpreted as a missed opportunity on Stanley's part. Those who had been concerned about the risks of Cheshire League football had been proved wrong, but neither was there much proof that Stanley had taken a great leap forward in terms of the quality of opposition they faced. Four of the top five clubs were ex-Combination, and of the Manchester clubs, only Curzon Ashton had made an impact.

Had Stanley secured one of the two promotion places, however, there were serious doubts as to whether the Crown pitch would have met the standards required by the First Division. There was little point in gearing up for promotion if the club would not be allowed into the higher tier. The depletion of the squad during the campaign was also a cause for concern. The club had lost Jack Brydon, forced to retire through injury, and other casualties had seen veterans such as John Hubberstey, Alex Smith and the manager himself, Dave Baron, called on to play during the course of the season. Reinforcements were obviously needed.

As the summer of 1979 approached, a team of volunteers once more set to work on the Crown pitch. One of the team, Peter McMillan, owned a mechanical digger, which greatly assisted the effort. The priority for the following season was clearly promotion, but the club needed to ensure that their facilities, including the playing surface, would be enough to satisfy Cheshire League officialdom. Manager Dave Baron also set about his task of building a squad with sufficient depth to cope with a bad crop of injuries.

Baron was helped by the return to the squad of Glyn Burr, who had been absent while completing a college degree in Chester, and Burr brought with him a young defender, Dave Mooney, another graduate of the college, with whom he had played college football. Baron signed Mooney, and also recruited Simon Clarke, a versatile footballer who could operate in both defence and midfield, and another defensive player in Ian Cookson.

The team were handed a tough opener at Middlewich Athletic, relegated the previous season, but Stanley dominated more than the 2-1 scoreline suggests and this set the tone for an excellent start to the season, with Stanley winning seven and drawing two of their opening ten league games. Established in the heart of the promotion race, the Stanley board invited the Cheshire League to inspect the facilities at the Crown. Fortuitously, the pitch was holding up slightly better than in previous seasons. Although the surface continued to retain water and was unfit on occasions, the club was able to host games at the Crown throughout the year.

In February, the Cheshire League president and a team of officials visited the Crown. Chairman John Prescott indicated to the press that a number of improvements had been demanded, but that none was insurmountable.

Nevertheless, the club appealed for help from their supporters to allow them to meet the ground improvements required – indeed, the very foundations of the club had been built on such a tradition of volunteerism. Two supporters who helped out at this time were George Duffy and Rod Kenyon, and they recalled:

> "There was a good backbone of helpers and volunteers there. And if someone dropped out of doing something, there would always be someone available who would be willing to step in and help out. You only had to go round the ground on a match day and say, 'Can you spare half an hour next week? We're doing a bit of painting' – and they would always agree to help."

With work at the Crown ongoing, the team's exploits in the various cup competitions meant yet another heavy end-of-season schedule, with the team playing ten games in April, seven of which were away from home.

The league had developed into a five-way battle for the two promotion places. A 2-0 home victory over Kirkby on April 4th represented ground gained, but injuries to key players again impacted on the team as the season approached its denouement.

Defeats at Eastwood Hanley (4-0) on April 7th and Congleton Town (1-0) on April 26th followed, but much more worrying was the 2-1 home defeat on May 5th at the hands of promotion rivals Prescot Town. Stanley could then only manage a goalless draw at Ford Motors before a vital 3-1 win at New Brighton on May 14th, where Stanley had trailed 1-0 at half-time but, facing disaster, had stormed back to win with goals from Ian Cookson, Mick Clark and Dave Hargreaves. The win, coupled with a defeat for Kirkby at Congleton, finally hoisted Stanley into the second promotion spot.

Kirkby needed to win by a five-goal margin in their final game to overhaul Stanley, but they could only manage a 2-1 result. The new Accrington Stanley had won its first promotion by the margin of four goals. It had been a desperately hard-fought battle, with yet another ridiculously congested run-in, but this time the players had seen off the challenge with a commendable display of spirit and determination.

The final action of the season was a one-off game on May 22nd at the home of the champions Prescot Town for the Second Division Challenge Shield. Due to the game being announced at short notice, Stanley were without four first-team regulars, and even manager Dave Baron could not make it. In a display that underlined the togetherness of the team, they defied Prescot pressure and eight minutes from time, Ian Warburton hit the winner to end the season with the unexpected bonus of a pot for the trophy cabinet. With a celebration dinner arranged for the middle of June, there was just one last hurdle to negotiate, and that was the ground inspection to confirm Stanley's promotion. It took place on June 9th. Chairman John Prescott takes up the story:

"There was no grading system in those days, so the president of the Cheshire League, a bloke called Eric Hinchcliffe, used to visit us and he'd say, 'You need to get this done, John, and you need to tidy that up,' and so on, but there was nothing ever put in writing. He came over half-a-dozen times and each time he'd point out different things and as a result there was a lot of work put in towards the end of that season and the close season to get the ground sorted as best we could.

"On June 9th they arrived, seven of them, and unfortunately there were about 30 people there as it was put in the press that they were coming. So they walked round the ground with me and then went back in the boardroom, asked me to wait outside and then asked me back in. They said: 'We're sorry, but we've decided by five votes to two that your ground isn't good enough to get into the First Division.' They then started to walk towards me to leave the ground and I said: 'I wouldn't go that way because there's 30 fans in there and if they find out you've turned us down, I'm not guaranteeing your safety.'

"We were all furious, the people who'd worked so hard on the ground, and it was so unfair the way they did it. We appealed against it and we went to an extremely opulent hotel for the hearing. There were ten people there from the FA along with Hinchcliffe. Hinchcliffe then levelled two charges at us, the two reasons why they'd rejected us: one was that the dressing rooms were too small and the other was that the pitch wasn't level – but he'd never mentioned the dressing rooms, so I immediately raised this point in front of the FA officials. I said to Hinchcliffe: 'You've never mentioned the dressing rooms once, never at any stage!' He claimed that he had, so I said, 'Don't call me a liar. You have never mentioned any problem with the dressing rooms at any time. And just answer me this. If the dressing rooms are big enough for the Second Division, why aren't they big enough for the First? Are we to have bigger players in the First Division?'

"It was a nonsense. The dressing rooms were small, but they had accepted us in the league so where was the problem? And about the pitch not being level, I said to him: 'What about Horwich RMI? It's on a hillside!' He defended Horwich because it was a 'level slope', in other words their pitch sloped evenly whereas ours was undulating, but again it didn't make sense.

"To be fair to the FA, they listened to what we had to say and then we were asked to leave. Hinchcliffe was in for half an hour and I think they told him in no uncertain terms that what had happened was unacceptable. The main problem was that there was no established procedure. He just assessed the grounds himself with the backing of the management committee. After our case, a grading system was introduced.

"I think another problem was that Bootle had been promoted the season before us and their ground was very heavily criticised by other teams, and the Cheshire League obviously thought that our ground was worse than Bootle's. With the benefit of hindsight it was a correct decision in that we would have been the worst ground in the First Division, but it sickened people when we were denied promotion. The way it was done was nasty."

Whilst the chairman and the board of directors could justifiably point with some anger to the lack of formal, codified arrangements for grading that had seen them fall short of requirements, the decision did indicate that the club could no longer ignore the more fundamental questions about the facilities at the Crown. Treasurer and company secretary John Alty had departed the club during the course of the season when his plan to borrow money from a brewery to develop the increasingly ramshackle clubhouse was turned down by a board still determined to avoid debt. Alty recalled:

"I made it clear that I wanted to borrow money and develop the ground. Mel Clay joined the board, and he was in the licensing trade as the manager of Wilson's Brewery, and he offered to lend us a few thousand pounds to do the clubhouse up, which was filthy and in a disgraceful state, really, nowhere to sell pies, no bar. But the rest of the board were reluctant to sign the documents and borrow money, they just didn't want to go down that road. So out of frustration I quit and left the club."

Prescott now faced a difficult decision. To discover that the ground was substandard was depressing news in its own right, but to have a hard-won promotion denied because of it was utterly demoralising to both fans and players. But there was hope.

The squad was a tight-knit group, and though disappointed and angry, the players stoically accepted the situation and set about preparing for the new season. There were at least no doubts about whether the squad was good enough. They had already won promotion once, and now the players had an added incentive to repeat the trick, if only to emphasise to the authorities that Stanley would not be denied what was rightfully theirs.

As if to hold to his side of an implicit bargain, John Prescott made the finance available for the club to meet the demands of the Cheshire League. Plans were drawn up to extend the dressing rooms, refurbish the clubhouse, and launch the biggest project yet on the playing surface at the Crown. In total, the redevelopment would cost over £10,000, a lot of money in those days, and this financial burden was borne mainly by the board and especially by the chairman. It was a significant investment in the future of Accrington Stanley.

And what might that future hold? The season just gone had seen the inauguration of the Alliance Premier League, the much-vaunted national division for the country's very best non-league sides. Altrincham had won the first Alliance Premier title to cement their reputation as the very best outfit outside the Football League, a team good enough to have taken Spurs and Everton to FA Cup replays in recent years. The next development seemed obvious – to promote the best non-league club to the Football League. It would not happen right away, but when, the following year, having won the Alliance Premier again, Altrincham were denied election to the Football League by a single vote, the media outcry in favour of the dynamic Cheshire club brought the prospects of automatic promotion to the Football League ever closer.

For Accrington Stanley, such opportunities would be an irrelevance for some time, but as the 1980–81 season began, some of the groundwork for a higher standard of football in the future started to be put down.

The clubhouse was in quite a state, which completely negated the chances of generating any income from match days. Former Stanley goalkeeper Derek Morris, by now an employee of the PermaSeal company, was brought in to fix the leaking roof. As someone around the club in the early 1970s, Morris might have remembered Dick Briggs taking some of the roof timber to build the wooden 'scratting' shed, but there had been consequences to old Dick's inventive use of the pavilion's resources. Directors Jack Tansey and Mel Clay were behind moves to sort the clubhouse out. Jack Tansey remembers:

"Mel asked me down to the club. He said, 'Come and have a look at this, see what you think.' We went into the clubhouse, and I've never seen anything like it. The rain had been coming through the roof and had brought the ceiling down. The ceiling was lying on the floor, which was wet through. So Derek Morris temporarily fixed the roof to prevent any more water coming in, then because they'd no money and we had a lot of material that was left over after finishing jobs, we re-fixed the hangers on the roof, reboarded it and plastered the ceiling up in the main room and the kitchen.

"Mel had a trestle table which he set up opposite where the bar is now, put the barrels under it – and that was the bar! And I went down to a second-hand shop and bought a fish fryer, about the size of a washing machine, and we put it in the kitchen and got another bloke who was a chef in the Accrington Victoria hospital at the time, Geoff Walmsley, and he came in and did some chips and beefburgers. So we got a kitchen going, whereas there was nothing before. We actually had a turnover and it was a start. People would start to come in before the game and have a pint and something to eat, and we might take £100 in total from the food and drink, so it was a start in generating some money at the game itself."

The first half of the season saw Stanley continue the promotion form of the previous year, but in order that work on the Crown be completed in time, the board made the decision to shut the ground altogether. A 3-0 defeat of Warrington Town on December 6th, a win that kept Stanley at the head of the table, was the last time that season that the team would turn out at the Crown until the end of March.

Between that time, Stanley played nine consecutive away league fixtures, and played all their cup-ties away from home, which included a 1-0 win at NPL side Morecambe in the Lancashire Junior Cup. It was not the ideal way of maintaining a promotion challenge, and the constant trips to unfamiliar grounds did have an effect as Stanley slid to unexpected defeats at places like Atherton Collieries and Skelmersdale. The team was also hindered by the absence of Dave Hargreaves, who underwent a knee operation. Another defeat on March 28th, this time at promotion rivals Glossop, saw the club slip to eighth in the table, but Stanley had games in hand.

Serious work on the pitch was about to begin, but Stanley had time to squeeze in six home league fixtures in three weeks before resuming their nomadic ways, winning four of them and drawing one. The drawn game, a 0-0 stalemate against Middlewich on April 14th, saw the return to action of Dave Hargreaves. It was a timely boost to a squad suffering from its usual spate of wear-and-tear injuries.

Stanley played their last game at the Crown on April 20th, a disappointing 3-1 reverse at the hands of Rhyl, who were themselves in contention for promotion. As the diggers moved in, the team arranged to play their final five home fixtures elsewhere. Darwen generously lent Stanley their ground for the fixtures at home to Irlam and Leyland Motors, while the final three games saw a return to the Accrington Amateurs' pitch, overlooking the Crown.

Having gone through a similar experience the year before, the players were ready for the demands of the run-in, and, having missed half of the season, Hargreaves was fresh and itching to resume his exploits in front of goal. However, Irlam shocked Stanley by scoring the only goal in the game played on Saturday May 2nd, and two days later in an evening kick-off against Leyland Motors, Stanley went in at half-time lucky to be level at 1-1, having been outplayed by their fellow promotion hopefuls. These were tense moments for everyone involved at the club, but particularly for John Prescott and his team of directors, having put in so much money to ensure promotion.

Manager Dave Baron rallied his troops and sent Stanley out in an aggressive mood, and just ten minutes into the second half, Dave Parr cut through the Leyland defence from the right and delivered a perfect centre for Hargreaves to head home for a textbook goal.

From that moment on, urged forward by hundreds of fans who had made the journey to Darwen, Stanley delivered a tour de force of attacking football which they maintained until the season's end. Hargreaves completed his hat-trick, and further goals from John Blackburn and Dave Parr earned a 5-1 win and a rapturous ovation at the end. The result sent Stanley to the top of the Cheshire League Second Division, a position that they would not relinquish.

Three days later, Skelmersdale were crushed 5-1 on Accrington Amateurs' ground, and on the evening of Monday May 11th, promotion was clinched with a 5-0 demolition of Salford. This game was the occasion of Dave Hargreaves' celebrated goal from the halfway line. It happened on the resumption of the second half, and was clearly preconceived, for Stanley were kicking with the wind behind them. Receiving the obligatory tap-back from Dave Parr, 'Haggis' sent his lofted shot over the entire Salford team.

It was such a well-measured effort that the ball crept in just under the bar, evading even the lunge of the back-peddalling Salford 'keeper, who could see perfectly well what Haggis intended. Had this been done at the highest levels of the game (as indeed, David Beckham did years later at Selhurst Park for Manchester United), it would have been heralded as a moment of footballing genius, so I see no reason why Haggis's effort shouldn't be included in such exalted company, for it was widely acknowledged that Hargreaves could have plied his trade at a much higher level. He just preferred life at Stanley.

The defeat of Salford sealed promotion, but Stanley had set their sights on the title, and for this they had to defeat Maghull in their final home game, played on May 14th. It was no contest – indeed, that Haggis goal reflected the supreme confidence that now ran through the squad. Stanley defeated Maghull 3-0 with the minimum of fuss to take the Cheshire League Second Division title. The season was finally completed on May 22nd when Stanley retained the Second Division Challenge Shield with a 1-0 defeat of Glossop at the ground of Rossendale United. The team were also presented with the Second Division trophy after the game.

Once again, Stanley had to await the decision of the Cheshire League's ground inspectors. After the fiasco last time, the authorities had introduced a formal system of grading, and Stanley had received specific feedback about which aspects of the Crown remained problematic. By now, the ground improvements were nearing completion. The dressing room extension had been finished at a cost of £1,500, and the roof above the small seating section at the front of the pavilion was extended and improved. To address concerns about security, another £1,000 had been invested in a concrete fence to enclose the ground.

The saga of the fence illustrates how much of a collective effort it had been to upgrade the Crown. It was a bargain at the price, but part of the deal was that it had to be dismantled from its current location at Whitworth Cricket Club and transported to the Crown. A small army of volunteers began the back-breaking work, and a lorry was commandeered from a business connection. The secretary of the new Supporters' Club, Rod Kenyon, remembers the task well:

"One of our members, Dave Stanley, called and said, 'There's a fence going at Rochdale, and we can have it provided we can dismantle it, get a lorry there to pick it up.' A friend of ours had a wagon, so we drove it there; there must have been around ten of us. The fence consisted of slot-in concrete sheets and posts. So we started loading the wagon up, but we had no idea about weight. By the time we'd got three-quarters of the way home over the tops, the clutch had gone! By some miracle we got the lorry back to the Crown, but we had to have a whip round to pay for a new clutch for the wagon, and it took a few journeys to get the whole thing across. It was very hard work, but as long as there were enough of you as a team, it was do-able."

Mark Turner, then a schoolboy who edited Stanley's programme but who would soon graduate to become club secretary, remembers that the fence was an important step in improving the whole appearance of the ground:

"There was a lot of land around three sides of the ground, and it was mostly unkempt scrubland. So the idea was to condense what we had to maintain, and it did look a lot tidier. One of the main criticisms of the Cheshire League when they wouldn't let us go up was the lack of security on the ground. They didn't like the fact that it was very open. The fence was useful as it was a means of keeping the club private. With the fence up, there were only two points of access, which was a big improvement."

When the Cheshire League officials visited the Crown at the beginning of June, the contractors hired to re-drain, rotovate and level the pitch had been unable to reseed the surface because of the wet Lancashire weather, but it was obvious that an enormous effort had been made to meet the league's demands. After meeting with the contractors and receiving assurances about the pitch, the officials gave the Crown Ground the official nod of approval. Accrington Stanley's promotion to the Cheshire League First Division was confirmed. It was a cause for celebration, but for chairman John Prescott, the feeling was just one of immense relief. He told the local press:

> "The mood was very tense on the day and to say that we were relieved when they gave their decision would be a vast understatement. It had been a weight on our shoulders because no matter what work we had put in, the final decision was always up to the league officials. This is the first step in a very long road back to Football League status…but it will take a lot of money to reach that standard again. All we can do in the meantime is to provide the best standard of football for the people of Accrington."

For Prescott, the investment he had overseen had been vindicated, as had the board's decision to move the club into the Cheshire League, but the pressure of trying to hoist the club upwards on a small budget was not about to relent. Although the pitch looked a lot better, the contractors had advised that ideally the surface be left for a whole year to settle, but that simply was not possible. Instead, Stanley asked for permission to rearrange their first batch of home games away from the Crown.

This would mean a lack of cash flow in the early part of the season, and so the club announced a set of initiatives designed to increase income in general, with the launch of a new lottery and a £25 loan scheme, as well as the appointment of a commercial manager, Alan Harker. The Supporters' Club, too, came up with a variety of schemes to raise cash.

As manager Dave Baron announced the retention of his squad and an increase in the number of contracted players from three to five, it seemed plausible to trust that Stanley's calculated gamble had paid off. But for those who believed in premonition, the first sign of impending trouble came in July when a fire gutted the canteen area of the pavilion. Although it meant more expense, the area was rebuilt with steel and concrete, beginning the much-needed process of replacing the old wooden structure, but it was just the first in a series of misfortunes that would bedevil the club during its first season in the top tier of the Cheshire League.

Stanley began the 1981–82 campaign with an unbeaten run of five away games in August, and the first fixture back at the Crown was quite an occasion with the visit of NPL side South Liverpool for an FA Cup preliminary tie. Goals from Dave Hargreaves and John Blackburn saw Stanley through to the first qualifying round in front of a healthy crowd, quite a few of whom were no doubt drawn by curiosity to the new-look Crown. As well as the improvements to the pitch, the whole ground itself looked a lot neater and tidier, and there was no mistaking the positive impression that the ground made on the supporters.

The midweek fixture that followed, a 2-2 draw with Horwich, attracted more than 700 spectators, this in spite of competition from an England World Cup qualifier on TV (no less than the infamous 2-1 defeat in Norway that prompted a delirious commentator to hit the rhetorical heights with "Maggie Thatcher, your boys took one hell of a beating!").

Unfortunately, the optimistic air around the club was soon to dissipate. In the FA Cup first qualifying round, Stanley drew Chorley. After two 0-0 draws, Stanley won the toss for the right to stage the third replay, but the pitch then failed to deal with the first heavy rainfall of the autumn. After two postponements because of the water-logged surface, Stanley reluctantly agreed to switch the tie to Chorley where they were convincingly beaten 4-0.

It was incredible to think that all the time and money spent on the pitch – installing a new central drain and more than twenty smaller herringbone drains – had failed to improve the drainage of rainwater from the playing surface. It was a deeply depressing outcome. There was nothing for it but for the club to again rearrange fixtures away from the Crown and call the contractors back in to investigate why the project had failed.

With the prospect of playing regular home games unlikely, the board announced that all five contracted players were being released. From earning some £12 a week, they were being asked to play for expenses only, and those players on expenses were asked if they could trim their costs too. Accrington Stanley's finances, stretched to meet the demands of the higher league, had become a matter of crisis. John Prescott remembers the time well:

"The lottery hadn't taken off and we'd no money. We were in October and we'd had just four home games all season and were down to having a fortnight's wages left and nothing else, it was that bad.

"One of the things that had happened was that I had proposed in a board meeting that each director should put £10 a week into the club, because the manager wanted to increase the players' wages. There were ten people present and the proposal was passed ten votes to nil. Within the week, six directors had resigned. To me it was so silly. They should have just said at the meeting, 'Sorry, I can't afford that'. One director did apologise afterwards, and he actually stayed on the board, but he'd been serving on the committee since 1970 and I wasn't going to force him off because he couldn't afford £10 a week. In those days, it was quite a lot of money. I suppose they might have felt that their hand had been forced, but they had all voted for it."

With a depleted board and faced with the prospect of losing their best players, who were now all free agents, the Supporters' Club intervened and offered to pay the players' wages. George Duffy recalled:

"It came to a point when it looked like the club was going to fold again. So we said the Supporters' Club would try and pay the wages, but we needed to know the bottom line. So we brought the players into this little room we had in the Crown Inn, one by one, and said 'You're on so much, but what will you play for? We're desperate for money.' And the players did understand where we were as a club, that the backroom staff were doing all they could to get the games on. Most of the players were on about £5 expenses and they agreed to drop it to £3. They were all prepared to play for less. But one or two of the players went back to the club and said that they didn't want the supporters putting their hands in their pockets, it wasn't the right way to run things to put that onus on the supporters. We used to pay to go on the ground and worked in our spare time for the club, so it wasn't right that we'd pay the wages as well! But the club was completely strapped for cash."

Though it was an ethical decision, the board's rejection of the supporters' offer made for some poor publicity, and did nothing to suggest that a solution to the financial crisis was in sight. Stanley quite simply needed a new source of investment, but where was it to come from? Things looked bleak, but events have a strange way of working out sometimes, proceeding not by reason or fair assumption, but by irony and unintended consequence. In a fine example of the latter, it was the cynical opportunism of one club that led to the return of someone who did have the resources and the willingness to see Stanley through their crisis: John Alty.

The news that Stanley's most admired players were free agents quickly travelled through the northern non-league network, and a few of the bigger outfits were soon circling, vulture-like, around the squad. One such club was Stalybridge Celtic, where ex-Stanley director Alty was treasurer. Stalybridge manager, Peter O'Brien, was a keen admirer of Dave Hargreaves, and in a calculated move, the club made offers for both Hargreaves and goalkeeper Mick Finn. They invited both players to Stalybridge's game at Prescot Cables with the intention of negotiating deals. In the event, only Finn turned up, but in the Prescot boardroom,

John Alty overheard a senior Stalybridge director boasting that Finn was, "the sprat to catch the mackerel".

This was an unwise thing to say, for Alty and Finn remained close from their time together at Stanley. Alty remembered:

"I was furious at that comment; I thought it was scandalous, so I stayed in the clubhouse with Mick as the game started. Mick then poured his heart out about the situation at Stanley and ended up by saying, 'I don't want to come to Stalybridge Celtic. Why don't you come back to Stanley?'

"I told Mick that I'd only come back if I was chairman. I wanted a major say. Well, Mick obviously went back to Accrington with this, and I made a phone call to Gerry King, who was on the board. He invited me to a meeting on the Sunday at the Crown pub. I said my piece at the meeting, and the board then had a discussion amongst themselves. A while later, Gerry came out and said: 'We've voted you in as chairman.'"

John Prescott remained on the board, but it was the end of his chairmanship – and he was glad that his time at the helm had finally come to an end:

"I was the last of the working chairmen. I was young, I wasn't an ideal chairman, I might have been one of the best candidates around at the time, but that's still doesn't mean that I was much good. I did my best and I enjoyed doing it, but I was very glad when John came back. The standard of playing that we'd established was gradually going down, and that was probably because standards elsewhere and around us were going up. The club was stagnating. It was difficult to know what to do. The number of people involved was declining, and there just wasn't the know-how there that we needed at that time. If one of the committee had come along and sold some advertising space around the pitch, you know, 100 boards at £50 each would have made a difference, but there was no one around with that kind of ability. John and Eric were more experienced businessmen who've used their financial know-how. But I've no regrets, and I still enjoy going on."

John Prescott's modesty doesn't do justice to what he did at the Crown. He was not the most gregarious of chairmen, but fellow board members at the time recall that his instinct was to find consensus and avoid conflict where it was possible to do so, undoubtedly the best thing for Stanley at the time. More people on the board meant more resources and expertise coming into the club, but it required a certain type of chairman to keep it together.

Aspects of Prescott's chairmanship were controversial, such as the sacking of Don Bramley, but he called it right when he led the club into the Cheshire League, and the significance of the ground investment cannot be over-estimated. They were the first concrete moves towards what had long been merely talked about – to return Stanley to the Football League. They were the first board to take a calculated risk towards fulfilling that dream.

The near-fatal reaction to Prescott's suggestion that the board put more money into the club was a clear indication that Stanley now required investment of a greater magnitude, and John Alty's return to the club could not have come at a more opportune moment. But all the same, Prescott had steered the club out of the cul-de-sac of the Lancashire Combination and into a decent level of non-league football in the Cheshire League First Division that provided an opportunity for further progress.

But that opportunity would not come about without more investment, and John Alty would very quickly find this out. The new chairman barely had time to order a celebratory pint that Sunday afternoon before he received a tap on the shoulder from Dave Baron. The Stanley manager gave his new chairman the unwelcome news that the Crown pitch simply was not fit for football. If you want the club to progress, said Baron, then you'll have to sort it out.

Alty had the opportunity to see for himself when the club played a rare home fixture on October 17th, the day after his return to the club as chairman was announced to the press. Stanley went down to a 2-1 defeat in the mud at the hands of Formby, and the surface was so bad that the team would not return to the Crown until the New Year.

John Alty immediately stabilised the club's finances, paying off an overdraft of around £3,000 and bringing players' wages up to date. The team, forced to play games away from the Crown, were battling mightily to maintain their mid-table position. An injury to Dave Hargreaves saw a less prolific Stanley, but they eked out points from tough fixtures at Chorley and Horwich, and scored vital victories at struggling clubs like Droylsden, Ashton United and Curzon Ashton. A superb Dave Parr hat-trick had also seen Stanley take both points at Formby, 3-2, having entered the closing stages 2-1 down.

Having seen all their December fixtures fall to the weather, Stanley finally made a return to the Crown on January 16th 1982, but could only manage a 0-0 draw with Leek Town. Of more concern was the crowd of barely 250, though having not been able to see their team in Accrington for three months, it perhaps was not surprising that a few Crown 'regulars' had fallen out of the habit. A better crowd turned up for the Lancashire Junior Cup replay against NPL side Netherfield three days later, and they saw a sumptuous second-half display from Stanley as they routed the Cumbrians, 5-0.

Chairman Alty had been busy in the meantime. Determined to resolve the pitch problem once and for all, he called on the expertise of Ian Brooks, who ran a local gardening and landscape firm. Brooks had helped with the previous attempt at a drainage system, but now Alty asked him to set out a more comprehensive plan. Brooks went back to Alty with a scheme to excavate some of the clay and slope the rest, re-installing the drains and using gravel and stone to further assist the drainage process. In the circumstances, it was as much as Stanley could hope to do, but it was not a cheap option. Even though put together at cost price, the quote from Brooks was around £20,000.

Alty decided to go ahead with the scheme at the end of January. For the second season running, the Crown Ground was closed as the diggers moved in. The closure also gave the opportunity for further ground development. Two of the Stanley faithful, Stan Spencer and Arthur McGilveray, worked at Huncoat power station on the outskirts of the town, which was in the process of closing down. The two salvaged a lot of steel from the site which was otherwise heading for the scrapheap, and more useful bits of hardware were recovered from Blackburn's dog track, which was being demolished to make way for a supermarket.

But for the Stanley faithful, it was yet more disruption to their simple wish to watch their team on a regular basis. At least the majority of the 16 'home' games were played nearby at the Showground. The old Great Harwood FC had been wound up, but a new club, Great Harwood Town FC, now played there in the Lancashire Combination. A game apiece was played at the homes of Darwen and Leyland Motors. For the fixtures against the Tameside clubs, Alty used his connections at Stalybridge to secure their Bowerfold ground, where Stanley played five times. The reasoning was sound. Stanley's faithful 100 or so would travel anywhere, and the hope was to attract 100 to 150 floaters plus 150 or so from the opposition, whose fans would travel to Stalybridge but who would not have travelled to Accrington. It worked, with gates for the Stalybridge games between 300 and 350.

In the programme for the game against Hyde United, played at Stalybridge on February 17th 1982, John Alty's column gave an impression of the activity at the Crown during this period:

"The state of the Crown and the unavailability of the local grounds have forced us to transfer our home games a distance of some 30 miles from our base. We are anxious to dig up our pitch next month and have the work completed by the end of the season. In the circumstances, we have had no alternative but to effectively close our ground. I apologise to all our supporters and in particular to our season ticket holders who will have had extremely poor value for money this season. In an attempt to compensate our season ticket holders, I'm happy to announce that they will be entitled to a free coach to Barrow on 6th March when we play our Lancashire Junior Cup tie. Work on the ground has gathered momentum with Stan Spencer, Sam Adams, Arthur McGilveray and other loyal supporters having done a tremendous job on terracing and stand renovating. Work is continuing, and with the application for re-grading due to be considered by the NPL grading committee next month, any volunteers for weekend work should contact Stan Spencer. We have just applied for a licence and I am sure all of you will agree that the interior of the clubhouse is unrecognisable from the days prior to the renovation. Brewery negotiations are in process."

But it was too much to expect that the team's performances would not suffer. Form was inconsistent at best, and manager Dave Baron resorted to tactical changes, such as playing Dave Hargreaves as an attacking midfielder, and drafting in youngsters from Stanley's successful reserve team, Altham, managed by former Stanley regular Ian Wilcox, as a means to pep up the team. At one point, Stanley went six league games without scoring.

A welcome respite came with a Lancashire Junior Cup semi-final at Barrow, but despite a much-improved performance the team ended up well beaten, 3-0. For John Alty, it was time for a change. He was not happy with the performances of the team, and manager Dave Baron was finding it increasingly difficult to combine the demands of the job with his professional career. Alty knew exactly who he wanted to take over, and he persuaded goalkeeper Mick Finn to take the job on a player-manager basis.

For Dave Baron, it was the end of a long association with the club. He had been an apprentice at Peel Park and was only denied his first team debut by the resignation of the club from the Football League. He had returned to the Crown in 1970, and had graduated from player to reserve team manager and assistant manager before taking charge in January 1978.

As manager, he had won two league titles and, of course, the promotion that never was. It was an excellent record, but four years was a fair term of service in non-league, and, at the time, Baron's resignation appeared nothing more than the usual shift in personnel that had seen Hinksman and Bramley move on before him.

In retrospect, Baron's departure was the end of a line. Hinksman, Bramley and Baron had been of a type – from the town, ex-Stanley players whose commitment to the club was reflected in the longevity of their service. All had played and managed over a number of years and had been central figures within Accrington football, with a good knowledge of the local leagues and the players within them. Stanley would never again return to that pattern of service, and not until the arrival of John Coleman in 1999 would the club find a manager who would serve as long as any of the triumvirate who had seen the club through its first twelve years of existence.

Mick Finn took charge for the game against Nantwich Town on March 23rd 1982, one of the 'home' fixtures played at Stalybridge, but Stanley were poor, going down to a 4-0 defeat that had the faithful seriously worried about the possibility of relegation; however four wins in the last nine games saw Stanley safe with some room to spare.

It had been a season of real upheaval, but there was one more change for Stanley fans to adjust to, and that was yet another switch of competition. This time, rather than being at the behest of the board, the move was part of a much-needed consolidation of north-west non-league football.

The Lancashire Combination and the two divisions of the Cheshire League were merged into a new three-tier structure called the North West Counties (NWC) League. Stanley would inevitably be somewhere in the new set-up, but for John Alty, it was of the utmost importance that Stanley were in the top division. Though the NPL still remained a closed shop without automatic promotion or relegation, the teams at the head of the NWC First Division were in pole position to replace any clubs resigning from the NPL – and vacancies were still a regular occurrence. In May 1982, Chorley and Hyde United were both celebrating successful applications to the NPL after the resignation of three clubs. They were the last to graduate from the Cheshire League.

Mark Turner, by now Stanley secretary (and the youngest football secretary in the country), was part of the club's negotiating team, and he recalled:

"One thing we fought long and hard for was that each club's rating was at least partly based on the previous two years' performances. That was vital, because we got an extra five points in the rating system due to having been champions of the old Cheshire League Second Division. Some clubs were arguing that the rating should have been done mainly on facilities – things like seating capacity and floodlights – not the playing record, and to put all the 'grade A' grounds in the First Division. It was all up for grabs."

In the end, Stanley made the NWC First Division comfortably, but the club was right to fight its case, for when the divisional memberships were announced, it was clear that a drop to NWC Division Two would have put Stanley back in the company of many old Lancashire Combination adversaries.

As it was, NWC Division One largely resembled the top tier of the Cheshire League, but there were some important differences. The system had been tidied up. The winners of the NPL were being admitted as a matter of routine to the Alliance Premier League, provided the ground met certain standards, so it seemed a logical development of the emerging pyramid system that the NPL would soon offer the top NWC club an automatic promotion place. If this happened, then for Stanley there was a clear route to the Alliance Premier, just one step below the Football League.

The problem for the Stanley board was that the Crown Ground was still some distance from being NPL standard. Floodlights would be needed at some point, and the seating capacity, then just 80, would also have to be addressed.

But by securing their place in the top tier of the NWC League, Stanley ensured that they could offer the highest standards of football possible to the people of Accrington with the facilities that then existed. From this point on, it was a case of consolidating and building towards a higher grade of football. Alty had departed from his predecessors by putting the club into debt to lift the look and feel of the Crown Ground. A lot of regulars did not approve, but it was a policy seen by the *Accrington Observer* as a very necessary progression for Stanley:

> "In a move that caused many a raised eyebrow, the club decided to borrow heavily from the bank to enable it to embark on a restructuring scheme which has seen internal changes and a massive facelift to the Crown Ground. The result of this bold step is that instead of going out of existence for the second time in 20 years, Accrington Stanley now find themselves on a new and exciting threshold."

There were other encouraging signs as well. The Supporters' Club had succeeded in raising £3,000 over the year for the club, and Stanley now boasted a brand new social club, opened in May by the town's MP, Arthur Davidson. An unexpected bonus was the new ground grading by the NWC League – the Crown had gone from an 'E' grading to a 'B'.

The chairman now desperately needed some success on the field to bring in the crowds, to raise the income-generating potential of the club, and, crucially, to manage the debt. But as John Alty was himself fully prepared to admit, you can't bank on winning games of football.

Chapter Five

1982–91
From Pipe Dream to Possibility

THE 1982–83 CAMPAIGN was something of a new beginning for Accrington Stanley. From being in an uncertain position within the football hierarchy, with no guaranteed or even obvious way forward, they were now perched just below halfway in an emerging pyramid system. Below them were their old adversaries in the Lancashire Combination, places that a club with any ambition really did not want to revisit. Above them was the challenge of the NPL, with its clutch of ex-Football League clubs and big non-league names.

The brief for Mick Finn was clear. Since Stanley did not yet boast the facilities required of an NPL club, he had to build a side that would attract the crowds and allow the club to accumulate. Relegation was unthinkable.

Finn was no football illiterate. He talked a good game and could call on some contacts from his days in the professional game. One such instance was when Stanley signed ex-Burnley midfielder Billy Ingham, but a far more significant recruit in terms of service and impact was striker Steve Parry, who arrived at the Crown from West Lancashire League side Haslingden.

A bright start saw just one defeat in the opening ten games, but behind the scenes, Finn was not having the happiest of times trying to juggle the demands of the manager's position with his work commitments and home life. On September 21st, Stanley suffered a demoralising

3-1 FA Cup exit at the hands of Harrogate Town in a replay in front of over 2,000 fans, this after being easily the better side in the initial encounter at the Crown. Contending also with an extensive injury list, Stanley began to lose games and after a 3-1 defeat at Bootle on October 9th, Finn called it a day.

It was a setback for John Alty, who had earmarked Finn for the manager's job from the start of his chairmanship. They got on well and Alty was convinced that Finn was a good manager in the making. Even as Finn was clearing out his desk, the chairman was being quoted in the press that he would be quite happy if his man changed his mind and decided to continue. Finn had lasted just seven months in the job, and for many years henceforth, John Alty and the board would struggle to find a manager who would stay at the Crown for any length of time.

It was around this time that Stanley announced a merger with Baxenden FC. Their chairman, Tony Noonan, had taken his club to the Accrington Combination title and already had a place on the Stanley board as vice-chairman. Alty told the press about his plans to have Stanley running five senior teams at different levels, but it emerged that the rationale for this extravagant set-up was as much about money as it was football. The move was at least partly aimed at expanding the pool of players whom Stanley could call on to sell lottery tickets. It was expected that all players should raise money for the club in this way, and Alty saw in running five teams the potential to greatly expand the club's income-generating capacity in conjunction with the new social facilities at the Crown.

The merger had little impact, but it served to underline the financial pressures of Stanley's debt, pressures which had forced a cut in players' expenses upon Finn's departure. Some squad members were released, including Billy Ingham, and Dave Parr left the club at his own request.

Dennis Cook, Finn's assistant, was promoted into the manager's chair. Publicly, Cook supported the economy cuts, but fans wondered who was in charge when it was the chairman, not the new manager, who announced team changes before the next game, an FA Trophy first qualifying round tie at Penrith.

Under Cook, Stanley had no luck in the cup competitions, losing 5-0 at Penrith and then suffering an horrendous 8-2 reverse at Horwich in the Lancashire Junior Cup. League form held up much better, and the emergence of Steve Parry as a striker of some distinction was the real dividend of a mid-table season. Parry was a target man, but was quicker and more agile than the typical hefty non-league centre-forward. Parry, in harness with a fully-fit Dave Hargreaves, would have been an exciting proposition, but though Hargreaves remained at the club, the years of opposition defenders hacking away had taken their toll on his ankles and knees, and Hargreaves' last couple of years at the club were injury-plagued.

At least the pitch had improved. There were fewer postponements and the club managed to avoid the traditional April fixture glut, though drainage problems still remained. Another £2,500 went on a sand-slitting project in May, a further cost, among others, that the club met with a £10,000 loan from the FA. To give the pitch more time to settle, Stanley played their final fixture, a home tie with Darwen, at Clitheroe.

Stanley finished tenth in a 20-team division. Champions Burscough opted not to pursue promotion to the NPL because of the increased costs this would involve – this from a club with floodlights and a 400-seat stand! It was a sobering reminder to the Stanley faithful just how far their club had to go to aspire to the next step up. More seating and floodlights were a prerequisite for the 'A' grading that Stanley sought, and for that they needed significant fundraising.

As it happened, the accession to the chair of John Alty had coincided with a renaissance of Stanley's Supporters' Club as a body with the capacity to raise decent sums of money. The role and operation of the official supporters' body has a curious history at Accrington Stanley, and this was the case even when the club was in the Football League. Sterling efforts at raising cash were invariably interrupted by clashes with the board, and this pattern was maintained at the Crown.

The Supporters' Club had been re-established in 1975, with Bill Parkinson in the chair. In the early 1980s, some new members had become involved and the club had started to raise significant amounts of cash. The Supporters' Club AGM in February 1983 gave a figure of around £1,500 for the year, though some activists claim that much more was passed to the club during the course of the season.

Whatever amounts the fans were raising, there was no denying that they had succeeded in building an efficient organisation with dedicated members and a real sense of camaraderie. Many of them had met when contributing to the upgrade of the ground. One of the more prominent figures was Ian Brooks, who owned the landscaping business that had worked on the Crown pitch.

Brooks was a strong character whose assertiveness caused some friction with the board, but this did not stop him becoming fully involved. Brooks installed the bar during the refurbishment of the clubhouse, and was behind some of the more imaginative fundraising events. He remembered it as a time when everyone was willing to do their bit, including first team and reserve team players who were often roped in to help with sponsored events.

But at the 1983 AGM, Brooks was elected as president of the Supporters' Club, and just ten days later, the organisation was mysteriously wound up at a special meeting. Both Brooks and Alty refused to comment on this strange turn of events; only Bill Parkinson would admit that there had been a "clash of personalities". A letter in the *Accrington Observer* claimed that one director had objected to Brooks' election.

More upheaval followed. The close-season period saw the departure of two of the more popular squad members, Kevin Twinney and Mick Moffitt, and in July, Dennis Cook became the third manager to leave in 18 months, citing boardroom interference in team affairs. This was followed shortly after by an article in the *Accrington Observer* about Stanley's appointment of a commercial manager in the light of debts totalling £40,000, and a veiled warning from John Alty about the future of the club:

"If fundraising can be stepped up substantially, our debts will continue to be repaid in line with the programme arranged and in due course further improvements, such as the installation of floodlights could seriously be contemplated. But if fundraising is not increased, the club will be fighting for its survival."

Given the recent closure of a supporters' club that was successfully raising funds, and on top of losing yet another manager, it perhaps was not surprising that at least one disgruntled supporter was moved to put pen to paper. A letter appeared in the pages of the local paper from an anonymous writer who claimed to be a Crown Ground regular:

"I would like to know what has happened to the friendly little club formed in 1968. Since this bunch of so-called directors came, we have had four managers in eighteen months, lost one of the only people who had any ideas on fundraising and lost a very good, loyal supporters' club which was raising £2,000 a year. The club is £40,000 in debt. Well, whose fault is that?"

The chairman exercised his right of reply, admitting responsibility for the string of failed managerial appointments, but arguing that things had changed from the days of the Lancashire Combination:

"...the economics of running a football club which is continually expected to improve its facilities in order to survive places both manager and directors under far greater pressure than was the case in the last decade. Decisions have to be taken regularly and will be made without fear of unpopularity if the board democratically believes them to be in the best interests of the club."

Alty also pointed out that the entire gate receipts of the previous season amounted to £2,706, compared to an annual figure of around £9,000 that was injected into the club by the twelve directors, including around £3,000 a year from him.

Those gate receipts were little improved on the Lancashire Combination days, and it laid bare the stark fact that more than £40,000 worth of investment in the ground and a higher grade of football had done little to entice more people to the Crown. It seemed a poor return on such an ambitious statement of intent, and further progress was dependent on ground developments that required more five-figure sums. John Alty quite simply needed to raise Stanley's income, and the only feasible hope of doing that was to forge a winning team.

The man entrusted with doing this for the 1983–84 season was Pat Lynch, formerly assistant to Dennis Cook. He added some new faces to the squad in Mick Higgins, Gerry Keenan (who would become Lynch's assistant during the season) and Pete O'Brien, but the biggest boost was the return of Dave Hargreaves to the team, where it was hoped he would form a productive partnership with Steve Parry.

Early season results were steady, with Stanley holding a mid-table position when they drew Gateshead in the second qualifying round of the FA Cup. The north-easterners were reigning NPL champions and enjoying their first season in the Alliance Premier League. It was a real test for Stanley, and in front of 420 at the Crown they held Gateshead to a 1-1 draw, with Steve Parry heading a second-half equaliser.

No one gave Stanley much chance in the midweek replay, but in what was subsequently billed as their greatest result since reforming, two superb Parry goals and a lot of stubborn defending saw them through 2-1. It gave the club a tremendous boost, but they were disappointingly eliminated at Bishop Auckland in the next qualifying round.

The League campaign that followed through the winter months saw Stanley firmly entrenched in the lower half of the table, but the team gained fresh confidence from good runs in the NWC League Cup and the Lancashire Junior Cup (known at the ATS Trophy after its sponsor). They reached the semi-finals of the former and the final of the latter, Stanley's first such county cup final appearance since reforming. The team's much improved form was reflected in their final league position of seventh, which represented the club's highest ever placing in non-league.

There were other signs, too, that the club was finally making real progress. Pat Lynch had added value to the squad with some astute signings, such as goalkeeper Glenn Johnson, midfielder Gerry Keenan and forward Errol Williams. Dave Hargreaves also proved that he was still a real asset to the team, scoring 35 goals in all competitions and surpassing both 300 games and 300 goals for the club. Stanley's run to the final of the Lancashire Junior Cup included three NPL scalps in the form of Southport, Horwich and, in the semi-final, Chorley, a game that saw all-out attack from Stanley pay off with a thrilling 3-2 win in front of 690 spectators at the Crown. The final, in which Stanley faced South Liverpool at Wigan's Springfield Park, was lost 2-1, but 400 made the journey from Accrington.

Little wonder that John Alty sounded confident that Stanley would hit their target of NPL football by the end of the decade. He told the *Lancashire Evening Telegraph*:

"It's not just an idle boast. We are going to do it. We have got the best board of directors we have ever had in number and quality, we have the most professional management team with Pat Lynch and Gerry Keenan; we have a full-time commercial manager, Rod Kenyon, and we are attracting the highest attendances in the League."

Another indication of the club's potential was the explosion of press interest – albeit of the nostalgic variety

– when Stanley played Gateshead in the FA Cup. The game, between two former Football League names, attracted the national media to the Crown, and though the resultant publicity did not reflect the image Alty wanted for the club, it was a definite sign that success on the pitch would bring rich pickings in terms of utilising the club's name and history.

Mark Turner remembered:

"John Alty had fantastic ideas and good ambitions. He wanted to raise the profile of the club and he understood the value of the name. He brought in a more professional attitude. He'd turn up in a suit, collar and tie, whereas most of the active folk around the club would come in straight from work. When we played Gateshead in 1983, he turned up in collar and tie and put a great spread on in the boardroom because the *Guardian* had said they were going to cover the game; he wanted to show that the club was going places. What do they publish photographs of? Stands full of pensioners, and one old chap with his Scottie terrier. John was frustrated at that, he didn't like the image we must have portrayed to the world."

More frustration for Stanley fans came in May with the departure of manager Pat Lynch, who cited family and work commitments for the decision. As with previous vacancies, the club appointed from within, with midfielder Gerry Keenan given a player-manager role. Of all the players at the Crown, Keenan, then still only 29, had the most impressive pedigree, having had a League career at Bury and Port Vale ended only by injury, and he retained good contacts around the Bury area.

Confidence was high that Keenan could build on the progress made under Lynch, but 1984–85 was an entirely forgettable season, as Stanley struggled from the outset, losing their first six matches and never finding consistent form. When Stanley conceded 16 goals in the first four matches of the New Year, including four at the hands of a Burscough striking partnership by the name of Coleman and Bell, there were qualms that Stanley might slip into the relegation zone.

Those fears were thankfully not realised, but it was an unhappy period with what appeared to be yet more friction between manager and chairman over wages and budgets. The club announced another cut in players' expenses, the result being that a number of players from the core of Lynch's squad moved on during the season, some of them rejoining their old manager in his new position at Darwen. Stanley began to rely more on reserve-team graduates and recruits from amateur football, one of whom was Paul Beck, who had fallen back into Accrington Combination football. Stanley even called on some old faces in Stuart Illingworth, Dave McDowell and Dave Parr, all of whom turned out as the season drew to a close.

The board now had to make a decision about the running costs of the team. Keenan had been pushing hard for significant new investment for months. Stanley's exit from the Lancashire Junior Cup via a 5-3 home defeat to Fleetwood on February 2nd had brought this public comment from the manager:

> "I now realise that the resources I need to strengthen the side just aren't here at the club. I have tried to bring in new faces from the reserves in a bid to get the right results, but it doesn't seem to have worked. Looking ahead to the next term, we are going to need new blood if we are to mount a serious title challenge. At the moment, the lads' morale is at rock bottom. With a first team squad that basically consists of 13 players including myself, it is hard work."

When, in April, Stanley were embarrassingly thrashed 5-0 at Eastwood Hanley for an eighth successive away defeat, Alty appeared to concede the argument. As Stanley limped to the end of the season and a final position of 15th, he wrote:

"It is clear that the present squad, no matter how hard they might try, are simply not good enough to give Stanley a chance of chasing honours next season. With the support of my co-directors, I have therefore decided that some money will be made available to enable Gerry Keenan to sign some quality players for next season. The club is £46,000 in debt and realistically I shall be happy if we can hold debts at this level whilst at the same time dramatically improving performances on the field. Despite our financial position, the club must go forward."

To his credit, Keenan took on the role of commercial manager from Rod Kenyon, and both had some success in their attempts to increase the club's income. Matthew Walker, one of the partners behind the local Hindle & Walker car dealership, was a keen fan and paid for his company to become Stanley's first shirt sponsor, and would go on to support the club financially for a number of years. Mafco Motor Products put their name on the tracksuits, and the club started to sell more advertising space around the pitch perimeter and in the programme. But it was never less than a struggle to convince businesses to invest in a non-league club. The general economic climate in the region didn't help, and the facilities at the Crown meant that Stanley could not offer much in the way of corporate hospitality, as Mark Turner points out:

"Nobody had any real expertise about raising money. In those days you could sponsor a match for £20. In the programmes, you'd find that we were selling boards around the pitch at £100 for three years. At that level, sponsorship was a strange concept. It wasn't impossible, but you had to remember where we were – at level seven, in the North West Counties League. Yes we had a famous name, but what could we offer them? We had no hospitality rooms, just a social club. We only had 80 seats. Admission was £1. We had lottery tickets and did weekly draws, but things were fairly low-key. Even players were expected to take £10 worth of raffle tickets every week. We'd have boardroom arguments about players not selling tickets, but try telling a player from Bury that he's on £12, but that he has to shift £10 of Accrington Stanley raffle tickets!"

It was not just business, either, that proved immune to the charms of an afternoon at the Crown. In December 1984, in his role as commercial manager, Keenan had handed out 150 free tickets to Accrington schoolchildren for a home game against Eastwood Hanley, but barely more than a dozen had taken up the offer on the day. By dropping out of the football world for those years in the 1960s, Stanley had missed out on a whole generation of local football fans. Accrington teenagers in the 1980s rarely lived in a household where parents would take them to the Crown in preference to either Ewood Park or Turf Moor.

Indeed, the number of adults attending the Crown became a cause for concern as form slumped in the New Year. The average attendance for the season would come in at a shockingly low 193, almost certainly the lowest levels of support since 1970, which at least reflected John Alty's opinion that Keenan's was the worst ever Stanley side. In February, the chairman had distributed questionnaires to the 150 or so fans who never missed a game at the Crown, but even among these diehards, interest seemed low, with only 30 bothering to reply. Nonetheless, there was strong support among the respondents for the club to continue the development of the Crown with floodlights, with two-thirds agreeing that the club should add to its debts to install them.

With money earmarked for new players, Keenan and Alty had started the process of drawing up a list of targets, but by the time of the club's annual presentation night, there had appeared to be a shift. Alty admitted that running the squad on a shoestring had not made for a good season, but he now stressed that the club had to find money for other things as well. It was the familiar problem of how to juggle insufficient resources between the three hungry mouths of team, ground and debt. Keenan thought he had won a promise for the team to be prioritised, but now Alty declared that the club would not "throw silly money around" on players, hinting that some wage demands had been excessive, and pledged instead to reduce the club's debt significantly and continue with ground developments:

"No-one will come to the club who only wants to play for us for the money, and we will be sticking to our youth policy. This is what the club is based on. I guarantee by the end of the coming season, our debts will have been reduced to less than £25,000 from the current figure of more than £45,000, and there is no way that we are not going to have floodlights within the next two years."

It was the last straw for Keenan, and in June he resigned. Though he had put a great deal of effort into the club both as team and commercial manager, it had not been a happy time for him, and he clearly was not convinced that he would receive the financial backing he thought was needed.

There was, however, something else in the equation that Alty had to take into consideration – a new regulation, passed by the NWC league committee, that First Division clubs would be expected to have floodlights by the start of the 1986–87 season. It meant an unavoidable financial commitment if Stanley were to comply, and the board had little option given their avowed intentions to take the club higher. And, quite by chance, Stanley director Alan Harker, in London on business, had discovered that Conference club Enfield were selling off some old floodlight pylons for around £10,000, and the club was keen to snap them up.

It was of little consolation to Gerry Keenan that his team-building plans had been stymied for a necessary investment in the ground, and his manner of departure was regrettable. Players at the club during his managership remember Keenan as a more sophisticated manager than usual in terms of tactical knowledge, but he struggled to motivate and maintain team spirit in the face of poor results, and in non-league perhaps the latter is more important. Dave Mooney, a regular under Keenan, also suspected, like Alty, that some of the players he brought to the club were not as committed as they should have been:

"I always remember going to Eastwood Hanley and getting beaten 5-0, and thinking that it was hard work, and we were poor. The playing standards had definitely gone down, and the atmosphere wasn't the same. It had become like a lot of non-league clubs that you hear about, with a lot of players coming in from all over the place and no real team spirit.

"The players that came in almost inevitably didn't have the commitment. You'd see them coming in and you'd think, 'Are you going to be here in three years' time, are you going to play 100 games for us?' I remember a left-back who Gerry brought in from Radcliffe. After a dozen or so games he'd gone, and that was the case with a lot of these guys. For someone like me who'd been at Stanley a number of years, it was another face just flitting through, whereas I wanted people there who were very committed, who'd be there next to me for the next three or four years. That was how I viewed things, I wanted that consistency and stability."

In a break from the established tradition of appointment from within, Stanley advertised for a new manager. The man to emerge with the job from a round of interviews was Frank O'Kane, who applied as the assistant manager of Radcliffe Borough, newly-crowned champions of the NWC First Division. Like Burscough before them, Radcliffe declined to enter the NPL. Instead, second-placed Caernarfon Town applied and were admitted.

Joining the First Division as NWC Second Division champions were Clitheroe. Under the managership of Eric Whalley, Clitheroe had won the Third and Second Division titles in consecutive seasons. Their elevation to the top tier at least provided Stanley with some local competition, but it was a couple of developments off the pitch for which the season was remembered.

Firstly, it was confirmed that, at long last, non-league clubs had earned the right to automatic promotion to the Football League. This had been the whole point behind the formation of the Alliance Premier, and had been long lobbied for, but the approval of the Fourth Division clubs had not been forthcoming. However, in the autumn of 1985, the Football League finally agreed that the winners of the 1986–87 title, the season the competition was rebranded as the Conference, would become the first team to be automatically promoted to the Football League, with the team at the foot of the Fourth Division relegated to the Conference.

Stanley were a long way from the Conference, but now a route existed for non-league sides to win a place in the Football League on merit, and the other major development at the Crown that year represented an important step along the way, and that was the deal with Enfield for their old floodlights.

Enfield FC, based in the heart of the North London district of the same name, were the pre-eminent non-league team in the south of England. They had won the Alliance Premier in 1982–83, and were on the way to winning the title again in 1985–86. They had the sort of non-league profile to which Stanley aspired, but when the Accrington delegation visited Enfield's vast Southbury Road ground to pay for the lights, they were open-mouthed at the facilities they saw. Jack Hudson remembered it well:

> "When we went down to Enfield to pay for the floodlights, we were taken into the club's

hospitality facilities. They had a big concert room with banisters and seating all around. It was palatial. They had waiters on at lunch time serving business people. The father of one of our players at the time had a haulage business, so he went down there shortly afterwards in one of his wagons and transported the pylons up to the Crown. We'd already done the groundwork for them, so we quickly put them up. But it was quite sobering to see what Enfield had. We had nothing like their set-up."

John Alty and the Stanley board secured the eight 60ft high pylons for £15,000, well below the estimated cost for brand new ones. It was an important step for the club in a number of ways. It meant that they could join the rest of the senior football fraternity in playing games at 3.00pm and 7.30pm all year round, the latter especially useful when players on shifts could not always guarantee making a 5.00pm or 6.00pm midweek kick-off.

They opened up a new competition to the club in the Lancashire Floodlit Trophy. But most importantly, the lights signalled that Stanley were gearing up for a higher grade of football. With illumination in place, all that remained for the Crown to be acceptable for the NPL was more covered seating – and even as the floodlights were being lowered into position, plans were being made for a new stand on the Clayton side of the clubhouse and for further extensions to the clubhouse itself.

If Stanley were preparing the Crown for NPL football and beyond, all that remained was for the team to earn its place there, but Frank O'Kane proved not to be the man for the job. Although Stanley improved on the mediocre outcome of the previous season, they made little headway, finishing the 1985–86 campaign in eleventh place without ever looking capable of mounting a title challenge.

The season did witness one of the biggest crowds at the Crown for some time for the visit of Alliance Premier side Runcorn in the FA Cup. Stanley had accounted for Darwen and Droylsden before drawing the Cheshire side, who were on their way to a top-six finish in what would become the Conference. Stanley held their visitors to a highly creditable 1-1 draw in front of over 900 at the Crown before crashing out 9-1 in the replay. Stanley also conceded seven against Stalybridge in the same week, and generally struggled defensively, conceding 60 goals in a season for the third successive year. Five of those goals were conceded against Clitheroe, who completed the double over Stanley on their way to yet another NWC title. In one of the most eagerly awaited clashes of the season, Stanley went to Clitheroe on New Year's Day. Against form, Stanley held a 3-1 lead with only 20 minutes remaining, but ended up losing 4-3, while a single goal was enough for Eric Whalley's side to win the Easter return in front of 550 spectators at the Crown.

By this time, Frank O'Kane had already handed in his resignation, but had been persuaded to stay by John Alty. In May, however, the manager resigned decisively, citing work commitments. Both O'Kane and Alty toed a diplomatic line in the press; it was certainly in the interests of neither party to suggest that there had been friction and trouble behind the scenes, but O'Kane had nevertheless become the sixth Stanley boss to leave the club in little over four years. It was a worrying record that begged the question as to why no Stanley manager could settle at the club, but from this point on, the revolving managerial door at the Crown would turn with slightly less velocity.

Though this was due in part to the incoming boss and the success he brought to the club, it was also the case that Alty himself knew well enough that it took time to build a winning team. His programme notes once mused over this football truism, stating: "Building a championship-winning side can take years rather than months and patience is an essential virtue for all of us." He fired that particular manager six months later, but after the resignation of Gerry Keenan, he told the press that he was looking for a manager to stay at the club for at least three years and put together a serious challenge for the NPL, a sign that he was prepared to put on the record an intention to be more patient with his team managers.

Even so, John Alty was without doubt a tough chairman who expected to see progress on the field. With a large debt to service and a ground to upgrade, increasing revenue through the turnstiles was vital. The *Accrington Observer* suggested that the club might make a move to reinstate in some form a managerial team from the club's recent past. It was a plausible suggestion, since Don Bramley and Jimmy Hinksman were looking after Stanley's reserve side, and Dave Baron was taking the occasional training session. In those three there was a veritable wealth of knowledge and experience.

In fact, Jimmy Hinksman had approached John Alty with an alternative proposal, which was to appoint ex-Stanley player Mike Ferguson in the hot seat, with Hinksman as his assistant. Ferguson was one of the few survivors of the 1961–62 squad who had gone on to have a decent career in the Football League. After retiring as a player, Ferguson had managed Rochdale, where he had offered full-time professional terms to Dave Hargreaves, and had gone on to manage in a number of countries. Back in the UK, Ferguson now expressed an interest in the Stanley position, and at another time Alty might have taken him on, but in May 1986 there was another outstanding candidate for the job who also happened to be the popular choice among the fans – Clitheroe manager Eric Whalley.

Whalley had just completed a unique hat-trick of NWC titles and a superb Lancashire Junior Cup triumph with the small Ribble Valley team. Since reforming, Stanley had been used to catching up and then overhauling their local rivals, but here for the first time was a team who had performed the trick on them. What is more, Whalley had done it on a tight budget using mainly local players. It was precisely the template Alty was looking for.

Just hours after Clitheroe's final, triumphant game, Whalley informed Clitheroe chairman Cyril Whiteside that he was resigning and taking the manager's job at Accrington Stanley. In the weeks that followed, Whalley offered terms to eight Clitheroe players, five of whom agreed to follow him to the Crown. Whalley also made an astute signing in Chris Grimshaw, an Accrington lad who had been released by Bury, and was able to play on the wing or in midfield. Goalkeeper Gary Pierce was released.

The recruitment of Whalley and his ex-Clitheroe players for the 1986–87 season had an immediate impact on the gates at the Crown, which jumped from an average of just under 300 to around 400, bringing in valuable additional revenue. Not that Eric always saw eye-to-eye with those on the terraces. When Goole Town arrived at the Crown for an FA Trophy tie, an above-average crowd of 451 turned up, but were disappointed to see Stanley pegged back in the second half and held to a 1-1 draw. As the teams left the pitch, there was a minor altercation between the manager and a small group in the crowd who were criticising Whalley for not making a substitution in an effort to find the winner.

The row was not helped by Stanley's 3-0 defeat in the replay a few days later, but in a letter in the following edition of the *Accrington Observer*, a Crown regular castigated the "senior citizen so-called supporters", pointing out that Stanley were top of the NWC First Division using a much smaller nucleus of players than before.

It was a fair point. Stanley had hit the ground running with a nine-match unbeaten run, and through September negotiated a period in which a number of the squad were suspended due to an arcane system used by the NWC. Stanley simply ground out the points in much the same way Clitheroe had done before.

As a manager, Eric Whalley based his teams round a strong rearguard and a combative midfield. It was not always pretty, but his record of achievement was indisputable. The fans also enjoyed the special atmosphere of a night match at the Crown Ground when the floodlights were used for the first time for the game against Penrith on October 10th.

It was around this time that rumours of another re-organisation of the non-league pyramid solidified. The North West Counties League had been running for four years, but on each occasion the First Division champions had been denied access to the NPL. Some of them, such as Clitheroe, had insufficient facilities, but this could not be said of clubs like Burscough and Stalybridge. Only one team from the NWC – Caernarfon Town – had made a successful application to the NPL who were still refusing to countenance automatic promotion between the two leagues.

Perhaps as a means of forcing the hand of the NPL, the NWC announced plans to form a 'Premier' division, with the winners automatically promoted to the NPL. The NPL countered with plans for its own feeder division, an NPL First Division, with automatic promotion to the top tier of the NPL. In October, it was confirmed that the 1987–88 season would see its launch.

John Alty enthusiastically endorsed the plans and in October announced that there would be Northern Premier League football at the Crown the following season. It was a slightly disingenuous claim, for the likelihood was that most of the senior NWC teams in Stanley's league would also transfer their allegiance to the NPL First Division. Alty sympathised with the NWC, but had to act in the interests of his club:

"The main issue is that the [proposed] NWC premier league would not have automatic promotion to the NPL because the latter will not entertain the idea. You can say it is unfair and unjust to the NWC league committee who have worked hard for four years, but at the end of the day you do what is best for your club. It is a higher standard of football and if we can gain promotion to the NPL we would be rubbing shoulders with teams like Southport, Barrow and Hyde United."

The irony of all this was that such a reorganisation made Stanley's valiant efforts to win the NWC First Division somewhat immaterial in terms of access to a higher league, as their facilities and playing standards made them a shoo-in for the new competition. But this did not deter Eric Whalley's team. Though a 1-0 victory at Burscough in early November was Stanley's first league win in a month, they were proving almost impossible to beat. A 16-game run of undefeated league games between October and February kept them well in touch with Stalybridge and Clitheroe in what had become a three-horse race for the title. The run included another memorable festive clash at Clitheroe on Boxing Day. In front of 1,152 spectators, Stanley found themselves 3-1 down with minutes remaining, but two late goals from centre-half Dave Mooney snatched an unlikely point. It was typical of the spirit Eric Whalley had forged among the players.

Progress was being made off the pitch as well. The new John Duckworth Stand was opened before the top-of-the-table derby return against Clitheroe on April 18th 1987, Easter Saturday, a game that drew 683 spectators. Goals from ex-Clitheroe heroes Mick Ashcroft and John Taylor gave Stanley a 2-0 victory that consolidated their second place in the table. With one game left, Stanley had to win at St Helens Town to take the handsome NWC runners-up shield. It was a tough assignment, for their hosts had a decent side, but Mick Robinson converted two first-half penalties to put Stanley in control of the game. Though they conceded a goal early in the second half, Stanley defended tenaciously to hold out for a 2-1 win. It was the club's first silverware for six seasons and had been thoroughly deserved. The team had lost just four league games all season, and had reached the semi-finals of the Lancashire Floodlit Trophy.

It had not, however, been an entirely easy ride. Eric Whalley was a combustible character who would brook no interference from the board, a fact highlighted by an incident after Stanley's 0-0 draw at Winsford United in December.

The local press reported that director Sam Adams had become involved in an argument with the manager. The precise source of the disagreement was unclear. Eric Whalley had dropped Adams' son Daryl, a long-serving player at the Crown, and had also sidelined centre-half Chris Chisholm in favour of Mick Ashcroft, one of Whalley's ex-Clitheroe men, so perhaps the director was querying team selection. Whatever the reason, reports suggested that Whalley had accused the board of not backing him fully, and that the manager had subsequently been sacked.

Alty admitted that there had been a row, but denied that it had ever escalated to the stage of a sacking. The matter quickly blew over, but there were other instances where the manager was fully prepared to have a go at those he thought were failing to give the team their total support, and this included the crowd. On one occasion, he gave a local radio interview, criticising supporters for not backing the team as much as Clitheroe fans had done during his time there.

Those looking in from the outside might have mistaken this simply for a manager with a quick temper, but those closer to the dressing room thought it was more to do with his general attitude to those who tried to undermine the confidence of the team. Eric Whalley demanded high standards and could administer a fearsome half-time roasting, but it was his policy not to criticise the team or individuals in public, and to defend them against outside critics, whether on the terraces or in the boardroom.

Dave Mooney said of him:

"Eric was a player's manager: win, lose or draw, as long as you'd done your best then you deserved a drink and to relax and enjoy what you'd achieved on the field. He looked after his players and didn't give a monkey's about anyone else. He was a magnanimous bloke who drew people towards him and made them want to play for him. He put his heart and soul into it and he expected everybody else to do the same, and it annoyed him if he saw someone slacking or not doing their job properly."

For all the mutual irritation that often erupted between the manager, the board and the fans, there was no doubting that Stanley was the place Whalley wanted to be. He had played as a youngster for Stanley's 'A' team in the late 1950s, and now as the club's manager, in a short space of time he had raised standards on the pitch and guided the club to a position where they could contemplate a serious assault on promotion to the NPL, long the aim of John Alty and many other fans whose memories went back to the days of the Lancashire Combination.

In the close season of 1987–88, while Eric Whalley plotted his assault on promotion, some of the club's faithful were ensuring that the Crown itself would be no obstacle to progress like it had been in the past. The development of the ground continued apace, with the construction of the two covered terraces along the side of the pitch opposite the clubhouse. As with so much of the building at the Crown, these were home-made constructions put up largely through the efforts of a small group of fans, particularly Stan Spencer and Arthur McGilveray, who gathered together the materials from a wide range of sources. Though elementary in design, the stands were utterly sturdy and provided cover for a thousand spectators, which invited much admiration from visiting directors.

In August 1987, Stanley took their place as founder members of the NPL First Division. Only 12 of the 20 NWC First Division teams made it to the new league, justification enough for Stanley's move. Of the other seven teams, five were from the Northern Counties East Premier League, and only two had made the leap from the NWC Second Division – champions Droylsden and, curiously, Lancaster City, who had finished only 13th. Former champions Clitheroe and Burscough stayed put.

Just before hostilities commenced, chairman Alty and manager Whalley had a pleasant weekend in London as guests of the Football League, who celebrated their centenary with a gala dinner and a match at Wembley between a World XI and a Football League XI. The Football League, in a rare moment of clarity, felt that the town of Accrington had to be represented as one of the twelve original towns who competed in the inaugural competition.

It had been a nice touch to invite Accrington, and both Alty and Whalley had enjoyed their weekend immensely, but now came the real business of promotion to the NPL. Eric Whalley largely stuck by the squad that had seen Stanley finish as runners-up the previous season. The team responded with a superb start that saw them top of the table after 10 games, and though form dipped slightly as the winter months loomed, it was clear that a promotion challenge to the top tier of the NPL was in the making.

The team had less luck in the national cup competitions. Particularly disappointing was a 1-0 FA Cup defeat at Northern Counties East side Bridlington Town in a preliminary qualifying round. Not only were Bridlington the sort of opposition that Stanley should have eliminated, but it transpired that the cash from an FA Cup run was badly needed. Despite the extended run of good results on the pitch, Stanley's debts were weighing more heavily than ever on the shoulders of the board. With the team still competing strongly at the head of the table, fans were shocked by a sudden headline in the *Accrington Observer* of January 26th 1988 which claimed that Stanley faced financial oblivion. Alty announced that losses were running at the equivalent of £6,000 a year that he alone was covering.

A set of measures was announced to alleviate the problem, which included a directors' subscription of £20 per week and increases in admission prices for the following season. Alty did point out quite reasonably that if Eric Whalley did achieve another promotion, costs at the club would inevitably rise anyway, and argued that he had to take tough action to maintain playing standards:

"Playing standards must be maintained and possibly improved, which means income will have to rise.

As long as I am chairman of this club, playing standards will not be sacrificed since this would be a recipe for disaster. If we are going to survive, it is going to cost more money. The only alternative is to allow the club to die."

Not so, argued some stalwarts, who knew that Stanley could comfortably survive at lower levels of non-league if need be. Not everyone around the Crown shared in the rhetoric of the club's leaders that Stanley had a rightful place somewhere much higher up the football ladder. Many Crown regulars remained happy just to have a team to watch. Former chairman John Prescott remembered a conversation with some supporters at a reserve team game around this time. They had asked him whether he thought Stanley could ever make it back to the Football League:

"The only answer I could give them was that things could change. I was thinking at the time that the likes of Rochdale and Bury could not carry on as full-time clubs given their gates. So I said: 'It could change. Possibly the Football League will split into the Fourth Division North and South, and there'd be an opportunity for Conference standard clubs to go in.' But for me it was not all-consuming to get Stanley back into the League, I was quite happy for us to try and make progress wherever we were."

Other fans, alienated by Alty's style, which they thought too domineering, wondered precisely who else ought to take responsibility for the debt if not the man who had got the club into it in the first place. Attendances remained relatively healthy for that level of football, so it hardly seemed right that the chairman was now telling the fans that they had to pay more or face losing their club.

In the midst of this apparent crisis at the club, help emerged in the shape of Terry Styring, a Yorkshire-based businessman who was a client of the chairman's accountancy practice. After a quite lengthy courtship, Styring agreed to Alty's entreaties to invest in the club in return for a place on the board. Styring remembered that although he was not instinctively a football man, he was looking for an interest outside of his business.

It was a new source of money at just the right time, but although Styring's investment and the other measures seemed to stabilise the situation, the episode had cost two of Stanley's most dedicated activists their directorships. Both Jack Hudson and Arthur McGilveray resigned in the light of the new directors' subscription, this in spite of work around the ground that had saved the club thousands of pounds. For those Stanley loyalists who remembered the Combination days, it seemed a changed club, one increasingly focused on the cost of everything, rather than the value of the contributions made to the well-being of the club.

A reminder of how effectively money could facilitate success came with the visit to the Crown of Colne Dynamoes for a Lancashire Junior Cup tie. Funded by the largesse of their owner and manager Graham White, Colne were runaway leaders of NWC Division One and on an irresistible rise up the non-league ladder. However, Stanley proved the better team on the day and deserved their 2-1 win in front of a gate of 675 at the Crown.

Stanley went on to reach the last four, where they were defeated 2-1 by Morecambe, leaving Eric Whalley and his men – who now included assistant manager Dave Thornley – with the sole focus of securing promotion. At the start of March, Stanley occupied the second promotion spot, but the team suddenly began to struggle in fixtures they would normally have approached with confidence.

A defeat at Farsley Celtic was compounded by a series of home draws that saw Stanley drop to fourth as Easter loomed. A 1-0 win against Harrogate on Easter Monday was a scrappy affair, and another dropped home point a week later led the *Accrington Observer* to lament that promotion hopes had gone. However, Stanley responded with three quick wins in what was a congested run-in, one vital victory being at promotion rivals Fleetwood Town.

With two games remaining, the maths was quite clear. Stanley needed to win one of their last two games to win the NPL First Division title and promotion to the NPL itself. Their chance to clinch the title at the Crown came and went with the visit of Fleetwood, who were the more enterprising team on the evening and went away with a 3-1 win in front of 1,110 spectators.

Stanley had one final opportunity with their last fixture at Eastwood Hanley, but everything went wrong on the day and Stanley suffered their worst defeat of the season, a 4-0 reverse. After spending most of the season in a promotion place, Stanley slipped to fourth in the final reckoning. They had succumbed in the end to the fatigue of a long season played on a heavy Crown pitch. It was a bitter disappointment, but no more so than when the club had been denied promotion eight years previously. Then the whole club from top to bottom had rallied round and determined to go one better the following year, but events played out very differently this time.

Before the game, the directors had brought a crate of champagne into the dressing room in anticipation of the post-match celebrations. It clearly had not turned out that way, but ever the players' champion, Eric Whalley sought the bubbly anyway. His lads had toiled long and hard for nine months and had come within a whisker of a second successive promotion. They deserved a drink for their efforts. One of the directors thought differently, however, and when the manager discovered that the champagne had been taken back and secreted in the hold of the coach, he was enraged at what he perceived as an insult to his players. Whalley told the directors what he thought in no uncertain terms.

Bust-ups in the heat of the moment were nothing new, but this time the ill-feeling simmered over the weekend. When Eric Whalley attended a board meeting on the Monday, he told John Alty and the directors of his decision to resign. And when a newspaper asked Whalley for his thoughts the day after, there was no recourse to diplomacy from the ex-manager, who accused the board of not being fully behind him or the players, and of behaving essentially like a "gentlemen's club who treat match days like days out." This sparked an angry exchange, all ventilated in the local press who did not shy from splashing the vitriol around their pages.

John Alty claimed that he did not want to be drawn into a public row, and he clearly had to defend his board, but he could not refrain either from a few digs at Whalley. This only gave the press something with which to prolong the row. Said Alty:

"The directors have given Eric Whalley their total support, and left him free to run the playing side of the club. They did not enter the dressing rooms, and have at all times behaved courteously and respectfully towards Eric. The board have never interfered in team matters. Indeed, the attitude of the board towards him has been exemplary. I suggest he carefully examines his own performance as far as co-operating with the directors and other individuals is concerned. He has asked me to sack two directors...tried to have our football secretary removed...publicly abused journalists and has also shouted abuse at spectators. His abuse of referees has landed him in serious trouble with the football authorities, and I have had letters of complaint about the language coming from our bench."

Defending his directors was one thing, but the rest of Alty's statement was hardly designed to avoid a public row. Whalley not surprisingly hit back, taking aim at one of the more sensitive aspects of John Alty's chairmanship:

"Mr Alty has to ask himself, if he really wants Accrington Stanley to progress to the position it should be in, why I am the longest-serving manager under his regime. The main issue here is why the club has gone through so many managers in a relatively short space of time."

For many Stanley fans, it was a pertinent question. Eric Whalley had very quickly lifted the club to the brink of the NPL, the highest league the club could aspire to without further ground development. He had used mainly local players retained on relatively modest wages or expenses – as had been the custom in the early days under Hinksman, Bramley and Baron. Whalley had proved that success was not necessarily about money, but about man-management, motivation and the unfashionable idea that you stuck together and took pride in wearing the shirt. It was the sort of mentality that resonated with Stanley fans and was the policy they wanted to see at the club, not contract players who travelled in from all corners of Lancashire, who, it was thought, rarely served the club well.

But there was a downside to Whalley's style, and that was an antagonistic relationship with the board that inevitably wound its way through the club: players and manager on one side, the chairman and directors on the other. It was hardly conducive to the stability the club needed. The divide was all too evident at the club's annual presentation evening. John Alty had appealed to the players to wait until Stanley's new manager had been appointed before deciding whether to move on, but not one of them turned up to the presentation evening. In front of the guest speaker, Dave Bassett, the various playing awards were picked up by a proxy. Alty remembered it as the lowest point of his chairmanship, and in the next few days it became clear that the entire squad assembled by Eric Whalley would move on from Stanley, including some players he had not recruited, such as Steve Parry and Neil Rowbotham, both utterly dependable stalwarts with well over 500 appearances between them. An era which had promised so much had come to a bitter, acrimonious end after just two years, and Accrington Stanley had been left a football club with no footballers. The new manager would have to assemble a squad from scratch.

In the circumstances, one might have expected the chairman to turn to a tried and trusted non-league hand, but he very quickly appointed ex-Wolves and Stanley goalkeeper Gary Pierce into his first managerial position. The speedy appointment was no doubt motivated by the formidable levels of recruitment that were required, and the chairman was determined that the tumult over Eric Whalley's departure had as minimal an impact as possible on the forward momentum of the club. The improvement of the team under Whalley had seen the town respond. Average gates had gone up by over 30% to around 450, an encouraging sign that a good NPL side could attract several hundred on a regular basis.

The support of the club was the angle highlighted by the *Accrington Observer*, which, in the midst of the turmoil after the Eastwood game, headed an editorial with the line "1,110 reasons for Stanley to succeed". The opinion piece lauded the levels of support that the club had attracted, and in what seemed to be a gentle nudge to the chairman, thought that the club ought to "recognise" their loyal fans, though quite how this was to be done was not made apparent.

One figure who did decide to stay at the Crown was Dave Thornley. He had applied for the manager's position, but John Alty preferred instead that he remain as an assistant to the untried Pierce. Thornley had the opportunity to rejoin Eric Whalley at Morecambe, but his decision to stay turned out to be a shrewd move. Whalley's move to Morecambe did not work out, and as assistant to a new manager, Thornley would have far more influence over team affairs at Stanley.

The recruitment of Pierce was a good example of the perils of choosing a manager by interview. John Prescott, Stanley chairman between 1975 and 1981, likened it to a contest of persuasion – successful interviewees tended to be those who could most believably sell the idea they had of themselves as a manager.

As such, the skills that won you a manager's job were somewhat different to those required to actually manage a squad of footballers. John Alty remembered that

Accrington Stanley president Sir William Cocker (left) and vice-president
Sam Pilkington pictured a month before the resignation. (Garth Dawson)

Harold Bodle (centre) captained the ground-breaking 1954-55 team but as manager he lasted just ten months. Jim Jamieson describes how to cut grass while long-serving Stanley secretary Jack Wigglesworth listens carefully. (Garth Dawson)

The Aldershot Military Tattoo stand in its original form. Its purchase and relocation cost Accrington Stanley £15,000 at a time when the club was barely breaking even in the Third Division (North). (Aldershot Military Museum)

Accrington v Glossop, January 8th 1966: the last 90 minutes for the old club before resigning from the Lancashire Combination and from the football world altogether. (Garth Dawson)

With Accrington Stanley no longer resident at Peel Park, the Burnley Road stand, source of so much financial stress, was quickly demolished and sold for scrap. Little wonder that this depressing scene finds a supporter in deep and sad reflection. (Garth Dawson)

Autumn 1970 – a small group of volunteers begin construction of the first standing cover at the Crown. From left, the adults are: Alf Band, George Buller, Harry Stevenson, Charlie Tuck, Bill Parkinson, Tom McColm and John Duckworth. (Lancashire Evening Telegraph)

The results of their efforts can be seen on the far left, with the makeshift stand providing protection from the elements for around 200 people. In the foreground is the original wooden pavilion. (Garth Dawson)

Without the dedication of Stanley volunteers, the club would never have been reborn. Here, one man helps to dig the makeshift drainage system at the Crown. (Garth Dawson)

Stanley, August 1970. Back row from left: John Nuttall, Alan Braithwaite, Mel Widdup, Dave Baron, Benny Newell, Dick Hartley. Front: Jimmy Hinksman, Franny Franks, Stuart Illingworth, David Bywater, Tommy Beard, Bryan Pemberton. (Garth Dawson)

The most prolific predator of them all: David Hargreaves, scorer of 316 goals in 355 appearances. (Garth Dawson)

Chairman John Alty, in jacket and tie, awaits the kick-off as Stanley face Gateshead in the FA Cup second qualifying round, October 1983.
(Don McPhee/Guardian Newspapers Ltd 1983)

Pierce came across extremely impressively at interview, convincing the chairman that he was ambitious and was in it for the long run. Pierce also had good contacts from some previous work he had done for the Professional Footballers' Association, as well as from his time as a player.

As things turned out, Thornley's presence was vital. Bizarrely, Pierce did not have a phone installed at his house, so Thornley became the hub of communication between management and players as they set about constructing a new team. Of the previous season's first team regulars, only Dave Tattersall and Gary Butcher remained, though some reserve team players with first team experience were also signed on, including Duncan Seddon, Mark Heys and goalkeeper Andy Cutts.

With so few players at the club, Pierce initially abolished the distinction between reserve team and first team, treating all the players as one squad and appealing in the local paper for Accrington Combination managers to recommend their better players. By the first week of July, Pierce had made fifteen signings, but few were local, with most from the Tameside area with which he was familiar, from clubs like Stalybridge, Mossley and Hyde. The most notable recruit was Gus Wilson, who was signed as a midfielder, but who would make an equally worthy contribution in defence.

With pre-season friendlies underway, Pierce had collected more than thirty players from which he could make his first team squad. As the management team continued in this task, the focus of the board shifted temporarily to other aspects of Stanley's progress up the non-league ladder. The club announced yet more developments to the ground with plans to extend the clubhouse and include a lounge to allow match sponsors to receive club hospitality while watching the game.

This was deemed especially important by Terry Styring, who convinced John Alty that developing match day sponsorship was crucial to the club's finances, while the extension would make the clubhouse less crowded on match days and enable the club to hold bigger functions.

Original builders' estimates came to £20,000, so the ever-willing volunteers behind the scenes offered to do the work themselves simply for the cost of the materials, estimated at £6,000. Stanley took out another brewery loan to cover these costs and the project was soon underway.

The PR offensive continued when, on August 4th 1988, Stanley launched the 'All the Way' campaign. The idea was to hang a promotion drive on the hook of the club's forthcoming centenary in 1993. John Alty revealed that Stanley were in debt to the tune of £60,000, and though he maintained that the sum owed was carefully scheduled, he nonetheless expressed the hope that some thousands could be raised for the club during the campaign. Said Alty:

"We are three promotions away from the Fourth Division. To achieve that we will have to improve our ground and be able to afford to pay wages to good players. This is a tremendously exciting time for Accrington Stanley and I just hope that people will support us."

There was little evidence for this. Gary Pierce was new to club management, and although he had decent contacts and maintained a link to the Football League by doing some coaching at Bolton, there was little to suggest that he would be able to bring about a miraculous transformation. The reality was that the best Stanley team of recent years had been completely dismantled and the club needed to rally the troops. Hyndburn MP Ken Hargreaves was brought in to front the campaign, and to the press at least, the club denied that they were setting themselves an unrealistic target:

"Three or four years ago, it would have been a pipe dream. But with the pyramid system it is now within reach, it is realistic. Not so long ago, a lot of people would have said that NPL football and getting an 'A' grading was pie in the sky. The secret is to match success on the pitch with the financial side and developments off the field. Without an initiative like this, there is no way the club could contemplate going beyond the NPL."

At the same time, the chairman was forced to admit that the bill for the club to be ready for League football could be close to £500,000, and the club was even then losing £5,000 a year. It was difficult not to see the 'All the Way' campaign as just another hand-to-mouth fundraising effort covered with a glossy coat of ambition.

A different picture was painted upon the release of the accounts for the previous season. The club announced it had broken even and reduced bank and brewery loans to £36,900. Gate receipts had gone up to £9,500 and sponsorship was also up. While gates had indeed increased during the exciting push for promotion to the NPL, the real reason for the small profit of £160 could be found in the small print of the share capital – £9,000 worth of new shares had recently been issued. It was no secret that the club relied on these periodic injections of cash to survive, but right now it suited the inclusive and positive feel of the 'All the Way' campaign not to draw attention to it.

There was, however, one real breakthrough at this time that proved well worth the £4,000 investment – the use of new 'verti-draining' technology on the Crown pitch. Though improved immeasurably from the Combination days, the surface still retained water and would be churned into mud well before the end of the year. Verti-draining involved boring small holes at regular intervals into the bed of the pitch and then filling them with sand and gravel. Not only did this avoid the far bigger task of digging up large areas of turf, but, as the rainy autumn season descended, it emerged to the delight of everyone that Stanley had finally discovered an effective method of drainage for the Crown Ground pitch. It remained playable throughout the season, and at last offered the prospect that decent players would not have their skills diluted by having to plough through mud for six months of the season.

A decent player very much on the minds of the Crown faithful at this time was Chris Grimshaw. With the season just getting into its stride, Stanley became embroiled in a row with Colne Dynamoes about Grimshaw. Though firmly established as a Crown favourite, he had followed Eric Whalley to Morecambe at the end of the 1987–88 season, but the move had not worked out. Now Grimshaw was eying a move back to Stanley, and rumours suggested that the deal was close to being completed. When Grimshaw then signed for Colne Dynamoes shortly afterwards, chairman John Alty wrote in the next home programme that Colne had deliberately priced Stanley out of the market for the player.

Though Grimshaw kept his counsel, the reality behind the scenes was quite different. After being made a free agent, Grimshaw had actively sought a return to the Crown, but found the club in no hurry to offer him a deal. Someone did eventually get round to seeing him, but by this time Colne had also come in for the player and unsurprisingly were able to better Stanley's offer. Grimshaw was not going to turn down the chance of joining Colne's remarkable adventure, but the reality of events was that Stanley had been negligent in not securing the player rather than being unfairly gazumped for him.

That was hardly the impression made by manager Pierce, who went to the press and fairly tore into Colne and their manager Graham White. He accused the Pendle club of trying to buy the title, of soaking up all the talent around, especially strikers, and of generally inflating wage demands within northern non-league football.

It was not that Pierce's analysis was necessarily wrong. Colne did have a large, well-paid squad and there was a knock-on effect with wages, but this had nothing to do with the Grimshaw case, and the incautious manner in which Pierce expressed himself on the record did not bode well. For example, he also accused Colne of having "spies everywhere" simply because they had tracked the same Bolton-based player, but there was no reason why Colne ought not to scout in the same places as Stanley. It was an early sign – and a worrying one for John Alty – that Pierce was not a character to bite his lip in the name of good relations, but instead would shoot from the hip and speak his mind.

The pattern of the 1988–89 season was established fairly quickly. Stanley proved a match for most opponents at home, playing stylish, attacking football and scoring freely, but struggled away from the Crown. Given the circumstances in which the new squad had been put together, it was understandable that Pierce would struggle to find a settled line-up with which he was satisfied, and this proved to be the case. There was a constant stream of players either leaving or arriving at the club during the season, and again, most came from the Tameside area.

One such arrival was midfielder Darren Scott, who came from NPL side Mossley for £250, becoming the first player for whom Stanley had paid a transfer fee, a policy agreed by the board during the summer. In response to a poor run of form in December, the management team brought in more players, including hefty forward Mel Tottoh from Bamber Bridge, creative midfielder Ken Quigg and defender Steve Guest.

Pierce had guided Stanley to the safety of mid-table, but the new manager was hugely frustrated with the inconsistency of his team, perfectly illustrated over the holiday period when Stanley crushed Radcliffe Borough 6-1 on Boxing Day at the Crown, but then were flattened themselves 5-0 at Colne on New Year's Day in front of 1,278 spectators. As exasperated as Pierce was by the defeat at Colne, they were by far the strongest side in the division, and onlookers doubted whether his public criticism of the side would help matters. He said of the team after the Colne game:

> "Make no mistake, changes will be made, we are not putting up with that rubbish. I feel cheated and I told them so. I just feel sorry for the Accrington supporters who made the trip. We trained on the morning of the match and they were told how to play it but they just couldn't do it. They didn't have the brains or the heart to go in there and battle."

When, shortly afterwards, Stanley were beaten at Darwen in the Lancashire Floodlit Trophy, Pierce appeared to distance himself from the efforts of his players when he said:

"When they finally got the ball in the net, nobody was more surprised than us on the bench. I want every player to think about how they are playing. I want every player to go out there and die for the club."

In reality, Pierce could not avoid accountability for any indiscipline on the part of the players, for problems with his managerial style had arisen quite early on in the season. On October 9th, Stanley had suffered a very poor defeat at lowly Sutton Town, and the manager's plans were disrupted when Mark Heys failed to turn up for the game. Heys said that he had not known that there had been a game on. The following Monday, Pierce had to hold a 'clear the air' meeting at the Crown with the players and clarify some of the rules and regulations to which he expected them to adhere, but the issue seemed equally to be one of organisation and communication on the part of the management.

The New Year saw an improvement in form that led to Pierce taking the division's Manager of the Month award for March, by which time Stanley had lost just once in twelve outings. In perhaps the two best performances of the season, Southport were put to the sword 4-0 in the Lancashire Junior Cup, and Burnley were soundly beaten 4-1 in the Floodlit Trophy. Easter Monday was also quite an occasion at the Crown when 2,015 spectators turned up for the clash with runaway leaders Colne Dynamoes, and Stanley fought hard for a creditable 2-2 draw in front of what was a record crowd, both for the club and for the NPL First Division.

But for all these signs of progress, there were other incidents to suggest that Pierce would not be a long-term occupant of the manager's seat. After a poor performance at Alfreton Town on March 3rd, Pierce admitted that some players had not turned up for training, and when, at the end of that month, Pierce won recognition for his team's form, John Alty had a tankard inscribed with the same honour for Dave Thornley, a discreet but clear sign that the chairman regarded Thornley's role at the club as being far from a mere assistant.

But even Thornley could not escape censure following the events of the Lancashire Floodlit Trophy tie at Great Harwood on April 19th. Great Harwood Town FC, two divisions below Stanley in the second tier of the NWC, were now being managed by Eric Whalley, so, inevitably, some personal animosities were thrown in alongside the usual local bragging rights. Stanley had edged the home fixture 1-0 in a close and hard-fought contest which could have been won by either side, so now, on their own patch, Harwood attacked Stanley from the off and played with the greater desire throughout. Stanley were thoroughly beaten long before the end, and the frustration of Pierce's men boiled over in a febrile second half that saw six Stanley players booked and two sent off, most as a result of the players criticising the referee.

Indiscipline on the pitch never reflects well on the management team, but on this occasion Pierce's own actions did his reputation irreparable damage. The worst incident was sparked by a red card shown to Stanley forward Mel Tottoh, who reacted furiously to his dismissal and had to be restrained by team-mates. Pierce ran onto the pitch to shepherd his man from the field, but then angrily remonstrated with the officials. Eric Whalley approached Pierce and said something, upon which Pierce made a lunge at Whalley and almost knocked him over. This was too much for John Alty, who ran onto the pitch himself, shouting "Think of the club!" in his efforts to calm Pierce down. Dave Thornley was also booked for running onto the pitch. Quite apart from the 3-0 defeat, it had been a shambolic and embarrassing episode.

Pierce later publicly apologised to all concerned, pointing out that it was out of character for him, but his actions had sown serious doubts about his suitability for the job, certainly as far as the board was concerned. Alty held a long meeting with Pierce and Thornley after the game, and admitted in the local paper that it had been a sad and shameful night for the club. Stanley pulled out of the competition immediately after this game.

There was, mercifully, little left of the season by this time, and Stanley played out their remaining fixtures to end the season in a creditable sixth position. Given that Pierce had arrived at the Crown to find just one surviving senior player from the previous squad, there could be no complaints about Stanley's final placing. Though they had suffered from inconsistency – the *Accrington Observer* commented that "Stanley have the frustrating habit of either raising their standards to match top class sides or lowering them to be on a par with inferior opposition," – they were one of the division's more prolific scorers.

However, it was off the field that the more notable events occurred. As part of the 'All the Way' campaign, a gala day was held at the club in October, with sponsored walkers arriving from four Football League grounds: Blackburn, Burnley, Preston and Bolton. John Alty and Hyndburn MP Ken Hargreaves had both raised around £1,000 in sponsorship, and another MP, Burnley's Peter Pike, had also walked from his constituency to the Crown Ground for the cause. With the Accrington Lions helping to run events around the ground, it was exactly the kind of family atmosphere that those around the club wanted to promote. Bill Parkinson was also involved, and he must have looked upon the proceedings with a proud eye.

By the end of the year, the 'All the Way' campaign had raised £6,000, and the board put another positive spin on the finances. John Alty announced that the club policy was now to pay transfer fees and to employ more contracted players, and some of the figures from the accounts were impressive. Income from commercial activities rose to over £53,000, and commission from a new home insurance initiative netted the club £10,000. However, the shift to Manchester-based players meant a steep rise in travelling expenses to over £22,000, and new liabilities had been incurred with loans from a brewery and the FA. Once again the club showed a small profit of £547, but this was underpinned by another £14,500 put into the club in the form of shares.

Just before Christmas, the extension to the clubhouse, the Hudson Lounge, was officially opened. In the ceremony, John Alty paid a well-deserved tribute to the people who had built the extension. They had saved the club over £15,000 in building expenses, and had created a facility that would in the future raise a lot more.

The chairman named Jack Hudson, after whom the Lounge was named, Arthur McGilveray, David Clarke, Stan Spencer, Jim Shaw, Derek Dixon, Norman Sumner and Frank Gallacher as the main volunteers behind the building effort. In another fitting tribute, the club made life vice-presidents of two stalwarts behind the scenes, Doris Moore and Lily Bullock, and bestowed the same on the first three Stanley managers, Jimmy Hinksman, Don Bramley and David Baron, who, said Alty, had put Stanley back on the map.

The first week in April 1989 also saw the premiere of a very significant twenty seconds of film – the now famous Milk Marketing Board television advert in which two youngsters knock back the white stuff after being told by Ian Rush that without it they'd "only" be good enough to play for Accrington Stanley. The advert was clearly a light-hearted reprise of the old music hall joke that poked fun at the club when Stanley were perennial strugglers in the old Third Division (North). Though few suspected it at the time, the advert has gone down as something of a classic of the genre, due in no small part to the performance of Carl Rice, the eight-year-old who memorably wrapped a broad, incredulous Liverpudlian accent around "Accrington Stanley" as if he was describing a particularly horrific form of mediaeval torture.

The club was paid £5,000 for the advert, though chairman John Alty ruefully confided to a director that he thought he might have got more had he bargained a little more forcefully. Ian Rush apparently received double this amount, and he was not being insulted! But at the time, that fee represented half a season's gate receipts, and it paid for more verti-draining and a new roof on the dressing rooms.

There were some at the Crown who thought that the advert was just another kick in the teeth for the town, but time has proved them wrong. The advert has cropped up regularly on television down the years, enough to have made it a handy publicity vehicle for Stanley, and the football team have had the last laugh. Today, no footy-mad eight-year-old worth his or her salt would have to ask: "Accrington Stanley: who are they?"

The 1988–89 season had, regrettably, been a season to rebuild and gather strength, but John Alty knew that it would only be a twelve month hiatus. The promotion of Colne Dynamoes to the NPL (and, no one doubted, to that title as well come the following May) meant that Stanley had once again been overtaken by a local non-league rival. Unlike Clitheroe, however, Colne were easily outspending Stanley thanks to the lavish funding of their owner, Graham White. Nonetheless, the 1989–90 season was Stanley's last chance to fulfil the pledge made by John Alty in 1984 that he would bring NPL football to the Crown by the end of the decade.

At least Pierce and Thornley now had another chance to fine tune the squad for a tilt at promotion. Most of the previous season's players were initially retained, and eight were added, including Chris Grimshaw, who rejoined the club from Colne Dynamoes, and big centre-forward Ian Blackstone, who arrived from Harrogate Railway Athletic. Most players, however, continued to commute to the club from the Tameside area, and this led to a row in which midfielder Ken Quigg walked out on Stanley after his demands for more travelling expenses were turned down.

Quigg had been something of a find, spotted as an amateur playing for Highfield United of the Manchester League, but ending the season the recipient of Stanley's young player of the year award. Keen to retain Quigg, the club had eventually come to an agreement with the young midfielder, but it was another reminder of something long suspected by Stanley fans – that it was unrealistic to expect too much loyalty from part-time players with no attachment to the town.

Nonetheless, on the eve of the new season both the chairman and manager sounded optimistic that they had put together a group of players, twenty in total, capable of challenging for promotion.

Despite early problems with injuries and suspensions, with forward Mel Tottoh out for a month for his antics at Great Harwood, Stanley began the season well.

When, on 20th September, they won 1-0 at Penrith on a foul evening of wind and rain, the *Accrington Observer* cautiously tipped Stanley to last the distance, noting the work ethic of the team and their adaptability to the conditions.

Defeat at Mossley in the second qualifying round of the FA Cup was Stanley's first major reversal of the season, and in October they strengthened the squad further with the acquisition of Tibor Szabo, signed from Buxton for around £900. On October 11th, Stanley's attacking prowess saw off Workington Town 4-2 at the Crown, and although the team had not played particularly well, it represented an impressive unbeaten start to the season; but things were about to change.

On Saturday 14th October, Stanley suffered their first league defeat at Eastwood Hanley, and, as it had been two seasons before, that journey back from the Potteries proved fateful. Pierce took exception to some comments from board members about the performance of the team, and he left the coach at Bury having resigned from the manager's position.

When news of Pierce's resignation became known in

203

the town, popular opinion appeared to back the manager, perhaps unsurprisingly given the position of the team in the heart of the promotion race. The editorial in the next edition of the *Accrington Observer* said:

"Without wishing to take sides, it's fair to say that most of the fans thought that Mr Pierce was well on the way to creating a team capable of winning promotion this season. A chairman like Mr Alty does, of course, have the right to express an opinion on playing matters but immediately after a game, when football people are notoriously touchy, may not be the right time to do it."

There were further suggestions that the club ought to make efforts to persuade Pierce to return, led by none other than Bill Parkinson, who echoed the sentiments of the newspaper that the manager had been taking the club in the right direction and that the club ought to ask him to reconsider.

The perspective of the board was quite different. The chairman turned immediately to Dave Thornley and asked him to take over. Thornley accepted without hesitation. Pierce's popularity among the supporters was partly explained by his heart-on-the-sleeve style. He said what he was thinking at the time and the supporters warmed to this, especially if it involved a local rival. Pierce was also an effortlessly egalitarian character who had time for everyone at the club. His popularity was well-earned. John Alty reflected that Pierce would have been an ideal commercial manager, some role that involved contact with the supporters. He was not, however, cut out for the role of team manager, and there is no evidence that John Alty or any of the directors thought for a moment to ask Pierce back.

The following Tuesday, October 17th, Dave Thornley took Stanley to Workington Town for his first game in charge, and Stanley were well worth their impressive 3-0 win. Striker Mel Tottoh announced his departure immediately after the game, but Thornley's Stanley continued regardless. In

November, the manager signed goalkeeper Martin White and the following month added experience to the squad in the form of ex-Chelsea midfielder Ian Britton.

On December 12th, the team reached the halfway stage of their league campaign, and they did it with a 2-0 home defeat of Irlam Town, a result that took Stanley to the top of the table with 12 wins and 7 draws from their 21 games. With the added bonus of the Crown Ground pitch now coping with everything the Lancashire elements could throw at it, things were looking very encouraging indeed. But hopes of a serene passage to the NPL would not survive the holiday period.

On Boxing Day, hundreds of Stanley fans converged on the Rawtenstall ground of Rossendale United, now Stanley's nearest league rivals. Rossendale were mid-table, but in front of 1,369 they succeeded in knocking Stanley out of their stride and inflicted a rare defeat on Thornley's men, Stanley going down 2-1. This was the precursor to a poor January, which also saw the manager sack three players, including Darren Scott, for missing a training session. Thornley assured the fans that the rest of the team were well motivated and determined to land promotion, but the manager also admitted that there had to be more discipline in general. It was a worrying shadow over what had been hitherto a time of uneventful progress.

Despite further defeats at the hands of promotion rivals Droylsden and Whitley Bay, Stanley ended January still clinging on to the second promotion spot. What was helping the Stanley cause was the evenness of the promotion race, with five teams vying for the two places and no single team able to put distance between themselves and the rest. It did, however, make games between the top teams particularly significant, and when, on March 3rd, Stanley lost at promotion rivals Leek Town, the *Accrington Observer* thought it the end of Stanley's challenge.

The paper had reckoned without the cheque book of John Alty. Stanley had gone to Harrogate Town in February and the defence had been given a torrid time by the home side's fast and powerful centre-forward, Andy Bondswell. After the game, a mightily impressed Dave Thornley conspired to get Bondswell's phone number on the back of a beer mat, and John Alty subsequently offered to make the big striker Accrington Stanley's first £100 a week player.

Bondswell was being courted by Blackpool, but with a good job as a chemical engineer and an aspiring career, he did not have to go full-time. Harrogate told Alty that he could make an offer for the player if he wanted, but that Stanley had no chance because a League club was in for him. It must therefore have been something of a shock when Bondswell announced he was moving to Stanley, but Harrogate were mollified by the £1,000 cheque that came their way for his services.

The recruitment of Bondswell was the clearest sign yet that no expense would be spared to get Stanley into the NPL, and the team responded with four wins and a draw in the next five games, a run that included an excellent double over Emley which put the Yorkshire side out of the promotion frame.

Stanley went into the Easter programme once more on top of the league, although with fewer games left than Leek and Droylsden below them. Stanley had to win their two home games, and though they won the first on the Saturday, they disastrously lost the second, an Easter Monday derby clash against Rossendale, where a late goal gave the visitors a shock 1-0 win in front of over 700 at the Crown. That the scorer was Paul Beck, an Accrington lad who had already left Stanley three times, made the result all the more maddening (as did Beck's celebration).

Leek had won their games in hand and were secure as champions. Stanley had 76 points from 40 games, Droylsden 74 points from 39 games – and so Stanley's visit to Droylsden on April 21st was virtually a promotion decider. The Butchers Arms was never the place to go for a pleasant gander at the finer aspects of the game, and now, filled with more than a thousand home fans, it was even less so. Under the guidance of Phil Staley, Droylsden attacked with pace and strength and succeeded in dictating the pattern of the game. Stanley were defeated, and their hopes of promotion to the NPL were effectively ended for another year. Stanley finished third, although their playing record was virtually the same as the year before.

It was a bitter disappointment to all concerned, but none more so than John Alty, whose pledge of NPL football by the end of the decade had been dashed at the very last, despite a record investment in playing staff. Wages for the season had totalled £3,500, with a further £28,000 on travelling and expenses. In the face of this, gate receipts remained stagnant at £13,000, although commercial activities had shown a vast improvement, with sponsorship bringing in £13,500 and the weekly draws and lotteries earning £16,000. Overall the club lost £3,500 on the season, the "price of ambition", according to the *Accrington Observer*.

For one director, it was too much. Terry Styring left the board citing differences over how to run the club. Styring argued that the club had to be given a budget and be run strictly within these means, essentially applying a classic business model to Stanley. Hauling out the cheque book for a player and putting him on record wages, as Alty did with Andy Bondswell, was not Styring's idea of how to do things. Alty disagreed. Experience had told him that it was impossible to budget accurately for a football club. Each season he had budgeted for mid-table and early Cup exits, but found that invariably he ended up putting money in for the good of the club. It was simply the nature of the business, he reasoned, that you gave things a boost when you had the opportunity to progress.

Alty was the boss, so there was little Styring could do other than either buy him out or resign. On this occasion, he chose the latter option, but this was just the first act of a fraught relationship between John Alty and Terry Styring that would continue for the next few seasons.

There was one happy ending in this anti-climactic season, and that was the success of the Accrington Stanley youth team in what was their inaugural season. Managed by David Hinksman, son of Jimmy, the youngsters won the Lancashire FA under-18 trophy with a 3-0 defeat of Lancaster City in the March final. Two of the players, David Bradshaw and Jamie Livesey, were awarded a Lancashire county cap after playing regularly for the county under-18 team.

Such was the impression made by Hinksman's team that he was asked to manage Stanley's reserve side, which had been competing with little success in the Lancashire League, playing against the 'A' sides of most of the area's strongest Football League clubs. The set-up below the first team thus had a familiar ring to it, with David Hinksman in charge, and both Jimmy Hinksman and Don Bramley assisting. None were claiming any money for their time, an increasingly disparate scenario to that surrounding the first team. For as Stanley prepared for another attempt at promotion, chairman Alty decided that the club would go the extra mile – he granted Dave Thornley the resources to gather the strongest squad in the division in an attempt to finally secure Stanley's place in the top tier of the NPL.

The 1990–91 season started off with the encouraging news that a major local business, Holland's Pies of Baxenden, had become the club's main sponsor with a deal worth around £10,000. It was just the financial tonic needed as Stanley added to the wage bill with a series of signings.

The most high profile of these was striker Paul Beck, signed for £1,000 from Rossendale in July. Beck had a long history with Stanley, having been first signed by Mick Finn in the 1982–83 pre-season. His first goal arrived shortly afterwards when he scored at Rhyl on September 25th 1982, but the striker's berth at Stanley in those days was difficult to wrest from Dave Hargreaves, and Beck soon left to play for Altham, then Stanley's reserve team, scoring a hat-trick in the final as they won the Accrington Combination Cup. A spell at Foxhill Old Boys ended with his return to Stanley in October 1984 under Gerry Keenan. Again, he did not last long, moving to Rossendale United in February 1985. He joined Clitheroe for the 1986–87 season, top-scoring with 20 league goals.

Rejoining Rossendale the following year, he helped them to the NWC First Division title in 1988–89, though he did briefly return to the Crown on loan under Eric Whalley. By this time, his talent was widely recognised, and he underlined it by ending the 1989–90 campaign as the top scorer in the NPL First Division. In his previous three spells at Stanley, Beck had scored five goals in 18 fitful appearances, but he returned now as a key first team player.

Thornley also signed a tough-tackling midfielder in Alan Crompton, and forward Clive Dunn from local side Great Harwood Town. But the sensational August events in Colne offered Stanley another source of talent. Colne Dynamoes, runaway NPL champions the previous season, had been unable to find a home acceptable to the Conference and had been wound up. Their large squad suddenly had to find other clubs, and Thornley swooped for full-back Duncan McFadyen and centre-half Simon Westwell. Another ex-Colne player arriving at the Crown was Jock Wylie, though he had signed before the fold-up.

Pre-season was a time of real optimism, and everyone agreed that Thornley's squad was one of the strongest ever seen at the club. One friendly involved the relaunch of Bradford Park Avenue in Bradford. After folding in 1973, they restarted in 1988 in the West Riding County Amateur League.

Now, just two seasons later, they were in the pyramid system, preparing for their first season in the NWC Second Division, and were ready to move to a new home within Bradford, having previously been located in Bramley. They asked Stanley to help them officially open their new ground, and the nostalgic quality of two ex-Football League clubs generated a great deal of publicity. Unfortunately, the game was marred by a dreadful tackle that put Stanley midfielder Alan Crompton out for the season.

With the season underway, good home league form saw Stanley well-placed in the promotion race, but what really caught the imagination of the town was the team's run in the FA Cup. Stanley had not been beyond the third qualifying round since 1974, when they had lost at Altrincham, so they entered the competition at the preliminary round stage, travelling to Blackpool Wren Rovers and defeating the NWC Second Division side 4-2. Stanley were then fortunate enough to draw four consecutive home ties.

West Auckland Town of the Northern League Second Division were seen off 3-0 in the first qualifying round before much tougher opposition arrived in the shape of legendary Cup fighters Blyth Spartans. Blyth's reputation and Stanley's history made it one of the more high-profile FA Cup ties of the day, with Stanley featured in the *Daily Telegraph* on the morning of the game.

Though Blyth's glory days in the Cup were behind them, they were Stanley's equals on the day, and only a late goal in a compelling game saw Stanley through 2-1. Another top Northern League side, Gretna, made the journey to the Crown for the third qualifying round. The game attracted 1,121 spectators, far more than a typical league fixture, and another last-gasp goal saw Stanley through 2-1, though this was a dour struggle far removed from the Blyth encounter.

Just one team now stood between Stanley and a return to the First Round proper for the first time since 1961, and the team out of the velvet bag was Fleetwood Town, a team one division higher than Stanley in the top tier of the NPL. Fleetwood were favourites for the tie, and Stanley's morale was not helped by a midweek 5-0 drubbing at Bridlington Town in the League Cup just days before the big game on Saturday October 27th.

A record crowd of 2,096 descended on the Crown on what was a chilly, miserable day, and things were not to improve for the home side.

A goal in each half saw the visitors through, and Stanley

never really got going on the day. The occasion was also ruined by crowd trouble, with the game stopped for twenty minutes in the first half because of fighting that spilled onto the pitch.

Though Stanley chalked up another league win against Lancaster City a few days after the Fleetwood game, the team began thereafter to struggle for form, with injuries to key players not helping the cause. Particularly noticeable was a tendency to concede, and when, in mid-November, Stanley could only manage a 1-1 draw at home to lowly Netherfield, Dave Thornley and his assistant Paul Webb were sacked. Thornley had been in charge for 13 months. Under his guidance, Stanley had won 32 and lost 20 of 65 games, and they had taken 23 points from the 15 league games of the current campaign. It was undeniably short of promotion form, something the board felt they had given him the resources to achieve.

The *Accrington Observer* agreed with the decision, commenting on the "remarkable haul of players" Thornley had been allowed to sign, and the "seemingly bottomless pot of money to bring in the players – and promotion". Thornley himself was philosophical about the decision. He was honest enough to admit that recent form had been below par, but behind the scenes there had been changes about which Thornley remained ambiguous.

One of these was the return to the board of Terry Styring, but this time in the much more central role of 'joint chairman'. Precisely what this entailed was not entirely clear, but it reflected a further investment in the club on Styring's part, the need for which was obvious given the recent commitment to players and wages. As joint chairman, Styring had a brief to resume what had been a successful role in increasing the commercial base of the club, and he also became more involved in the football side of things.

Styring himself argued that assisting the manager in terms of bringing in players for him to assess was not necessarily interference, provided all involved were focused on the same goals and moving in the same direction. Whilst this view undoubtedly had merit in theory, the reality was rather different. As the one person who was ultimately accountable for the team's performance, Dave Thornley had to insist that, over team affairs, his word was final. The relationship between the two had not been helped by a row over Stanley's injured midfielder Alan Crompton. Thornley insisted that the club honour its contract to the player, but Styring was equally adamant that the club could not afford to pay wages to those who were not playing.

In the press, Styring, Alty and Sam Adams were the named board members who had taken the decision. They issued this statement:

> "Since Terry Styring became joint chairman, he has worked tirelessly with Dave in an effort to ensure that Dave's job as manager was secured so that continuity as far as management was concerned could be maintained. But results have not enabled this to happen and the directors took the view that the change had to be made if results were to be improved. We are the best supported team in our division and the sixth best in the whole of the NPL."

Given how quickly the board found a replacement, there was little doubt that they had earmarked Thornley's replacement in advance. Their target was Phil Staley, the manager who had steered Droylsden to promotion the previous season at Stanley's expense. Staley was one of the most colourful characters in non-league. He had a string of disciplinary offences to his name, mainly for blowing his top at referees, but the season before he had been found guilty of bringing the game into disrepute after the league had discovered a forged signature on the registration form of a recent signing, although Staley himself maintained that he had not done it.

But for all the misdemeanours, Staley also had a track record of dragging up teams by the collar and achieving success. He also had a remarkable network of contacts in the game, all listed in his legendary black book, which one chairman described as containing more numbers than a telephone directory.

From Staley's point of view, the approach from Stanley was completely unexpected, but his recollection of the first meeting with John Alty and Terry Styring was instructive:

"That night, I had my eyes well and truly opened by the determination and ambition of the two guys from Accrington who told me they wanted a new manager to come in and get them promotion as quickly as possible. They believed that, having done it once with Droylsden, I could do it again with Accrington Stanley. They made me an offer there and then which saw my meagre pay packet treble overnight, and the wage bill available to me was twice that at Droylsden."

This impression might reflect the financial limits that Staley worked under at Droylsden as much as the relative affluence of Stanley, but Staley could hardly refuse the offer as it was presented to him. He accepted the post almost immediately. John Alty told the local press:

"We've chosen him because he is a winner and has done it all before. The most important thing to Stanley at the moment is getting out of the First Division. The sooner we go up the better. This division is getting tougher every year. Better teams are coming in and the weaker ones dropping out. Promotion is a must and we believe Phil can get it for us."

It was a tall order for the new manager. As December approached, Stanley held a mid-table position, 14 points adrift of the promotion places, but with games in hand. Staley took a few weeks to assess the squad, during which time Andy Bondswell won the division's player of the month award, cementing his place in the side at least.

Just before Christmas, Staley announced that he needed at least five new recruits, and he set about reshaping the side to his specifications. Nine players were either moved on or put on the transfer list, and the first major recruit arrived in the formidable frame of striker Bernie Hughes, signed from Droylsden for a club record £2,250, with Terry Styring personally funding the transfer. (At the same time, a Hyndburn teenager by the name of Brett Ormerod was being signed on schoolboy forms by Blackburn Rovers.)

Just as Alty had hoped he would do, Staley succeeded in geeing up the side. Stanley won seven of their first eight games under his command, including a 4-0 demolition of Rossendale United on Boxing Day. By mid-January, the team had risen from thirteenth to sixth.

On January 23rd, a Wednesday evening, a Lancashire Junior Cup tie at the Crown was postponed because of a frozen patch in front of the stand, and in doing so it became the first senior home game to be called off for nearly three years, an uninterrupted run of 89 games played on schedule. For those who remembered the mud heap that once masqueraded as a pitch at the Crown, it was a remarkable transformation and some vindication for those who had grappled with the clay bed for many long and hard hours.

In the event, a cold snap put paid to most non-league football for a few weeks, and it denied Stanley action just when the team had built up momentum. Far more serious was the sudden interruption to the cash flow of the club. The absence of a home game through late January and most of February brought on a serious crisis with Stanley having exhausted their financial reserves. There was no other solution than for those board members who could afford it to inject more money (Styring later reckoned to have put in another £15,000 at this point) and manager Staley was forced to make some economies. It caused a lot of disharmony both among the directors and between them and the manager, and raised serious questions about the viability of running the club on the very edge of its financial means.

When the weather did relent, the team could not pick up from where they had left off, and when they slumped to a shock 3-2 home defeat to lowly Irlam Town on February 29th, there were concerns that Stanley were going to miss out again. But Phil Staley earned his tripled wage now, guiding the team to another solid run of form. Stanley won at promotion rivals Rhyl, and the point earned from a 2-2 draw at Netherfield on March 27th sent Stanley to the top of the table.

A few more victories would have sent Stanley clear at the top and on their way to the title, but to the exasperation of all concerned, the team now started to draw games they should on paper have won. To heighten the anxiety, the two teams below them with games in hand – Emley and Whitley Bay – maintained their winning form and overhauled Stanley, just as Droylsden had done a year before. For the rapidly greying John Alty, it must have seemed as though Stanley were somehow destined not to reach the top tier of the NPL.

By mid-April, Stanley had to win their final four games to stand any chance of going up. They won the first two, but on May 3rd, the eve of Stanley's final home game, results elsewhere confirmed that Stanley could not win promotion automatically. They had lost just that one league game in the 24 they had played under Phil Staley, but too many draws had condemned Stanley to a final position of fourth.

There was, however, hope that Stanley might yet find salvation from another season of near-misses. The rumours had, in fact, started well before the season's end. The talk was that there might be up to two more vacancies in the NPL premier division, with doubts over the future of both South Liverpool and Shepshed Charterhouse. South Liverpool's ground had been deemed unfit for the NPL and they had not upgraded it as they were obliged to, and the man behind Shepshed had withdrawn his backing.

John Alty initially dead-batted the rumours. Shepshed were soon reprieved, reforming as Shepshed Albion and maintaining their status. Furthermore, the club in line for South Liverpool's berth was Worksop, who had finished third. But there was another complicating factor. Worksop were building a new ground that would not be ready in time to be graded for the NPL top tier, but they had the option of continuing a ground share arrangement with Gainsborough for another season. If they continued at

Gainsborough, the NPL place would be theirs.

On June 15th, it was confirmed. Worksop were playing the following season at their own ground. Accrington Stanley – with their NPL-approved stadium, complete with floodlights, 200 seats and covered standing for 1,500 – had finally made it to the top table of northern non-league, and no one gave a hoot that they had done it by the back door. Stanley had been the victims themselves of unpredictable league officialdom in the past, and all the thousands of pounds and thousands of hours invested since in the Crown Ground had been for this very eventuality. Stanley had ensured that they were ready to go up, and they had reaped the reward for their ambition and foresight.

Dave Thornley could be excused for thinking himself hard done by. He had guided Stanley to third the year before with no reward, and now his successor had won promotion with a fourth place finish. It hardly seemed fair, but Thornley knew that he had played his part in the club's finally achieving its long-held ambition of NPL football. Some of the players he had brought to the club had made vital contributions to the cause, none more so than Paul Beck, whose return of 28 league and cup goals was the best return since the days of Dave Hargreaves.

The following few days were to be savoured by all Stanley fans as the team, the board and the supporters all celebrated together. The club had achieved what everyone had wanted, and so it was right that divisions could be momentarily forgotten, but it would be a brief respite from what had been an embattled period for John Alty. The chairman had delivered what he had promised, but it had not been an easy or harmonious time, though Alty himself would be the first to admit that he did not always make life easy for himself.

One such instance came after the Lancashire FA under-18 Cup final, contested for the second successive year by Stanley's youth team. On this occasion they had to settle for runners-up, but Alty caused a storm when he caustically criticised the lack of support for the youngsters:

"I was disgusted. For a team of our status in the non-league pyramid it was a terrible turn out. Apart from Ruth Chadwick, I can't remember one other member of the official supporters' club who attended the game, a county cup final. If that is the encouragement that our best young players are going to get, then we are wasting our time. Only recently, Terry Styring and myself came under criticism for paying transfer fees and bringing players from outside the area to the club. We were told there were not enough locally based players. But if supporters want to see more local players come through they have got to support the youth team. They can't have it both ways."

Alty undeniably had a point, but his tone did not go down well, especially with the official supporters' club. His outburst provoked at least one printable reply in the local paper, but it was dripping with contempt, calling Alty the "great white chief of the Crown Ground".

Although for a different reason, there was little sympathy either from Phil Staley. He had little time for youth or reserve teams, preferring instead to focus all resources on the first team squad. No doubt as a result of Staley's attitude, David Hinksman resigned from managing the reserves and then found himself sacked from his role with the youth team. In May, Alty decisively ended all the friction by disbanding the reserve team, arguing that too few players were coming through the ranks for the club to justify the annual £6,000 expenditure on running the side.

Money was clearly uppermost in the chairman's mind during the summer. Promotion had been achieved, but at a cost. When the accounts were released later in the year, it was revealed that Stanley had incurred a huge £25,687 loss over the season, with a 500 per cent rise in the amount paid to players, from £3,575 to £22,477. Losses on that scale were unsustainable, but now Stanley needed investment to compete at a higher level.

For all these concerns, John Alty could at least reflect

with satisfaction on a mission accomplished. When he first arrived at the Crown in 1975, the ground consisted of little more than a field and a pavilion. The first major ground investment happened under John Prescott, but it was Alty who oversaw the most significant developments from 1982 onwards.

By the time Stanley's promotion to the NPL was confirmed, the Crown looked like a proper football ground. There was still scope for further development, but from the most rudimentary of surroundings had grown the outline of a small stadium. It was possible to look around the Crown in 1991 and see how, with a bit of work here and there, the ground could be upgraded to the standards required by the Conference and the Football League. In exactly ten years of leadership under Alty, for all the doubts about his style and the periodic financial crises, it represented quite an achievement.

Stanley were now just one promotion away from a return to nationwide football in the Conference, but the real question as the 1991–92 season approached was whether Stanley could survive at the higher level. Other clubs before Stanley had declined NPL football, fearful of the financial pressures the league generated, but for Alty there could be no such circumspection. His chairmanship had been geared up for this moment for years; he simply had to find the resources to fund Accrington Stanley as a competitive Northern Premier League club.

Chapter Six

1991–99
Cup Drama,
League Decline

AS PREPARATIONS BEGAN for Stanley's first season in the top flight of the NPL, the key issue for the board and manager to resolve was how to both rein in the finances and allow the team to compete. It was not a question with an easy solution, and before a ball had been kicked there was a casualty. On July 19th, Terry Styring resigned from the Accrington Stanley board for the second time.

Ostensibly, Styring's departure revolved around a pre-season friendly against Blackpool that had been arranged for the Crown. It was an attractive fixture that held the prospect of bringing decent away support, but John Alty remembered all too clearly the crowd trouble during the Fleetwood FA Cup tie in 1990, and suspected that the troublemakers that day had been Blackpool fans. He contacted the local police about the friendly, and they recommended a police presence at the game. For Alty, the additional cost this would entail made the game a non-starter and so he cancelled the fixture, a decision that Styring disagreed with and which, on the record at least, led to his departure.

Styring would later disclose to the *Accrington Observer* that there was another source of conflict between the two and that the pre-season period of 1991 was a time of great debate within the club. Styring had drafted a stringent budget designed to keep the club on an even keel and prevent it from sliding any further into debt. According to Styring, he insisted that this could be the only way to run the club in the light of the previous season's losses. But for Phil Staley, it meant a cut in his budget and all the consequences – lower wages and a smaller squad. Not surprisingly, he objected.

With the demands of NPL football pointing to the need for a big squad and Styring insisting upon financial restraint, something had to give, and in this instance it was the joint chairman who resigned. At the time, other excuses – such as the row over the Blackpool friendly – were offered for the split, but Styring would later put the blame squarely on the refusal of John Alty to countenance the tight financial discipline that his budget demanded. Styring recalled: "It was quickly evident that my joint chairman could not stomach the medicine," and saw this as a clear signal that his role at the club, which was to balance the books, was at an end.

In hindsight, perhaps it had been a mistake for the two of them to give Phil Staley the impression that Stanley would spend whatever was required to bring success, for Staley, like all managers, was keen to recruit a big squad and was prepared to offer players good wages to come and play for him. That £25,000 deficit was not entirely the result of Staley's team-building, but it did indicate that the club were paying more than ever to their players, though it is also the case that wage inflation had hit the non-league scene, partly a legacy of big spenders like Colne Dynamoes.

The admission price for the Crown was raised to £2.80 for adults, but at a game a fortnight this equated roughly to just £600 per week, and it did not help the club either that three senior players, Bernie Hughes, Chris Grimshaw and Andy Bondswell were holding out for more money. Hughes and Grimshaw soon settled, but Bondswell ended up on the transfer list before finally agreeing terms. Also signed, among others, were goalkeeper Mark Pye, midfielder Jimmy Collins, winger Darren Lyons (for a £500 fee), and Neil Dunleavy, one of the few youth team players to graduate to the senior squad.

On the eve of the start, John Alty sounded unsure as to Stanley's prospects: "I'm looking forward to our first ever season in the NPL. There are new pastures to see and new clubs to visit but I approach the season with some trepidation too because I think it is going to be hard. If we are mid-table after seven or eight matches I will be happy because we have a difficult start."

Adding to the unease was a rash of injuries, suspensions and holiday absences at the beginning of the season. Even so, with a large squad of 21 players, there were still rumours that some players would have to leave to bring down the wage bill, but Staley moved quickly to quash any speculation. With a hint of the debate that had ensued during the summer, he told the *Accrington Observer*: "Under no circumstances is anyone leaving the club. Experience has told me that it's important to have a big squad. With the current problems, that policy has now been fully justified."

All the fears proved unfounded, however, as Stanley enjoyed a good start to their inaugural NPL season. Opening games included a vibrant 3-1 defeat of Morecambe in front of a 750 gate at the Crown, and a hard-fought 2-2 draw at Southport, two excellent results against a pair of the more fancied teams in the division.

John Alty quickly began to sound a lot more upbeat about Stanley's prospects and talked in the press about the club's plans to extend the Duckworth Stand around the corner and along the entire Clayton end, and also to renovate the clubhouse, where part of the old wooden structure remained. Some work had to be completed anyway. The NPL ground inspectors instructed the club to add more seating to the Duckworth Stand, and though the regulations gave clubs one full season to complete the work, Stanley had the situation well in hand having already bought some tip-up seats from Blackburn Rovers.

Stanley's good form continued throughout September. The increased levels of interest could be gauged by the increasing numbers travelling regularly on the coach to away games, so much so that the club had to institute a pre-booking arrangement. On the pitch, an unexpected bonus was the form of winger Darren Lyons. Having been expected to supply crosses to the likes of Hughes and Beck up front, Lyons also developed an eye for goal himself. His skill quickly endeared him to the Crown faithful and by mid-September his eight goals made him the club's top scorer. Also impressed were Bury, who were rumoured to be on the verge of a bid, but things were about to change for both Lyons and Stanley.

As the autumn months closed in, Staley's squad was decimated by injuries, two of the longer term casualties being the central attacking figures of Bernie Hughes and Andy Bondswell. Jimmy Collins, a busy midfielder, was also ruled out for a couple of months. Understandably, form began to suffer. Cracks also started to appear in the managerial team, and on November 15th, Staley sacked his assistant John Bendon, telling the press that "I gave way to John on one or two matters, but in the end you can't have two managers."

A cold snap in mid-November, accompanied by an early snowfall, reduced a midweek crowd to just 281 for a league clash with Chorley. Those who did brave the chill witnessed a 3-2 Stanley victory, their first in six league games. In the programme, Staley made the comment that he had enjoyed the "luxury" of a 15-man squad for the game, an indication of the injury crisis that the team had struggled through in the preceding weeks.

Unfortunately, the return of players from injury did not immediately reap rewards on the pitch, with the following few weeks being perhaps the most difficult of Staley's time at the Crown. He did strengthen the squad with the acquisition of Rossendale United's left-back Steve Lampkin, but on December 1st Stanley were soundly thrashed 4-0 at Blyth Spartans in the third qualifying round of the FA Trophy. So inept was this performance against a team not even in the pyramid system that it provoked quite a response in the *Accrington Observer* from fans bewildered by some of Staley's decisions.

One fan wrote: "To be thrashed by a team from a lower league is bad enough, but hardly surprising to those of us who have watched the team in steady decline over the past few months. Once injuries were the excuse, but what is it now? John Bendon hit the nail on the head when he said he did not agree with Phil Staley on either tactics or team selection. If by tactics he meant teamwork, he is quite correct. The teamwork is non-existent."

The suggestion that John Bendon had been the better managerial bet was a barb carefully aimed at Staley's fleshier parts, but the manager had also invited hostility from the more parochial elements of the crowd by sidelining the two local players in the squad, Paul Beck and Chris Grimshaw. There was always an element that instinctively disliked the fact that players travelled in from all points of the compass, but in this case the critics did seem to have a point. Grimshaw had smashed a hat-trick in an earlier FA Trophy tie at the Crown against Shildon after coming on as a second-half substitute, but he was back on the bench for the following game. One fan contended that: "Management have to play their expensive mistakes week after week in the hope that one day they might justify themselves." At least club sponsors Holland's had cause for satisfaction. Another regular wrote: "The most enjoyable thing at the Crown recently has been the pies."

The undoubted nadir of the season arrived on January 17th, when Stanley lost at Shepshed Albion, a team anchored to the bottom of the league with 23 defeats from their 26 games. The result left Stanley in danger of the relegation zone themselves. Morale had not been helped either by the departure of Darren Lyons, who had walked out of the club, unhappy at what he perceived to be excessive criticism from the Crown faithful. He nonetheless left with the impressive record of 15 goals in 24 appearances.

Gradually, the team turned around their fortunes. The injured core of the squad recovered and slowly regained match fitness, with the return of Jimmy Collins from a nine-week absence appearing to especially lift the side. The first sign of the resurgence was a run to the semi-finals of the

Lancashire Junior Cup, and though Stanley were eliminated by Southport in the last four, the team continued their good form with successive away wins at Goole Town and Buxton. It was enough to earn Staley the February NPL manager of the month award.

The team were set the target of a top nine finish so as to qualify for the following season's President's Cup. Stanley thus tackled the final two months of the season with a purpose, exemplified by a stunning 6-0 win at Bishop Auckland. This result forced the historians at the famous County Durham club to rewrite their record books, for it was the heaviest defeat ever inflicted at Kingsway, one of the country's oldest football grounds.

Stanley finished in eighth position for an entirely satisfactory first campaign in the NPL. Happy with the way the manager had rallied the side in the New Year, John Alty gave Staley a two-year extension to his contract, this in addition to having also invited Staley onto the board, an invitation that the manager had accepted. The extended Duckworth Stand had been completed well before the season's end, and the Crown now had an 'A' grading with the NPL.

Staley announced his intention to retain the majority of the squad. The five contract players, Pye, Lampkin, Beck, Hughes and Cunningham were re-signed, and Jimmy Collins also accepted a contract.

On the way out was Chris Grimshaw, given a free after taking his Stanley record to 254 appearances and 48 goals, and placed on the transfer list at his own request was Andy Bondswell, having scored 36 goals in 99 games.

Staley told the press that he was confident he could take the club up to the Conference provided he was given the resources to bring in the reinforcements he had targeted. The rest of the club, too, both directors and fans, were looking onwards and upwards, but there was an emerging problem. The financial situation was fast assuming critical status. At the club's annual presentation evening, John Alty hinted as much when he said:

"We are now at the crossroads. We can get into the Conference but to do so we need a good side on the pitch and a ground that is up to standard, but we need to stay in, too, because history shows that is an extremely difficult thing to do. Together we can get there, but it will take a lot of hard work."

Others had also sensed Stanley's financial vulnerability. In the depths of the January slump at the Crown, Rossendale United had made an audacious £1,500 double bid for Paul Beck and Chris Grimshaw. The two were allowed to speak to their suitors, but thankfully they decided to stay at Stanley. Their departure would have been a PR catastrophe for the club, and would no doubt have had a real impact both on gates and on the morale of a squad that was, at the time, struggling for form.

But as the chairman set about completing the club's accounts for the season, the actual cost of the club's move to the NPL became apparent. Accrington Stanley had lost the alarming total of £35,000 over the course of the season. Although total expenditure had actually fallen to £97,000, the combined wages and expenses remained high, just under £50,000. Most worryingly, the total debt of the club had risen to £92,000, some of which was short-term and due.

The biggest contributing factor to the loss was a significant fall in income, and to this end the club appointed a commercial manager during the summer. But there could no longer be any denial about the state of the club. Stanley had lost £60,000 during the last two seasons, and were clearly failing to establish their financial viability at the more rarefied levels of non-league football.

On July 17th, John Alty went to the press with the figures and made an appeal for help in the starkest of terms:

"The club is now literally at the crossroads. The present squad looks to be an extremely strong one. It is, however, essential that our income is increased substantially if we are to fund the payments to the quality players which we possess. In past years I have personally injected thousands of pounds into the club, but quite simply I am no longer in a position to do this. It is essential that supporters are not complacent. If they want Stanley to survive at this level, they must come forward and help."

The chairman went on to say that neither would he preside over a club slowly sinking down the pyramid. If no help was forthcoming, then he would sell up to someone else. At least no one could accuse Alty of not laying the cards squarely on the table.

The extremely strong squad to which Alty alluded was the result of yet more transfer activity on the part of Phil Staley. He signed Darren Schofield and John Burns from Droylsden, and Terry Williams arrived from Grove United, both clubs Staley had managed previously. Eddie Johnston was recruited from Bangor City and Charlie Cooper from Emley. Staley had also gone to the press with a plan to sign ex-Manchester United player Gary Worrell, securing a big headline in the local paper: 'Stanley High Hopes for Former Red Devil.' For those familiar with the manager's style, it was uncannily reminiscent of the time that Ashton United, then managed by Staley, had sensationally signed Peter Coyne from Manchester United.

With the financial problems at the club showing no sign of curbing Staley's acquisitive habits, one bit of good news at this time was the new shirt deal with Gibson's Sports, with the company given a franchise deal to produce a range of clothing featuring the club's name and crest. The summer ended on a sad note, however, with the death of Stanley secretary Joe Daly, not long after the club had received the news that both Jimmy Harrower and Harry Hubbick had also passed away. These two men had struggled to keep the old Accrington Stanley going during the early 1960s, and it was sad to relate, but as the 1992–93 season approached, the new Stanley faced similar financial uncertainties.

Cup Drama, League Decline

With the 1992–93 pre-season underway, John Alty announced that he was disbanding the Stanley reserve team. The decision to revive the reserves had been taken in February, with the board apparently persuaded by the argument that it encouraged the sale of season tickets since holders could gain free admission to reserve team games, a privilege that quite a few Crown regulars exercised. Season tickets had thus been sold on this basis, and Stanley had even paid the registration fee for the reserves to the East Lancashire League. Letters of complaint winged in to the *Accrington Observer*, but Alty was unrepentant. He revealed that the finances were still a grave problem and he could not justify the cost of running a reserve team. No one had come forward to join the board in the light of his appeal.

On August 21st, Alty called a general meeting of supporters at the Crown for the Monday after the opening league game. He promised that he would put them in the picture in no uncertain terms about the financial situation at the club. In the event, there were few surprises. The club was still haemorrhaging cash, and no one had come forward to join the board and inject money into the club. Alty announced the formation of a new body, 'Save Accrington Stanley', a supporters' organisation. The inaugural attendance was good, and Alty distributed application forms to those present for the purchase of shares in the club.

As the season kicked off, Staley expressed his confidence in his 17-strong squad, to which he had made two late additions, signing Martin Clark from Lancaster City and Paul Burns from Altrincham. Stanley did not enjoy the most fluent of starts, however, and a poor performance in a defeat at Barrow saw Staley make a few changes. He dropped goalkeeper Mark Pye, and replaced him with a loan signing, Paul Collings. Officially on the staff at Tranmere Rovers, Collings had arrived at Stanley from a trial period at Shrewsbury Town where he had played in the first team. Although he was hoping for a full-time deal at a League club, Collings agreed to a loan period at the Crown while he awaited an offer. It was quite a move by

Staley, for the big 'keeper proved to be a real asset in the months that followed.

With Stanley in such financial straits, the idea of promotion to the Conference was a non-starter. The club could not afford the required ground improvements, and neither could they fund a squad of sufficient strength. What the club really needed was a Cup run, but having never proceeded beyond the fourth qualifying round, the notion of Stanley in the velvet bag come December was fanciful at the very least, and would necessitate something out of the ordinary.

With timing that could not have been bettered, the team delivered something out of the ordinary. It needs to be said that by the time the FA Cup campaign was underway, Staley's side were looking good. The manager had beefed up the forward line with the recruitment of Mike Lutkevitch from Witton Albion, and the defence was surer with Collings behind them. Their progress was therefore no fluke, but then again this was Cup football, and Stanley fans had seen their side capitulate to lesser opposition too many times to take anything for granted.

Stanley had already thumped Hyde 6-2 in the league when they returned shortly after for the first qualifying round. The unpredictability of knock-out football suggested a much closer game, but Stanley defied conventional wisdom with another spectacular win, 5-1, with a goal apiece for Burns, Beck, Hughes, Collins and Owen. A more routine win followed in the second qualifying round at home to NWC First Division side Bradford Park Avenue, though the national media again honed in on the nostalgic angle of the tie. Goals from Beck and Hughes saw Stanley through 2-0 in front of over 700 spectators.

That Stanley's progress was not just down to the alleged magic of the FA Cup could be seen in the form of the team between the cup games. On the Monday after the Bradford tie, Stanley won easily at Guiseley in the President's Cup, and on the eve of the third qualifying round defeated Barrow 2-0 at the Crown in front of 841 spectators, not one of whom went home unimpressed by the speed, movement and imagination of Stanley's football.

There was little doubt, therefore, that Stanley could do well, but they had received a tough draw in the third qualifying round at Conference side Stalybridge Celtic. The game was to prove the value in the old adage of 'setting out your stall', for within two minutes of the start Stanley had hit a Stalybridge post and had the home 'keeper scrambling to cover an audacious long-range effort. Stanley's message was clear: they were not frightened and they were out to win. The confidence of the team survived the dismissal of Jimmy Collins for two bookable offences, and just after the hour, centre-half Stuart Owen headed in the opening goal. Then, with 15 minutes remaining, a neat passing move carved out a chance for Mike Lutkevitch, who finished precisely. A late Stalybridge consolation goal made no difference – Stanley had outplayed their hosts with an all-round display of passing, movement and determination.

It was not the first time that Stanley had beaten Conference opposition away from home. The 1983 side had done it at Gateshead in similar circumstances, but that result was more like a typical cup upset, achieved in the face of inconsistent league form. Staley's team was playing some of the best football ever seen at the Crown.

In the fourth and final qualifying round, Stanley were given a home draw against Northern League side Northallerton Town. On paper it looked a relatively easy tie, but the North Yorkshire team had already beaten one NPL side on their Cup run – a 2-1 win at Fleetwood – so it was destined to be a tough game, and so it proved. In front of 1,159 at the Crown, the game was deadlocked at 1-1 for a lengthy spell with chances at a premium before Paul Beck scored from close range with little more than 15 minutes remaining. Stanley made sure with a third in the last minute.

After 21 years of trying, Stanley had finally made it to the first round proper of the FA Cup. For John Alty, the additional revenue was a lifeline. In the *Accrington*

Observer of October 16th, the chairman revealed that the amount owed to pressing creditors was £10,000, but urged the town to continue supporting the club, as the additional gate receipts were considerable. The club had taken £1,500 at the Barrow league match and received £1,200 from their share of the Stalybridge FA Cup tie; 22 people had bought just under £4,000 in shares and another £420 had been donated. The club had also raised £1,200 from the sale of three fringe squad members. The senior squad had been pared to just 13 players; it was an incongruous situation in which the team had discovered its best form when the squad had been stripped down to the barest of essentials.

With Stanley given a home draw in the first round proper against Conference side Gateshead, a sell-out Crown Ground crowd of 2,500 was assured, as were record receipts. On October 30th, John Alty announced that enough cash had been raised to see the club through its immediate financial problems. The admission price for the Gateshead cup tie was put up from £3 to £4, but when the logistics of the tie were finalised, Stanley raised the price again to £5. The club had to pay for 30 police officers at the game, including some on horseback, and the away fans were to be segregated, slicing around 200 from the ground capacity. The club also found that the media interest in the game was such that a section of seating had to be reserved for journalists.

The £5 was not far short of double what Stanley fans were used to paying to watch a game at the Crown, but this was no ordinary game – it was a historic occasion and the town recognised the fact. Tickets for the game soon sold out, and the drama that ensued was well worth the admission price.

After taking an early lead from a deft Paul Beck header at the back post, Stanley were pegged back, and for the first time in the cup run they looked like a team from a lower division. Gateshead soon equalised and then proceeded to dominate the rest of the half. Vitally, the Stanley defence – without the suspended Eddie Johnston – stood firm until half-time, though there were few in the pie queue who thought Stanley would go on to win it.

To compound matters, Mike Lutkevitch had pulled up with an injury, so Staley had little option than to put Paul Burns on the right wing. With this enforced tactical switch, the tie was turned. Burns had a superb second half down the right, where he provided an outlet for Stanley to counter-attack. The second half was barely five minutes old when a pass from Collins sent Burns scampering down the flank. Beck was the only striker to go with the counter, but he timed his arrival perfectly and crisply turned Burns' low cross past the 'keeper for a beautifully executed goal.

It was a sucker punch straight out of the textbook. Gateshead had recklessly pushed up and left the flanks exposed, and now they had to come forward to find an equaliser. The Crown was abuzz. Infused with a new sense of belief, Stanley were now looking like the team from a higher league. Another 15 minutes passed, and then Burns again found space to advance down the right and sent the ball across. This time there were more bodies in the box, but Beck was first to the ball once more. This time the bounce was more awkward for the Stanley striker, but with the deftest of touches he flicked the ball first time over the oncoming 'keeper.

The Crown exploded with delight. The second round of the FA Cup was just 25 minutes away. Now Gateshead attacked with purpose, and Stanley started to defend in depth. With 15 minutes left, Stanley's marking went awry and Gateshead scored with a free header from a corner. The Crown was in a rare state of tumult. Darkness had descended, and the 2,270 squeezed into the ground swayed together in the sharp November wind, roaring with anguish and encouragement.

Stanley were defending as tenaciously as ever, but with just minutes remaining a Gateshead striker found room in the inside-right channel and sent a fierce shot goalwards. Collings sprang to his left and beat the ball away; the Crown erupted in relief.

With the clock nudging ten to five, and 2,000 Accringtonians urging the referee to bring to an end a mystifyingly long period of added time, the final whistle brought unheralded scenes of celebration. Paul Beck, the hat-trick hero of the hour, fell to the ground completely drained. He was instantly engulfed by fans and helped to his feet. Hundreds poured onto the pitch to congratulate the team, and as the players finally made it to the dressing rooms, the fans turned to the *Match of the Day* camera perched on the roof of the clubhouse. As one they pointed and roared "Stanley are back!" in an impressive display of pride and support. And with the club in the second round of the FA Cup for the first time since 1960, few were going to argue with them.

Stanley received another home draw, and when the opponents were revealed to be Crewe Alexandra, the club knew that the occasion would be on a bigger scale than the Gateshead tie. John Alty made his way to the police station and he was told, as he suspected, that the tie could not go ahead at the Crown. He wasted little time in phoning Blackburn Rovers to ask whether Stanley could play the tie at Ewood Park. Blackburn agreed, and decently asked for no fee other than the expenses incurred on the day.

As the tie drew closer, Alty predicted a gate in excess of 10,000. Some thought this exaggerated, but even the chairman had been taken aback by the degree of interest in the tie. It far surpassed the media circus that had gathered before the Gateshead game. With such an occasion looming, it would have been forgivable for the team to lose their edge in the humdrum of the league, but form continued to be good.

The team had lost the pace and power of Mike Lutkevitch to a long-term injury, giving Staley the ammunition to justify more signings. Winger Ashley Hoskin arrived from Burnley Bank Hall, and the manager also persuaded Jim McCluskie, a highly-regarded striker in non-league circles, to sign on at the Crown. Though McCluskie arrived from Conference side Witton Albion on a free transfer, his capture was seen as something of a coup for Staley, though it made sense in that Stanley were far too reliant on Paul Beck to score the goals. McCluskie made his debut at the Crown as Stanley convincingly beat Droylsden 4-1 in front of Crewe manager Dario Gradi, who left the ground impressed by what he had seen.

As the big day approached, Stanley squeezed every last drop of enjoyment from the FA Cup experience. Television cameras again visited the Crown to document the team's last training session, and the Milk Marketing Board decided they would exploit the opportunity by uniting the team with Carl Rice, the young lad from the now famous milk advert. The team stayed the night before the game in a hotel, before travelling to the ground in a luxury coach.

Awaiting them there was a multitude of 10,801 fans, easily the biggest attendance of the second round. Stanley started brightly and forced a series of corners, but Crewe defended solidly and broke with pace. On his scouting mission to the Crown, Dario Gradi had been surprised at the fluidity of Stanley's attacking moves, but he had also spotted that the central defensive pairing of Owen and Johnston lacked pace. His game plan was thus for his team to hit on the break through the middle, and once Crewe had established a lead, Stanley never looked like retrieving the tie. Staley admitted later that he should have played with a sweeper, though the final 6-1 scoreline was an injustice to Stanley who had competed well for most of the game.

The end of Stanley's FA Cup adventure of 1992 also coincided with a truce in the struggle going on at the club behind the scenes. Whilst the team had been sweeping all before them on the field of play, off the pitch the latest episode of the saga involving John Alty and Terry Styring had been playing out. Most of it remained off the record, but in the *Accrington Observer* of October 2nd, Terry Styring had suddenly gone public with his version of events.

Styring claimed that he had been invited back to the Crown in August 1992. He had received a phone call and learned that all was not well at Stanley, with creditors pressing for due payments the club could not meet. A series of meetings ensued, during which time Styring claimed to have had an in-depth look at the club accounts. He stated:

"The more I studied the figures, the more I realised the depth of the financial tragedy of the club's affairs. Events moved quickly, with pressure being placed on me to cover the most pressing creditors' demands in return for a substantial number of shares."

By mid-September, according to Styring, he was ready to take the plunge. He had decided to make an investment sufficient enough for John Alty to hand over the reins as club chairman. Styring explained that this was not a takeover in the sense of him buying up John Alty's shareholding and becoming the sole owner, but it was a total commitment on his part to rescuing the club's finances, and as such he wanted full executive power:

"It would not happen overnight – indeed with debts of over £100,000 this was to be the hardest decision I had taken in my life. It required my total commitment even at the expense of the smooth running of my own business interests."

Monday September 21st was the date that Styring remembered arriving at the club with, as he put it, "a cheque in my pocket", expecting in return to be confirmed as club chairman, but John Alty decided not to take him up on the offer. Said Styring:

"It highlighted the same problem that arose at the time of our joint chairmanship. It was not possible to hand over the reins and lose status. Although desperate times call for desperate actions, it just was not to be."

Styring claimed that the club's financial situation was "frightening" and possibly beyond the abilities of one man to solve. Though this was just Styring's version of things, an incident that blew up around the same time illustrated the club's desperate need for cash. A butcher had contacted Stanley about using their car park to sell cheap meat from a truck and offered £100 a week for the privilege. Precisely how the club responded is not clear. The fact that the butcher in question went ahead and advertised the event may not be indicative, but it forced the council to intervene, for the car park was the council's land and could not be used for such activities without planning permission. The town's butchers were not impressed either. The fuss quickly died down, but it did not make for good publicity.

Just when it seemed that Styring's return to the club had been vetoed once and for all, a small, unobtrusive block of text in the *Accrington Observer* at the end of November announced that he would, after all, be returning to Accrington Stanley as a director, and Styring did indeed take his place on the board just before the Crewe FA Cup game.

With money in the bank from the FA Cup run, the hope now was that these two strong and opinionated characters could cohabit harmoniously enough to steer the club into safer financial waters.

On the pitch, the team continued to do well, and with interest still in the FA Trophy and the Lancashire Junior Cup, there was reason to believe that Stanley could end the season with some silverware to show for their efforts. On Boxing Day, the team thrashed Emley 6-1 at the Crown in front of a crowd of 1,049, and by the turn of the year, Stanley had still lost only three league games. Their FA Cup exploits had left them with a fearsome backlog, however, having played up to eight games fewer than some of the sides above them.

January was the month when the autumn exertions finally caught up with the squad, as key members of the FA Cup side – a tightly-knit group of only 14 players or so – succumbed to injury. At one stage, Staley found himself without Collings, McCluskie, Hughes, Owen, Collins and Burns, with the last suffering a serious neck injury at work. Full-back Martin Clark also left the club at the end of January after agreeing a move to Crewe Alexandra, with Stanley receiving around £10,000.

With so many absences, and with a bit of money in the bank, the board gave Phil Staley the nod to sign some reinforcements, and there were no shortages of names in Staley's contacts book. In hindsight, this was a period that John Alty had reason most to regret. Although Staley did bring in some very necessary players, such as goalkeeper John Armfield, he also signed a number of players who did not add value to the squad and who would contribute little on the field of play, all of whom, nonetheless, cost the club money in fees and wages.

By the end of March, a whole string of players had been signed for very little return. Stanley again reached the last four of the Lancashire Junior Cup, eliminating holders Great Harwood on the way, but they were beaten 5-3 at home in the semi-final against Chorley, this despite by now having most of their senior players back from injury.

Paul Beck also reached 30 goals for the season with a hat-trick in a 3-3 draw at Droylsden, clinching a £200 bet made with Phil Staley, who ruefully quipped: "I'll have to go round the ground with a cap!" Beck became the first Stanley player to score 30 in a season since Dave Hargreaves in 1983–84.

Further injuries to Jim McCluskie and Charlie Cooper saw the team limp towards the end of the season. Their final league position of sixth was Stanley's highest ever placing in non-league, but there was some regret that the team, playing such fine, flowing football in those early months of the season, had not managed to put their name on some silverware. But they had rewritten the Accrington Stanley record book with their FA Cup exploits, and had certainly raised enough money to keep the club going just when a re-run of 1962 had seemed possible.

For all the cash raised by the famous 1992 Cup run, however, the problems with the club's finances were not even close to being solved. As John Alty had reason to later regret, too much of the cash raised had gone on players who had failed to make any impact on the field. Having gone through half of the season with a squad of around

15 players, by the season's end, a total of 40 players had donned the red jersey, few of whom would remain at the club for any length of time.

Another issue was that of ground regulation. In response to the improving standards in the Conference, the NPL had raised the bar for its clubs, stipulating a minimum capacity of 3,000 along with other directives that meant Stanley had to start planning for terracing behind the goals, an extension to the dressing rooms and better floodlighting. It all meant more resources being found for the Crown Ground when evidence suggested that Stanley needed to plough everything they had into the team.

But such longer-term considerations were put a considerable distance behind the back burner when the latest episode of the Styring–Alty affair came to light in May, with the season only just over. The details that emerged hinted at real turmoil in the boardroom during this most successful of seasons on the pitch, and by the end of the month the dispute had become headline news in the town. Alty had called an Emergency General Meeting of the club's shareholders with just one item on the agenda – the removal of Styring from the board. In the course of announcing the EGM, Alty admitted that it had been a mistake to invite Styring's return, as the two could not work together.

Since John Alty owned a controlling stake in the club, there was little that Styring could do other than appeal to the shareholders to back him in a symbolic show of support for his leadership rather than that of Alty. To this end, a petition emerged in Styring's support. Inevitably, a number of supporters had, down the years, taken exception to John Alty's chairmanship, so they were willing signatories.

Disgruntled fans were one thing, but a claim aired in the *Accrington Observer* of May 28th was far more explosive, for now Styring reckoned to have the support of not just 150 Crown regulars, but also of Phil Staley and the Accrington Stanley players. The paper had received a copy of the petition, and attached on a separate page were the signatures of the management and the playing squad.

Now the whole future leadership of the club was in the air. Some supporters were horrified that such an unseemly personal clash had been exposed in the pages of the local press. Others smelled a rat, pointing out that it would be easy to obtain a sheet of autographs that could then be used for an ulterior purpose. Confronted with the petition, Alty shrugged and merely confirmed that either he or Styring would have to go, suggesting that he was not going to hang around at the Crown if the shareholders were overwhelmingly hostile. Although many fans had their gripes about Alty, they were now forced to think seriously about his chairmanship.

It was at this moment that another key shareholder exercised his authority. Ex-chairman John Prescott had no doubts as to whom the shareholders should support. Prescott sent a letter to each of them strongly defending John Alty and also enclosed a proxy voting slip in favour of the chairman. Prescott had been in the chair when an earlier financial crisis had threatened to engulf the club, and he knew that only the intervention of Alty had saved Stanley on that occasion. As he argued in the letter:

> "John Alty has been very good to the club, inject-
> ing substantial amounts of money and time with-
> out which the club would not have survived. There
> was nobody else either willing or able to do what
> John Alty has done for Accrington Stanley."

Prescott also pointed out that the affair had made for a regretful end to what should have been a celebratory year, with the FA Cup run and the good league campaign having coincided with the centenary of the club. As the *Accrington Observer* also revealed from a document leaked to it, the cup run had netted the club something in the region of £30,000. The disclosure forced John Alty to confirm the amounts involved and to remind the fans that the club made a loss of £35,000 on the previous season.

Prescott's letter had the desired effect as far as the ex-chairman was concerned. At the EGM, held in the first week of June, John Alty received a substantial show of support from shareholders. It was not, however, an entirely comfortable evening for the chairman.

It emerged that Alty had asked the club to start paying him back interest on outstanding loans to the tune of £2,400 a year. In defence of his action, the chairman told the meeting that he had put into the club £60,000 in shares, £33,000 in loans and had written off £50,000 in sponsorship, and now he needed a little back due to the impact of the economic recession on his business:

> "At one stage I seriously wondered whether my business was going to survive. I thought it was reasonable to ask for the club to start paying me interest of around £2,400 a year as I guarantee every debt with the FA, Barclays Bank and Midland Bank. I have put my entire finances at risk and I was just seeking a reasonable rate of interest at a time of need."

It was thought that Terry Styring had refused to support Alty's request for interest payments on his loans to the club, and it later emerged that Styring was also making a renewed effort to succeed John Alty in the chair. Little wonder, then, that a climactic clash between the two ensued. The vote at the EGM brought the matter to an end. Styring departed the board, but not before he had spoken at the meeting and asserted that Stanley ought to be a cash-rich club with the commercial opportunities at their disposal.

On one of the more intriguing aspects of the affair – the role of Phil Staley – there was no public comment at all, but events had manured the fertile imaginations of the conspiracy theorists. In March, Staley had resigned as a director, apparently because the club discovered he was breaking a regulation that stated a director could not be paid a weekly wage if he or she was not a full-time employee of the club. At the time little was thought of this, but in the light of the subsequent row, Staley's departure from the board appeared less to do with a league regulation and more in line with cloak-and-dagger manoeuvrings in the boardroom. After all, if the leaked petition to the local paper was anything to go by, the manager had tried to use his influence against the chairman, suggesting that Styring and Staley had joined forces to oust Alty from the chair.

It is nonetheless difficult to credit that Staley would have remained at the club if he had indeed so blatantly tried to dethrone Alty. As it was, Staley remained firmly in the managerial chair, and, along with Paul Beck, was representing the club in Norway as guests of the Norwegian supporters' club when the EGM took place.

Although Terry Styring was no longer part of the board, his financial policy appeared very much in place when, on July 2nd, John Alty announced that the days of borrowing money to meet the wage bill were over. The squad would be funded by gate receipts and fundraising, and a pamphlet was produced detailing the various fundraising schemes at the club. It seemed to herald a new, more frugal and businesslike regime at the club.

It was hardly music to the ears of Phil Staley. He had retained the bulk of his squad from the previous campaign, but with the 1993–94 pre-season well into its stride, he was told to cut his numbers. The finance company sponsoring the NPL had withdrawn from the deal, meaning that clubs would no longer receive their share of the sponsorship money. Staley had already spent £1,000 on midfielder Jon Senior when the news came through, so Alty passed some of the loss onto the fans, as admission prices were raised again to £3.50. The sale of striker Jim McCluskie to Morecambe realised £1,500, money Staley spent on further reinforcements to the squad, including £500 on defender Paul Moss. Joining Staley on the bench as assistant manager was Ken Wright, who had just resigned from Horwich, and newly installed on the board was John DeMaine, who would soon take over as commercial director.

The club certainly needed some fresh energy in that direction. On the eve of the season, John Alty had offered a thought-provoking sketch of Stanley's position as a final appeal for more people to get involved in the club lottery scheme. The Conference, said the chairman, was a pipe dream given the current state of the club's finances. Even with the fine tradition of voluntary labour at the Crown, the bill for a Conference ground was £100,000, since the facilities now demanded by the higher leagues were such that only Leek Town and Boston United of the NPL teams had Conference standard grounds. No one could accuse the chairman of not being straight with the fans, but it all sounded rather depressing and hardly seemed likely to encourage potential sponsors or fundraisers.

Stanley began the 1993–94 league campaign well, easily defeating Hyde away from home and then prevailing 3-2 in another high-quality Crown encounter against Morecambe, but it was a deceptive start. In September, the first sign of problems surfaced when the players, management and directors met in the dressing room before the home game against Marine. The manager explained that the club had revised their pay scales and had introduced new rules that had caused some unrest, with several players demanding to know where they stood financially.

The row seemed to hasten a sharp decline in playing fortunes. The Marine game was lost 2-0, and for the first time in a while, Stanley began to misfire up front. Staley was not helped by another long injury list that saw such central performers as Hughes, Cooper, Lutkevitch, Hoskin, Burns and Lampkin all out at various points during the opening couple of months. But where Staley had previously been able to coax results out of weakened teams, he now struggled to halt Stanley's slide down the table.

Frustratingly, a few of the more fancied teams in the league, such as Boston, Morecambe and Barrow, were also struggling and some unlikely names, such as Bridlington, headed the table, so Stanley's malaise seemed like a missed opportunity to put some distance between themselves and some of their stronger competitors.

When, on October 13th, Stanley lost 1-0 at home to Whitley Bay, a downcast Phil Staley admitted it was the worst spell of his managerial career. It was Stanley's seventh defeat in nine matches and the gate had dropped to 317. John Alty noted that the club had lost 250 people from the average home gate, a £750 reduction in income each time, and that this had affected the club lottery. The chairman held out the prospect once again of financial trouble if things did not improve.

Alty's grim outlook was not improved when the club received an instruction from Lancashire County Council that the railings behind the goals would have to be improved before the club could again host a capacity crowd at the Crown. One of the railings had buckled at the Gateshead FA Cup game, and in an indication of how acute finances had again become, Alty claimed that the £6,000 bill for the repairs was money that the club did not have.

A few days after the home defeat to Whitley Bay, Stanley lost at the Crown again, this time to Frickley Athletic. It was a fifth successive league defeat, and with Stanley heading for the foot of the table, a board meeting after the game decided to end Phil Staley's managerial time at the Crown Ground. John Alty told the press:

> "We have had some good times in the last two sea-
> sons and we have happy memories of our ties with
> Phil Staley and Tony Keyes. It is a sad day because
> Phil has brought great success to the club. Up until
> the end of last season, the club was well placed and
> this season we were all looking forward to success,
> but things have not gone to plan."

It was the end of a managerial reign just short of three years – not a bad innings by Crown standards – and Phil Staley achieved a lot for Accrington Stanley. He established the club comfortably in the top tier of the NPL, and will always be remembered for those wonderful FA Cup occasions. For once, Accrington Stanley were in the headlines for all the right reasons – footballing ones – and the Crown faithful still recall with affection just how well Staley's side played the beautiful game in those ground-breaking opening months of the 1992–93 season.

But there was a more problematic side to Staley's management that proved a real headache for John Alty. Staley was, to use the parlance, a 'character', someone not averse to a bit of wheeling and dealing to land his targets. No one doubted that as a manager he had produced attractive, attacking teams, but they had come at a cost – and by the time Staley's reign was approaching its end, the club could no longer afford it. The meeting before the Marine game in September was significant, for here the players were told firmly that the club had to enforce a strict and prudent wage policy. It is perhaps instructive that it was from this moment that the manager seemed to lose his ability to extract the optimum performance from his players.

The board placed Staley's assistant Ken Wright in charge, and on the face of it, he was an ideal replacement. He was an experienced hand in non-league, and had a reputation for producing solid and competitive teams, if a little on the workmanlike side. It was just what Stanley needed in the circumstances if they were to grind their way to league safety, but just as pertinent was the FA Cup and the opportunity it brought of another life-saving cash windfall.

Wright's first game in charge was a midweek league fixture at Chorley, and a 4-1 defeat merely underlined the new manager's task, but this was the prelude to a much bigger occasion on the Saturday, Stanley's first FA Cup tie. This was an absolutely crucial game for the club. The previous season's exploits had given the team a bye until the fourth and final qualifying round, a real perk given the poor form of the side. Even so, Stanley had been handed the toughest of draws at Conference side Altrincham, and the new manager had severe selection problems. Burns, Lampkin and Hoskin were injured, and three recent signings were all cup-tied.

Thus it was that Accrington Stanley went into their most important game of the season with just one fit sub, and a crocked Ashley Hoskin on the bench in case of an emergency. Football, of course, would not be half the game it is without its unpredictability, and that afternoon, Stanley breathed life into the myth of the FA Cup.

Though playing with a makeshift side, Stanley at least came out with the right attitude, determined to make Altrincham work for the victory that virtually everyone assumed would be theirs. By the simple expedient of jutting out jaws and not budging an inch, Stanley repelled each and every Altrincham attack. Time did its thing – first half-time and then the hour mark passed with the Conference side unable to make the breakthrough. With twenty minutes left, the travelling Stanley faithful began to sniff a result – not a victory, but a replay, with the chance of bringing Altrincham back to the Crown, the scene of so many great cup exploits in recent seasons.

Stanley themselves, however, had a different idea. With the clock nudging half past four, Stanley cleared their lines to Paul Beck. The Stanley striker was much admired for his predatory instincts in and around the box, but now he ran at the Altrincham defence, and with a drop of the shoulder he went past two defenders on the edge of the area before finishing emphatically in the opposite top corner, in front of the Stanley contingent.

The 100 or so Stanley fans who had made the journey erupted with joy, surging towards Beck as he ran to the terracing behind the goal to celebrate. Now a real FA Cup shock was on. The sense that it might be Stanley's day was further heightened when Altrincham hit a post from a free kick, with the ball rebounding sharply onto goalkeeper John Armfield's knee and looping into the air, and Stanley finally clearing the ball after a frantic goalmouth melee.

With just minutes remaining, Beck further enhanced his heroic status by repeating his earlier trick, picking up the ball deeper than usual, and advancing past a defender before finishing coolly in the corner. The raucous Stanley following prepared for a serious party. It was Beck's 100th goal for the club, and it could hardly have been more important. Stanley were once again in the hat for the First Round proper, with the chance of earning more life-giving FA Cup cash.

Stanley were given another home tie, this time against Football League opposition in Fourth Division Scunthorpe United. Hopes that the inspirational display at Altrincham and the forthcoming first round tie would lift the side were sadly misplaced. Though Ken Wright acted quickly to reshape the side, he had little luck in turning round its immediate fortunes.

Staley's side was rapidly dispersed, with some core figures leaving, such as Eddie Johnston and Bernie Hughes, along with several fringe players. Joining the club were players who were to prove strong and committed performers, such as Lee Rogerson and Darren Quick, and the return of terrace favourite Chris Grimshaw for his third spell at the club. Wright brought in further defensive experience with Colin Methven and Jim Connor. Despite a victory against Great Harwood in the President's Cup, Stanley fell to two more league defeats, including a 5-0 mauling at the Crown from Barrow, a game covered by the television cameras who were there to record the visit to the club of a group of Norwegian supporters.

The first round tie against Scunthorpe was therefore played against the gloomy background of eight successive league defeats, and the contrast with the previous season's big FA Cup day out could not have been greater. There were no media blitzes, no overnight hotel stays or police escorts to the ground. The team simply trained on the morning of the game and quietly made their way to Turf Moor for the kick-off.

Despite the league form and an average home attendance of little more than 400, the tie attracted 5,879 spectators and they saw Stanley once again raise their game for the big occasion. Stanley competed for every ball, and though it wasn't an encounter for the aesthetes, they traded blows pound for pound with the League side. Having cancelled out Scunthorpe's opening goal, Stanley fell behind again but battled on and were rewarded when centre-back Joe Connor squeezed the ball over the line for a hotly disputed 88th-minute equaliser.

The Scunthorpe players protested furiously to the referee that the ball had not fully crossed the line, and perhaps enraged by what they perceived as an injustice, the visitors poured forward in search of the winner. With time almost up and every Stanley fan dreaming of a visit to a Football League ground for the midweek replay, Scunthorpe broke Stanley hearts. Stanley 'keeper John Armfield spilled a near-post corner, and amidst the bodies throwing themselves in front of the ball, a Scunthorpe player lashed a shot into the roof of the net from close range. Stanley had lost their defensive cool at a vital moment and had paid a cruel and heavy price.

Though Stanley had played admirably and had again succeeded in staving off impending financial crisis with another money-spinning tie, there was no mistaking the gloom at the last-minute defeat. A replay would have brought in yet more thousands of pounds, but now Ken Wright had to buckle down to the arduous task of plotting a route to league safety.

Unfortunately, he just could not get the side going, and by the New Year they had fallen to third from bottom with just one league win in 15 attempts, despite the influx of new players. When, on January 8th, the club crashed 4-2 at home to Gainsborough, there were signs of real crisis both on and off the field. In the league table, an alarming gap was developing between the bottom three and the rest, and in the programme that day, John Alty had stated bluntly that he would sell his stake in the club if Stanley were to be relegated.

Events moved quickly from thereon in. Following speculation in the *Lancashire Evening Telegraph* that proved to be on the mark, manager Ken Wright was sacked after just 10 weeks and 16 games in charge to make way for the return to the Crown Ground of Eric Whalley. Alty admitted that the decision was not unanimous among the board, but the chairman's judgement was that something had to happen quickly if the club was to survive in the NPL and there was no sign of such a transformation under Ken Wright.

Wright himself was understandably angry at the decision, arguing that he had not been given time to do the job properly. He accused Alty of panicking, but the chairman's thinking was clear:

> "Morale is low at the moment and the team has no confidence. It needs someone to take things by the scruff of the neck in a backs-to-the-wall situation, and I think there is no finer manager than Eric to do that. He is manager until the end of the season and his brief is to keep us up."

Alty also expanded on comments made in the programme a week earlier. In an *Accrington Observer* interview, he stated his continued disappointment that the club could not break even by raising more money from the club draw. There was no denying, from the tone of the comments, that the chairman saw his time at the helm drawing to a close:

> "During my years as chairman, I have sunk all my surplus cash and indeed much more into the club. Now, at the age of 50, I have a duty to look after my future after my income as an accountant has ceased, and this is likely to involve me putting my controlling interest up for sale. I have done as much as I can."

Eric Whalley, who had resigned as manager of Great Harwood at the same time that Ken Wright had taken over at Stanley, pronounced himself refreshed and ready for the challenge, and shrugged off those who reminded him of his problematic relationship with the Stanley board when he had been manager at the club in the late 1980s. That was then, said Whalley, this is now – and he had quite a task on his hands.

Whalley announced his intention that the team would play attacking football, and he was helped a little by the fact that his first game in charge was an eminently winnable Lancashire Junior Cup tie at home to NWC League side Nelson. Sent out to play positively, the team responded with a resounding 4-1 win and followed this with their first league win of the year, defeating Knowsley at the Crown.

Whalley drafted in young striker Phil Hutchinson, who had returned to the club, recalled Paul Beck to the starting line-up and welcomed Mike Lutkevitch back from injury. With these three attacking players in harness, Stanley never looked back and within half-a-dozen games had remarkably hoisted themselves clear of the relegation zone. A 4-2 defeat of Winsford at the Crown on March 19th meant that Eric Whalley's team had claimed 17 points from the nine league games under his direction, compared to 17 points from the previous 24 under Staley and Wright.

It represented quite a turnaround in playing fortunes, and even included a run to the semi-finals of the League Cup, though they were well beaten by an emerging Spennymoor side. Nonetheless, John Alty had been proved right when he reasoned that Whalley was the man to give the side the boost it badly needed.

Stanley guaranteed their NPL status with four games to spare, and celebrated with a superb 1-0 win at Boston United. The winner that day was scored by Paul Beck, and his return to form was undoubtedly a major factor in Stanley's renaissance. He hit a hat-trick against Hyde and a brace at Horwich to retain his position as the club's leading goalscorer with 16 goals, though he also cultivated a decent partnership with Phil Hutchinson, who himself scored 13 goals from 27 games.

There was even ground for cautious optimism on the financial front when the profits from the weekly draw pushed upwards to £650 per week, and the local Greyhound car dealership announced their sponsorship of the club's player of the month award.

Having made such an impact in his first few months back at the club, Eric Whalley announced that he was staying on for the following 1994–95 season, and at his behest, the board agreed to revive Stanley's reserve side. Where Phil Staley had deemed the reserve side an irrelevance, Whalley argued that it was imperative, a clear sign of the contrasting approaches of the two men.

The season ended, however, with an ultra-realistic

appraisal by John Alty at the club's AGM. He stated that the Conference was out of the question, and that the club had to consolidate in the NPL until they could afford another set of improvements at the Crown. The reason was a new NPL ground grading document, the implications of which were that Stanley would have to make improvements during the following two years just to stay where they were.

The club accounts also made for a worrying read, with the club losing another £5,000 on the year. If income from commercial activities remained sluggish, said Alty, then the club would lose £10,000 a year, losses which he had already indicated were now unsustainable and had only been bridged in the previous two years by the FA Cup ties. Relegation had been avoided – as had John Alty's resignation – but with the chairman no longer prepared to cover what appeared to be inevitable losses, the future of his chairmanship remained in doubt.

The squad for the 1994–95 season reflected the manager's decision to clear out most of the players that remained from the Staley era, including Steve Lampkin, who left having played 106 games for the club. Goalkeeper Rob Mulloy had been an early acquisition, and Whalley's preference for local players saw the return to the club of Simon Westwell and Paul Whalley, who joined from Great Harwood, and Mick Seddon, who arrived from Clitheroe. Striker Brian Welch was signed from Burnley, and David Hamilton, a veteran midfielder with League experience, moved to the club from Barrow.

As had been the case under his previous stewardship, Eric Whalley's Accrington Stanley relied on a core of players who hailed from the immediate area, and another familiar face returned with Dave Thornley's appointment as assistant manager.

At first, Eric Whalley's defiantly home-grown team held their own. After slipping to defeats against Boston and Spennymoor, the team put together a seven-match unbeaten run. Paul Beck responded well to the competition from Welch and Hutchinson, grabbing both goals in a 2-2 draw at Barrow after having been dropped to the subs' bench. In mid-September, Chris Grimshaw reached the rare milestone of 300 appearances for Stanley, and Whalley further strengthened the squad at the end of the month with the recruitment of defender Les Thompson, who had been a regular for Burnley just the previous season.

After 10 games, Stanley had won 11 points and were mid-table, but then things started to go wrong. As had happened under Phil Staley twelve months before, Stanley suddenly struggled for any kind of result. Early October saw heavy successive defeats at home to Bishop Auckland (4-1) and at Marine (4-1) and Guiseley (4-0). It was a turn of form the club could have done without, for as well as starting to slip down the league table, the all-important FA Cup loomed once more.

As non-league participants in the first round proper the previous year, Stanley again enjoyed a bye to the fourth qualifying round and had received a home draw, but opponents Spennymoor had proved tough opponents in the past and had already won at the Crown in the league. To compound matters, the squad was hit by injuries and suspensions for the tie. In a tight game of few chances, it was the visitors who scored the only goal in front of 750 spectators at the Crown, the biggest gate of a season that had seen attendances drop back to the 450 mark.

When Stanley then had to visit Spennymoor in the league three days later, the 5-1 defeat suggested that all was not well at the club. The team had conceded five goals in the opening half-hour, and though Whalley could point out that he had been forced to rely on some reserve team players for the fixture, he felt also that he had done all he could for the side, which had gone eleven matches without a win.

Eric Whalley therefore agreed to move up to the boardroom in a 'director of football' role, with Dave

Thornley and David Hamilton taking over first team affairs, the former in a player-coach capacity.

Alty revealed that Whalley had not taken any payment for his services since he returned to the club and thanked him for his efforts, but the chairman also warned about a serious downturn in the income of the club, mainly caused by poor results: "We clearly have serious problems both on and off the pitch, and once again we are sustaining losses."

The impact of the FA Cup defeat had been resounding, and made all the worse when Spennymoor drew Wigan Athletic away from home in the First Round proper, an attractive tie that would have guaranteed Stanley another sizeable windfall. Figures released for the previous season demonstrated that just one big Cup game could make all the difference. The game at Turf Moor against Scunthorpe had taken the season's gate receipts to £47,139, well above the normal figure of around £20,000.

The new managerial team succeeded in halting Stanley's freefall down the table and stabilised the club's position. Although the side never really hit their straps, the introduction of big centre-half Graham Sanders seemed to stem the flow of goals the team were conceding, and Stanley began to eke out some narrow victories that saw them reach the New Year having avoided the eye of the relegation storm. A squall of a different kind, however, blew up over the release of young striker Phil Hutchinson to Lancaster for just £500.

There had been a minor and uneventful clearout of players upon Whalley's move upstairs, but the January sale of Hutchinson provoked a response in the *Accrington Observer* from fans who accused the club of lacking ambition. Their mood had darkened over the holiday period when Morecambe thrashed Stanley 4-0 at the Crown, a game that saw a virtuoso display of forward play from their two strikers, John Coleman and Jim McCluskie. Why, Stanley fans wondered, could the club not get the best out of the obviously talented players that they possessed? McCluskie had laboured ineffectively at

Stanley, yet here he was in fine fettle for Morecambe: trim, sharp and hungry.

A letter in the local paper asserted that Stanley fans were fed up of seeing players being released and then achieving at other clubs, a fate that could be envisaged with Hutchinson:

"I'm sure that Hutchinson will join the increasingly large number of ex-Stanley players who will come back to haunt us."

A 1-0 defeat of Hyde at the Crown on January 14th was grim to watch, but the final whistle was greeted with a roar – it was a crucial victory at a time when the future of the club had once more become the subject of media speculation.

The *Accrington Observer* of January 13th reported that a consortium had approached John Alty with plans for a takeover of the club, and the paper claimed that the figures behind the bid were Terry Styring, Phil Staley and Droylsden chairman David Sterling. No doubt sensing from his public pronouncements that Alty wanted out, this time it seemed that Styring's approach was for a wholesale takeover of the club. There was, however, a sticking point. The consortium wanted Alty to write off the £40,000 he had loaned to the club, but Alty refused. A lot of that money had been invested in the ground and remained on the balance sheet as assets in hand. Furthermore, Alty had just persuaded Blackburn Rovers to host the club for a midweek centenary game with all the profits going to Stanley – an estimated £50,000 in guaranteed income. Alty, therefore, felt that Styring would not be paying the full price for what he would get if the loans were written off. But the chairman also admitted that he was looking to sell:

"I have been at the helm for 14 years and the time is probably right for a new leader to come along. The present consortium has failed to convince me that they are fit and proper to take over our great club."

Who else, then, had the money and motivation to take up the challenge? There was only one other possible candidate, and within a few days the deal was announced. Eric Whalley

was the new chairman of Accrington Stanley, only the third
incumbent to take the position since John Prescott in 1975.
As forthright as ever, Whalley talked of the deal as simply
being a case of him putting his money where his mouth was,
and pledged that he would be in it for the long haul:

> "The club needs a spark to get things going. John
> Alty has brought the club a long, long way and I
> hope I can take it further. One of my main ambitions
> is to see Stanley play at Wembley and be promoted
> to the Conference. I will be happy with that."

For John Alty, it was the end of a marathon 13 years and
three months in the chair, and he was ready to go. He told
the local press:

> "You get stale after 13 years and it is time for a new
> approach. I have been a bit laid back and it needs
> a more hands-on approach and a change of direc-
> tion. Eric is right for the club, and I think it will be
> in good hands. I have done as much as I can and
> I cannot take the club any further. It would have
> been nice to take the club into the Conference, but
> I have assessed that and, being realistic, we are still
> some way from that."

There was an obvious tinge of regret in Alty's tone, a
sense that things could have been run a little tighter and
perhaps more progress made, but his chairmanship had
seen the transformation of the Crown Ground and the
progress of the team from the Cheshire League, through
the North West Counties League and then up to the top tier
of the Northern Premier League. It is worth remembering
that the top tier of the NPL was on the distant horizon when
Alty took his place in the chair, and to get there progress
on the pitch had to be matched by even more significant
developments off it. Mark Turner, club secretary for a
number of years under Alty in the early 1980s, thinks that
this aspect of Alty's chairmanship is often overlooked:

> "Things came on a hell of a lot under John Alty. We
> could never have envisaged playing in the NPL
> with the ground as it was in the 1970s and most of

the 1980s, and it was difficult to move on when you had a big debt around your neck. But it worked in one respect, which is that the infrastructure which did not exist in the 1970s was put in by John – the drainage system in the pitch, the stands and the floodlights. But the debt that this expenditure incurred held the team back massively, without a doubt, but there was no other way."

John Prescott, another figure who put in years of service at the Crown, also argues that Alty laid the foundations for the more recent progress of the club:

"First of all, John Alty saved the club from folding, because when he came back as chairman we were down to four people on the board. And then things got better very quickly when John came on board. Things became more professional – any paperwork was quickly dealt with, and he dealt confidently with money matters, he was able to borrow money and he started to put money in. The pity for John was that while he started to improve things at Stanley, other clubs were moving faster on the playing side, and John was always hamstrung by the fact that the pitch and the surroundings were so bad. Had they been up to scratch when he took over then he would have achieved far more on the playing side. Of the money that he had for the club, he had to spend half on the team and half on the ground."

Today, John Alty is happy to have played his part in the return of Accrington Stanley to the Football League, but still remembers the stress of those final few years in the chair:

"The pressure was at its greatest in the last couple of years because expectations had risen and we had to kick on from the FA Cup runs. But the problem was that even if we had won the NPL, we would not have gone up, and there's nothing worse than winning promotion and being denied; that's a killer.

There was no terracing behind the goals, and the ground was short of requirements in other areas. I had been putting money in throughout, but I could not see the club taking the next step on that it needed to take. I was spending too much time there and was neglecting clients that I'd had for 30 years, and it gets to you after a while – you start arguing and falling out with people who previously had been your friends and colleagues.

"But I'm pleased and proud of what we did, and I have some great memories. We started building with steel and concrete at the Crown, we got rid of all the wood. I remember an early game I went to, when I looked up there was barbed wire holding the roof timbers together. But those people at the meeting in 1968 must take the credit, because they had the guts to start a new club, they'd no money, no tools, nothing, working with bent nails, but they got it off the ground."

The other impulse behind Alty's desire to sell also informed his legendary impatience with managers – he was convinced that Accrington Stanley could not afford to stand still, because the club would soon be overtaken and outflanked by better-resourced clubs coming up through the pyramid if things were allowed to stagnate for too long. While this led to boardroom interference in the work of managers who failed to deliver immediate success on the field, it also led Alty to recognise that his time was up; he had done all he could, and the club had to move on.

But barely had Eric Whalley got used to his new role at the club than he was looking for a new manager. David Hamilton left for a position at Preston North End towards the end of January, so the new owner set about sifting through the various applications that arrived at the club. He told the local paper:

"The thing I want to bring to Accrington Stanley is stability, not changing personnel every two minutes. I want to have somebody who is going to be able to plan for the long-term future, and this hasn't happened."

Though few would argue with Whalley's sentiment, it would prove more difficult in practice. He chose Stan Allan, an experienced non-league manager who had guided Witton Albion to the Conference. Allan diagnosed a lack of firepower as the main problem, having scored just 29 goals in 27 league games, but the problems seemed to run deeper when Stanley suffered a 2-0 home defeat to relegation rivals Matlock on February 11th. Though Matlock's opener was a speculative long-range effort that no one could do anything about, there was no denying the paucity of Stanley's performance. They looked like a team on their way down, and the display was enough to bring this reaction in the pages of the *Accrington Observer*:

"Of the five clubs who finished above Stanley at the end of the 1992–93 season, four have gone on to greater things. Supporters of Stanley are entitled to ask why it is that they have managed to plan ahead and sensibly build up the playing strengths of their respective teams, while Stanley have allowed theirs to disintegrate to their present level."

Things barely improved in the following weeks, and when Stanley fell to a 3-0 defeat in the semi-final of the Lancashire Junior Cup to Bamber Bridge, a team from the division below, the performance was so abject that the chairman saw fit to apologise to the fans who had travelled to Preston for the tie:

"It was the most embarrassing display I have ever seen by a team I have been connected with. The players on the park were a disgrace and some are certainly not proud to play for Accrington Stanley. I could not believe the lack of commitment in a cup semi-final. I will not put up with it, because I think our supporters are entitled to better than that."

A 4-1 home defeat to a good Guiseley side left Stanley firmly entrenched in a relegation battle, but this proved to be the nadir of the season. Allan coaxed more determined displays from the team at Winsford and Emley, with a point earned from both encounters, followed by a 2-1 victory at Chorley, and then a more handsome 5-2 defeat of Barrow at the Crown.

By the end of the season, Stanley were placed comfortably enough to have made the concerns of February seem something of an over-reaction, but the campaign was another in which the team had found its legs only when faced with a very real threat of relegation. At least the new Stanley reserve side had proved their worth, bringing home the North West Alliance Cup after a 4-0 aggregate defeat of Southport Reserves.

The team was able to put aside its difficulties for at least one night when, on March 22nd, Stanley were the guests at the revamped Ewood Park for the centenary match against soon-to-be Premiership champions Blackburn Rovers. The match attracted 7,741, enough to virtually fill the new two-tiered stand along the length of the pitch, and Stanley took home all the profits from the game. The team battled gamely to restrict Blackburn to just the two goals.

Another first for the club was a June trip to Barbados. The idea had been first put to Stanley a year before as part of a more substantial tournament involving three non-league clubs. These plans had fallen through, but Stanley were nonetheless invited to compete with two Barbadian teams for the Anglo-Barbados Cup. The squad eagerly accepted the invitation, and on June 13th, they won their first game against Lambada FC 3-2, where they hung on in the midsummer heat after leading 3-0 at half-time. Stanley then recorded another narrow victory, 2-1, against Barbados Cup holders Gall Hill, and so, despite the generous hospitality of their hosts, Stanley had won the inaugural Anglo-Barbados Cup.

If Eric Whalley had any doubts about the vast commercial potential of the club he had just bought, the Barbados trip banished them for good. The public acclaim and media attention lavished on Stanley more than 4,000 miles from home was beyond all expectations and showed him the magnitude of the name and the history that he now owned. Whalley even got to see a game at the famous Barbados Oval test cricket ground. Seven Stanley fans also made the journey.

When the accounts were released for the season, the impact of Eric Whalley's takeover became apparent. For the first time in a while, the club had made a profit without the help of an FA Cup run, with a surplus of £4,600 on the year. Whalley innocently professed himself baffled, telling the press:

"It's difficult to understand where the profit came
    from. We've just tried to run the club as a business."

What that really meant was that the belt had been tightened from John Alty's self-professed "laid-back" style of financial management. Waste was cut wherever it was seen, and the club started to chip away at its millstone of debt. Wages were reduced from £6,500 to just under £3,000, with Whalley insisting that the social club be run on a voluntary basis. Expenses for the playing squad were also reduced from £14,197 to £10,920, taking overall costs down from £97,797 to £76,196.

Income, however, had risen, and this was ploughed back into the Crown Ground, where improvements were almost immediately restarted after a few years of inactivity. The first major project was the terracing behind the goals, which was started during the summer and would raise the certified capacity of the Crown Ground to 5,000. The club also built a new medical room and a new visitors' dugout. It was an impressive start in the chair for Whalley, who was quite clearly preparing the club for bigger and better things. The question was – could the team earn them?

In addition to striker John McNally, who had been snapped up just before the transfer deadline day of the previous campaign, manager Stan Allan made a host of new signings as he started to mould the side to his preferences for the forthcoming 1995–96 season. Receiving the most attention were Chris Molloy, Stuart Anderson and Steve Shaughnessy, the latter signed for a club record fee, but two other players arrived at the Crown under the radar of the press who were to have a far greater impact at the club than any of Allan's other recruits: Paul Mullin and Brett Ormerod.

Both were local players, but with diverse backgrounds. Mullin had made the squad for the British Universities team, and had returned home to embark on a career outside the game, with part-time football the only plan. Ormerod, however, had been in the professional game since his teens, coming through the apprentice ranks at Blackburn Rovers before being released in the summer of 1995. Ormerod's mission was to prove to the Ewood Park hierarchy that they had made a mistake. Both arrived as reserve team players.

By the beginning of August, Allan had amassed a squad of 24 players, too many for Eric Whalley's liking, and the manager was told to trim his group. One casualty was Les Thompson, but not before Stan had made what sounded a mild complaint that he was not able to compete in the transfer market, commenting to a journalist that:

"I'm way down the list of people trying to spend money and I can't believe what some are paying out."

But for all of Allan's frustrations, he had his own team now and if sales of season tickets were any reflection, the fans were optimistic, with record numbers sold at £70 each. That optimism seemed well placed when the team made an extremely bright start to the season, winning 3-0 at Barrow and 2-0 at Witton Albion. The *Accrington Observer* was highly impressed with the all-round teamwork on display, and when Stanley prevailed by the odd goal in seven at Spennymoor, they went third in the table, having won six of their opening nine games.

It was, unfortunately, as good as it got, and the problem that emerged was an unusual one for Stanley – the team could not win at the Crown. Normally this would mean a relegation battle, but curiously, away form was excellent.

By the end of October, Stanley had won just three out of ten at home, but had emerged victorious six times out of eight on their travels. The poor home form saw the team slip from their early season high to mid-table, and things were not helped when the club were deducted three points because of an administrative error made during a transfer.

Another setback occurred in the FA Cup. Starting back in the first qualifying round, Stanley negotiated an away tie at Ossett Town thanks to a Brett Ormerod winner, with both he and Paul Mullin given a chance up front after impressing in the reserves. Though Stanley probably had mixed feelings about their home draw in the second qualifying round, opponents Bradford Park Avenue were eminently beatable, but the Crown jinx struck again and Stanley were eliminated 2-1.

Stanley ended the year in ninth position, with eight home defeats and nine away wins. The team clearly was not going to have an impact on the promotion race. Irritatingly for Stanley fans, Preston minnows Bamber Bridge were leading the way, a club with fewer resources who could not even go up because of inadequate ground facilities. If they could put together a title-challenging side on their meagre rations, why could not Stanley?

This question gained added weight when, in December, Chris Grimshaw was allowed to leave the club. By this time, 'Grimmy' had made 362 appearances and scored 52 goals, and was a firm terrace favourite, with the regulars unable to understand why he was not being used more regularly. Grimshaw argued that he had effectively been forced out because the manager had refused to play him, and his decision to retire at the age of just 30 prompted some of the Crown faithful to write in to voice their disappointment with how the season was unfolding. One letter in the *Accrington Observer* stated:

> "...perhaps Mr Allan ought to be more objective in his choice of players. Although Chris Grimshaw may not be Mr Allan's favourite person, he can still

be selected to play for Stanley because he remains Stanley's best right-sided player. Come on Stan, don't let one of Stanley's best players disappear. If he needs a swift kick up the backside give him one and let's get on with Accrington Stanley's progress."

Another was more critical of the team's style of play under Allan, and it was indeed the case that many, like this writer, saw the manager as an advocate of the long ball game:

"Most of the team's displays at home this season have been totally inept, with ineffective balls being played straight down the middle and the wings ignored. At least two or three of the players who continue to be selected are not good enough. If skilful popular players continue to leave, then gates will plummet..."

John DeMaine, in his new role at the club of commercial director, replied and appealed for more patience, pointing out that Allan had been brought in to put together a side to reach the Conference, with those on the non-playing side readying the ground for the higher level, and that both would take a little time.

In fact, the ground was being rapidly transformed. By the turn of the year, the terracing behind both goals had been completed, and Whalley revealed he was planning to utilise the space between the pitch and the clubhouse by installing 200 seats in front of the sponsors' lounge, taking the overall seating capacity to more than 500, in line with Conference grading standards.

On New Year's Day, the team drew 0-0 at home to Marine in front of 622, one of the biggest gates of the season. By this time the prowess of Brett Ormerod, long appreciated by those who watched the reserves, had finally been rewarded by promotion to the first team squad, and the presence of Stuart Anderson, Rob Mulloy and Chris Molloy in the representative side of the NPL (by now sponsored by Unibond) was evidence that Allan had raised the standards within the squad.

Results, however, proved stubbornly difficult to improve. Three consecutive goalless draws were followed by a disappointing elimination from the Lancashire Junior Cup at Radcliffe.

By mid-February, the team were around ninth in the table without hope of much further progress, and Allan set the team the uninspiring target of a top eight finish to qualify for the following season's President's Cup. Stanley's interest in the League Cup was ended at home to Leek in front of just 201, a performance that led to some criticism from the fans and one comment in the paper that Allan's tactics were "a poor substitute for football".

The run-in to the season's end was distinguished by a couple of oddities. On March 19th, Stanley were beaten at Knowsley in front of just 42 people, probably the lowest gate ever to witness a Stanley first team game. Less frivolous were the events of April 23rd, when the wife of goalkeeper Rob Mulloy went into labour on the afternoon of Stanley's fixture at Chorley. With the other two registered goalkeepers at work, veteran striker Paul Beck pulled on the gloves and amazingly managed to keep a clean sheet.

For Beck, it represented a most unlikely and bizarre swansong at the club. He had been made reserve team manager earlier in the season in recognition of the fact that he was no longer a first team choice, this after 299 appearances. His valiant effort in goal at Chorley not only earned the team a point, but booked his place in that most distinguished elite of Crown Ground servants to have played 300 times for Accrington Stanley.

He retired at the end of the season, having five times won the Jack Brydon trophy awarded to the season's highest scorer, and with 132 Stanley goals to his credit, none more memorable than the five in the two FA Cup ties against Gateshead and Altrincham.

The presentation night at the end of the season saw Eric Whalley in a bullish mood. He told the gathering:

"We're making a big effort to get into the Conference next season. I can assure everyone that Stan

has been given the go-ahead to go out next year
and, if he thinks we need them, get three or four
new players."

It was a bold statement of intent in the light of the
season just ended. Stanley had won just nine out of 27
games at the Crown. In another sign that the club was
expanding its operations, Whalley also revealed that
the youth team was to be revived to play in the LFA
under-18 Floodlit League. The club received around 60
applications each year from youngsters hoping for trials,
but the reserve league was too physical for kids and
Whalley contended that it was a source of embarrassment
that he could not offer them anything else.

On the financial front, the money from the centenary
game helped the club to a more healthy profit for the
year, and also included in the accounts was £25,189 of
non-trading income, with more than £21,000 of this being
directors' and other donations. It was not just the fans
who were putting their hands in their pockets in the hope
of providing Stanley with a brighter future, but the board
as well.

The fruits of this investment could be seen as the players
returned for training before the 1996–97 season, with work
well underway on the seating in front of the sponsors' lounge.
On the pitch, there was an equally significant development
when Brent Peters joined the board as 'director of football'.
Pressed as to what this meant, the club explained that Stan
Allan was still in charge of team affairs and would recruit
the playing and coaching staff, but that Peters would assist
him due to his "wide knowledge of local players".

The ambiguity of the relationship was obvious from the
start, and it did not take long for conflict to arise over the
signing of ex-Manchester United and England defender
Mike Duxbury who had been born in Accrington. He
joined Stanley on a trial basis in the first week of August, by

which time Stan had already made a number of signings. The following week, with around 24 players having been assessed pre-season, Allan had to decide which 18 players would comprise his first team squad.

Peters was keen for Duxbury to be offered terms, but Allan was most certainly not. The manager told the local press:

> "The lad is 36. I can't see any mileage in it. Whose place is he going to take? I have to look at what we have got at the back, and it is exciting – young lads who are hungry for the game."

Unwisely, Peters publicly disagreed with the manager, claiming Duxbury had not been given a fair chance. Despite Peters' assertions to the contrary, there was clearly a rift between the two, and Allan had every right to wonder quite what the director of football was playing at.

Tales of persistent boardroom interference were legendary at the Crown, but here a director was openly disagreeing with the manager about the squad before a ball had been kicked.

Towards the end of July, the club were as confident about their prospects as perhaps they had ever been. Eric Whalley declared:

> "Stanley will be applying to join the Conference for the 1997–98 season. We are as ambitious as anyone in non-league football, which is why we've spent so much money on the ground. We also now have probably the strongest squad that the club has ever had. Hopefully the stand will be ready for the start of the new season. With the seats in, the capacity will be well over 3,000, which will put us well within the Conference limit."

As applicants to their league, the Conference thus pencilled in an October visit to the Crown Ground to advise the club on any work that had to be done by the end of the year if Stanley were to be admitted to the Conference in the event of the team winning the NPL. To be fair to Whalley and the board, this procedure was what any club hoping to reach the Conference had to do, and it would have been disastrous had Stanley not gone through this and then topped the league. But what was noticeable was the confidence of the club in declaring that they were all dressed up and ready to move on.

An impressive 3-0 defeat of a young Liverpool reserve team in front of 2,028 at the Crown was as good a way as any to convince the town that the team was indeed gearing up for a tilt at promotion. The signing of ex-Manchester City striker Paul Moulden also generated some column inches in the press, and the club splashed £1,500 on Stuart Taylor, another prolific goalscorer who was signed from Guiseley.

Just as everything seemed from the outside to be set fair, events within the club revealed that the reality was anything but. On August 26th, after a poor performance and a 2-1 defeat at the Crown in front of 882, Stan Allan was sacked, just two games into the new season. The board were unhappy that only one of Allan's new signings had made the starting eleven for the opening game, and the manager's decision to release Lee Rogerson had been an unpopular one. Eric Whalley said:

"It's not just two disappointing performances; it's the lack of communication the board feels he has had with the players. We have not been happy for some time."

A furious Stan Allan lambasted the decision as ridiculous, but barely had the news sunk in than Stanley were revealing their new manager. He was Tony Greenwood, the man who had guided Bamber Bridge to the NPL title the season before. On that occasion, Greenwood had not reaped the reward of promotion since Bamber Bridge had not upgraded their ground in time, but there would be no such obstacle at Stanley. Conference officials visiting the ground confirmed that the Crown was virtually ready for Conference football. All Greenwood had to do now was win the title for Stanley as he had done the season before with Bamber Bridge.

The problem for Greenwood was that he had taken charge of someone else's squad. The club took the opportunity to re-sign Rogerson, but there was little else Greenwood could do other than to take the time to assess the players he had inherited. His patience, however, was sorely tested by results. On September 11th, Stanley lost 4-1 at home to Bishop Auckland in front of just over 300 spectators, a dreadful performance that had Greenwood incandescent and determined to make some signings of his own. Too many of the players, he maintained, were simply not up to standard.

Whalley backed Greenwood's judgement, and had a mild swipe at Stan Allan in the process, when he told the local paper:

"I think one of the statements made by the outgoing manager was that he had left Tony Greenwood a good squad. I think if you look at what has happened at this stage of the season, it was not as good as he thought. Tony is desperate to bring new players in."

This clearly was not going to do the confidence of those that remained much good, and one player at whom the charge could emphatically not be levelled was Brett Ormerod, for the months that followed were most notable for the emergence of this very real talent at the club. He was partnered up front mainly by one of Greenwood's first signings, Peter Smith, with the other strikers at the club – Moulden, Taylor and Welch – gradually eased out of the picture.

November saw the end of Stanley's experiment with a director of football after Brent Peters was told to leave. Sidelined after Greenwood's arrival, Peters had irritated Eric Whalley by applying for a managerial position elsewhere, apparently in contravention of an agreement with the chairman, who found out when he received a request for a reference. In full crowd-pleasing mode, Whalley told the *Accrington Observer*:

"I thought that somebody who wanted to move on

without first speaking to me obviously was not dedicated to the club. Whether it is players, committee or directors, if they are not 100% dedicated to the cause they will be asked to leave and there are no exceptions. If they aren't dedicated, they won't be with us much longer."

With the holiday season approaching, Greenwood had guided Stanley to a mid-table position with 29 points from 22 games, and progress had been made in both the NPL League Cup and the Lancashire Junior Cup, but league form was plagued with inconsistency. The manager's contention that the side were poor defensively was borne out by an exasperating 5-4 defeat at Barrow after an Ormerod hat-trick had given Stanley a 4-1 half-time lead, and when Southern League Midland side Bedworth United knocked Stanley out of the FA Trophy, Greenwood put a number of the squad on the transfer list, though he was hardly inundated with offers.

Some thought that the manager needed to reappraise his approach. If the Crown faithful had not been especially enamoured of Stan Allan's style of football, neither were they that much happier with Greenwood's. Many thought it relied too much on the long ball over the top for Ormerod to chase, though this did often reap dividends. The youngster bagged a brace in the League Cup win against Flixton (4-1) and then another to earn a point at Bishop Auckland (1-1) before a barnstorming performance at home to Bamber Bridge on Boxing Day, where another Ormerod double secured a 4-1 win in front of 768 spectators.

The New Year began unpromisingly with the listing of striker Brian Welch under a cloud, accused by the manager of being a disruptive influence; £1,500 summer signing Stuart Taylor also left the club. Stanley were trounced 4-0 at home by Gainsborough Trinity, and even their progress to the quarter-finals of the Lancashire Junior Cup at the expense of Skelmersdale (3-0) did not represent a drastic improvement in form. A supporter wrote to the local press with a sardonic line about the pantomime season at the

Crown, but made a more serious point about the lack of offers for Stanley's transfer-listed players.

Greenwood openly mused on the difficulties of arriving at a club two games into the season, and told the Stanley faithful to give him more time. "Give me 12 months to see what I can do," suggested the manager. "If we're not winning games you can judge me fairly then."

One wonders what Eric Whalley thought of that, but Greenwood's stock recovered through February, for not only did results generally improve but it became apparent that Stanley had a good chance of landing some silverware, with progress maintained into the latter stages of two cup competitions. Good league wins at Lancaster and at home to Marine were the prelude to the quarter-final of the Lancashire Junior Cup against Barrow, where a more confident Stanley won 4-1, with Ormerod adding another two goals to his tally.

Certain that confidence was the key to further success, Greenwood talked his team up in the press, saying that they were now generating a head of steam that would see them through to the season's end. A pairing with local rivals Great Harwood in the semi-final of the Lancashire Junior Cup was a further incentive to maintain form, but the win against Barrow was followed by a 7-2 thrashing at Hyde and a 3-1 reverse at Emley.

With a mid-table league position inevitable, all attention focused on the cups. On February 26th, a large midweek gathering of 644 watched Stanley come from behind to edge past Great Harwood, 2-1, to reach the Lancashire Junior Cup final. Two goals from the manager's brother Nigel, a recent signing, were the decisive moments in a physical game that brought post-match complaints from Great Harwood about Stanley's strong-arm tactics. Shortly afterwards, Stanley progressed to the semi-finals of the League Cup with a 3-0 win at Radcliffe, a game in which Brett Ormerod again shone with two goals, one a spectacular long-range effort worthy of a grander stage.

As it happened, Ormerod was about to graduate. It was

an open secret that a number of Football League clubs had been tracking his progress, and finally Stanley received a firm bid from Blackpool. Never one to undersell by jumping into a deal, Whalley began negotiations, while manager Greenwood admitted that he was tempted to rest key players for "meaningless" league games and save them for the cups.

It was obvious where priorities now lay, but Stanley's hopes of League Cup glory were dashed at Gainsborough by an injury-time goal. This tie was Ormerod's final appearance in an Accrington Stanley shirt. On March 19th, it was announced that a deal had been concluded and Stanley were to receive £50,000 for the young striker, with £40,000 of that paid immediately. It was easily the largest fee that Stanley had ever received for a player, but there was more to the deal than that. Whalley revealed that he had turned down Blackpool's initial offer, and had agreed the £50,000 fee only after insisting on a twenty per cent sell-on clause in the event of Ormerod moving again. It would prove a crucial piece of bargaining.

Ormerod departed with the thanks and best wishes of everyone at the club, from chairman downwards. He had scored 27 goals during the season, enough to land him the Jack Brydon trophy, and his overall Stanley record stood at 31 goals from 57 appearances. Although Stanley's finances were now more stable, debts remained, and the £50,000 would do no harm at all. Ormerod's move also helped the club in terms of recruitment, for no ambitious youngster could now claim that a move to Stanley was a dead end.

As the Lancashire Junior Cup Final loomed form was good, with Stanley registering 3-1 victories at home to Boston and at Runcorn, but the final itself proved to be something of a letdown. Playing in front of 1,345 at Deepdale, Stanley never got going and were defeated 3-0 by Conference side Southport. It was a disappointing performance in what was a rare appearance in a county cup final for Stanley, though the team had not been helped by the loss of Ormerod and the absence of Jez Baldwin and Darren Quick through suspension and injury.

With the cup campaigns over, Greenwood assured the fans through the local press that work had already begun in preparation for the next season, and to this end he brought a number of new players in, enlarging the squad for the final few league games. He admitted that his first season in charge had been a disappointment, especially the FA Trophy defeat at Bedworth and the equally feeble FA Cup exit at Ossett Albion. In the league, Stanley finished 11th, roughly in the mid-table position they had occupied since Christmas.

Greenwood knew that the team for the 1997–98 campaign would be one of his own making and that he was expected to guide the team to a strong promotion challenge. Nothing reflected these new expectations at the club more than the Crown Ground itself, whose development now overtook those on the field of play. For the first time ever, Stanley had a ground fit enough for a higher league than that occupied by the team.

In November, the Conference officials had given the Crown a 'B' grading, enough to be accepted in the event of promotion as long as specified jobs were completed. The one major change to the plans for the Crown was done at the behest of the Conference, who insisted on a single construction to cover the new seats in front of the lounge and the old Duckworth stand. The club had intended on building a separate roof for the new seats, but now a much grander structure extending half the length of the pitch was needed.

Stanley had also started to take advantage of the grants that were now available for ground development, and had received £21,000 to build the retaining walls behind the goals. At the club's presentation night, Whalley thanked those who had helped upgrade the Crown:

"In dealing with the ground improvements, I should

pay tribute to the people who have made donations to cover the cost of the work. Clubs like us can't survive without people donating, and we have had a lot of help this season for various reasons. Everything you see has been paid for, we don't owe a penny."

The chairman also revealed that the club was in a position to pay off the debts that remained from the old regime of John Alty. This burgeoning financial health was assisted, no doubt, by the Ormerod money, but was nonetheless part and parcel of Eric Whalley's fiscal policy at the Crown. The club would not be allowed to go into debt.

The accounts for the year underlined how carefully the club was now being run. Expenditure had been allowed to increase – wages, for example, were up to just short of £25,000 – but only in the light of expanded income, which included £10,000 in bar profits and another £12,000 in donations.

Commercial operations, under the stewardship of John DeMaine, had also increased the club's income. In May, Stanley announced a shirt sponsorship deal with Accrington's ASDA store, and a separate deal with Nield Distribution for the reserve team shirts. Overall profits had come in at £46,639, easily the largest surplus Stanley had ever made over a year.

With the club given the go-ahead in June to start work on an ambitious cantilever roof structure, it seemed that everything off the pitch had been readied for Stanley to make a go of life in the Conference. Attention now turned to Tony Greenwood. Could he build a team to take them there?

Greenwood laid out his philosophy to the *Accrington Observer*: he was not interested in ageing ex-Football League players, but wanted some experienced Conference campaigners to shore up a team of hungry and ambitious youngsters. He also wanted plenty of physical presence in the team, players who could look after themselves and each other.

One new recruit was familiar – striker Jim McCluskie

began his second spell at the Crown Ground. His first spell at the club had been marred by a broken leg, and he had then been cashed in to Morecambe. To the great frustration of the Stanley faithful, he had been a resounding success there, helping the Shrimps to promotion in 1995 with 39 goals, and it was hoped that this time he could reproduce that form. Greg Challender was another recruit, signed from Stalybridge, who had experience of the Conference.

With reserve and youth teams operational, Greenwood talked of a 35-strong squad of players, with fringe first-teamers turning out for the reserves. On the eve of the kick-off, Whalley declared: "We are going for the top, nothing but", and a glance at the league table after three games would have appeared to bear out his confidence. After victories over Winsford, Radcliffe and Altrincham, Stanley topped the table.

There were, however, more troublesome undercurrents. Striker Peter Smith had been lost to a broken leg in the opening game, and the team had not played well throughout, and had been particularly fortunate to defeat Altrincham. Greenwood sounded defiant to the local press:

"If we are pretty and win, great. If we are raggy and score in the last minute, great. Pretty teams don't win championships. I think the fans will be more satisfied with picking up points on their travels rather than being entertained and losing."

Winning ugly was no doubt a useful thing for a team to be able to fall back on, but it hardly seemed likely that Stanley could go through the season relying on it. Sure enough, things were about to take a severe turn for the worse. In the fourth league game of the season, at home to Runcorn, Stanley were resoundingly beaten 3-0, and Greenwood admitted that his team were well short of what was required:

"That result has been coming for the last three games, and I knew the outcome after two minutes. The team is not good enough. We can absorb pressure, nick a goal and then defend it, but we can't

grab the initiative and open defences up. We have
to get the balance right; there is not enough experience in the side."

Greenwood targeted Southport striker Steve Haw – a
prolific non-league goalscorer – as a replacement for Peter
Smith, but Stanley started to struggle desperately in the
meantime. A home defeat to Colwyn Bay on September
16th attracted barely 300 to the Crown, less than half the
attendance for the Runcorn game, leaving Tony Greenwood
sounding a forlorn man, and, more worryingly, one who
could not extract from the players the performance that
he wanted:

"I can't give it any more than I am giving it. We've
been going on at them for four games and there
was nothing more we could say."

It sounded terminal, and after a home defeat to
Guiseley on September 20th, Stanley's fifth successive
loss, Greenwood was relieved of his duties just 13 months
after taking over. Jim McCluskie was made the caretaker
manager for the midweek game at home to Leigh RMI.
Stanley suffered another defeat, but reports suggested that
McCluskie had instructed the team to try and play more
constructive football than the predominantly long-ball
game practised under Greenwood. Steve Haw had arrived
at the club, and hopes were high that he would form a
decent striking partnership with McCluskie – certainly
both had the pedigree to succeed within the NPL.

The club received more than 30 applications for the
vacant manager's post. Keenly aware that he had already
sacked two managers in less than three years, Whalley
defended his previous choices, pointing out that one
was very experienced in non-league, and the other was
manager of the champions the previous year. All the same,
the experience of the club under Allan and Greenwood was
a harsh lesson in the essential unpredictability of the job.

Perhaps with this in mind, the chairman took a new
tack in appointing Tony Greenwood's successor. For if
Stan Allan had non-league experience and Greenwood the

recent success, the latest recruit had neither. On Monday September 29th, ex-Welsh international winger Leighton James was revealed as Accrington Stanley's new manager. Once again, Eric Whalley spoke of his latest appointment in grand and glowing terms:

"This is a new era. We have a high-profile manager for a high-profile non-league club, so hopefully he can attract better players than the previous two managers have done. It's not every club that has a former Welsh international as a manager."

The former Burnley winger certainly brought a tremendous pedigree to the club in terms of his own playing career, but his profile as a non-league manager was somewhat less illustrious. Since taking up his first position at Gainsborough in October 1993, he had gone to Morecambe in January 1994, and then on to Netherfield just four months later. It was hardly a convincing CV, but then again, past deeds had ultimately counted for nothing with the last two managers.

James appointed Jim McCluskie in the role of player-coach and assistant manager, and promised, sensibly, to give everyone at the club a fair chance to impress. But like Greenwood before him, James had inherited someone else's players – and, moreover, a squad with a chronic lack of confidence and in desperate need of a win. He really could not afford to spend too long assessing if, ultimately, radical surgery was required. In his first game in charge, James at least halted the run of six successive defeats with a 1-1 draw at home to Lancaster, but the elusive win would take longer to arrive. When, on October 21st, Stanley went down to a 1-0 defeat at Barrow, it was the club's 13th game without a win, the longest such run in the club's history, and this unwanted record was accompanied by another broken leg in Stanley colours for poor Jim McCluskie.

By this time, James had started to make changes to the squad, with one of the outgoing players being Lee Rogerson, after 148 appearances and 15 goals for Stanley. Rogerson played during a difficult and highly volatile period of the club's history, rarely enjoying the luxury of an entirely settled side or a long-term manager. But he was an infectious character who always gave of his best, and is fondly remembered by Stanley fans for those reasons. James was also lining up returns to the Crown for striker Brian Welch and David Hamilton, the latter as reserve team coach.

A midweek 4-4 draw in the League Cup on October 27th was Stanley's 15th game without a win, but the team had fought back from 3-1 down and James was encouraged enough by the performance to tell the local press:

"If I was a player at Accrington Stanley I would be very excited and would very much want to be part of what's up ahead. I honestly think there are some good times around the corner for this club."

Just a few days later, Stanley defeated Emley to end their winless streak, and in the goalless draw that followed at Gainsborough the team looked solid and competitive in keeping a rare clean sheet. They could not, however, maintain the improvement.

On December 9th, a 3-1 midweek defeat at the hands of Marine provoked a frustrated outburst from James that Stanley were not too good to go down, and the manager made the valid point that he had inherited a poor team at a stage in the season where the only players on the market were those on the fringes of other first team squads.

James, though happy with the engine room of his team, wanted a passer, someone who could pick the ball up, distribute it and keep play going, but the theory that James would be able to attract decent players to the club looked flawed in the timing. A bid for Tony Kelly of Altrincham, for example, came to nothing; indeed, which club would be prepared to sell such a prized asset as a midfield playmaker at such a juncture of the season?

Stanley's 3-0 defeat of Spennymoor on December 20th in front of 409 at the Crown was only the sixth league win of a campaign that had started with three straight wins. Thankfully, as far as Stanley were concerned, two teams,

Radcliffe Borough and Alfreton Town, were having an even worse time of it, and looked halfway to relegation already. In spite of Stanley's struggles, they remained ninth from bottom, seemingly clear of the relegation zone.

The New Year brought another tumultuous Lancashire Junior Cup tie against Great Harwood, with Stanley again eliminating their local rivals.

The Harwood manager could not hide his anger at what he viewed as vicious tackling from the Stanley defence, and James rose to the bait, deriding Harwood as an "alehouse team". It was all mildly embarrassing.

Although Stanley recorded their seventh win of the season with a defeat of Blyth on January 17th, Whalley announced the following week that he had cut the wages of several players since their performances had not justified the money they were being paid.

The chairman stressed that there were no money problems at the club and that it was purely a football decision, but James said nothing. It could hardly have helped his efforts to motivate the players, and after a defeat against Chorley on January 31st, James tendered his resignation, which was accepted by the club.

James was gracious in resignation. He said that he had just received a promotion at work which made the two jobs almost impossible to combine, but he admitted also that his managership had not gone well in spite of receiving the full backing of the chairman:

> "The club have been nothing but fair with me. I haven't got a bad word to say about Stanley, the club has treated me absolutely marvellously."

Whalley told the press that, as far as he was concerned, it was in the best interests of the club since the 'new era' under James simply had not worked. For the chairman it was another frustrating outcome to a carefully considered appointment. With David Hamilton at the club as reserve team manager, there was a readymade replacement to step up, and Hamilton made the move jointly with Jim McCluskie.

The new managerial team, however, struggled to make

an impact. February was a poor month, with Stanley losing their first two league fixtures under the new regime, and a two-week break from league fixtures saw Stanley end the month in the bottom four. Bamber Bridge occupied the second relegation spot eight points behind Stanley but with three games in hand.

After having advanced to the quarter-final of the Lancashire Junior Cup at the expense of Ramsbottom United (a game which saw defender Darren Quick reach 200 appearances for the club), Stanley were eliminated 1-0 at home to Southport, leaving the team to focus solely on survival. Whalley set the players a target of ten points for safety, and they responded with an excellent win at Boston United on March 7th which dented the Lincolnshire team's own promotion hopes, but a defeat at home to Leigh RMI the following Saturday saw the sacking of McCluskie and Hamilton, the third and fourth managers of the season.

To infuse the situation with an even greater air of chaos, the decision to sack the managerial pair after just six weeks in the job was (publicly at any rate) made not by Whalley, who was on holiday, but by directors Frank Martindale and John DeMaine. The statement they issued sounded somewhat defensive:

"This is relegation form. Six games from the end of the season we must gain enough points to keep ourselves in the Premier division. How many games can you give somebody? Do we wait and do nothing?"

Even seasoned Crown Ground regulars could not remember a state of affairs like this, and few believed that Whalley had delegated such a crucial decision. Neither Hamilton nor McCluskie was happy with the situation either, and the latter handed in a transfer request with both adamant that they had improved the performance of the team and dismayed that they had not been given more time to see the job through.

It quickly emerged that both McCluskie and Hamilton had resigned after their first game in charge, which had been the Ramsbottom cup tie, but had been persuaded to return. A statement to the press from the pair read:

"We resigned because of interference. We were not setting off on that footing. I think they saw two lads who were not 'yes-men' and were not prepared to put up with it. We never really had a chance to make a go of it."

Although the Crown faithful appreciated the progress made with the development of the ground under Eric Whalley, this represented the chairman's stickiest moment yet. Four managers had come and gone in six months, and now there were accusations in the press that the board routinely interfered to the point of sacking managers who resisted them.

In response to the allegations of interference, Whalley responded:

"Every manager we have had I have personally backed 100 per cent. If anybody has said they have not been able to sign a player, that is not true – I have not agreed with some of the signings, but they have been the manager's decisions."

Steve Haw, scorer of 11 goals in 33 games during the season, was given the task of guiding the team to safety in what remained of the season. On April 2nd, with the club still not safe from the drop, Whalley explained his strategy for making a new managerial appointment. The club were not going to advertise but would consider the possible candidates and approach an individual to appoint as a long-term manager, proven at this level:

"The one thing we need to bring to this club is stability, and certainly over the last twelve months, as far as managers go, I am really embarrassed that we are on our fifth."

Whalley also maintained he knew nothing about the sacking of McCluskie and Hamilton, but defended the decision with the argument that Stanley's meagre points total would have seen them occupying a relegation place in a typical season.

In his only foray into the market before transfer deadline day, Haw signed winger Ashley Hoskin, an old crowd favourite who had made 131 appearances in his previous spell at the club. Easter Monday saw Stanley lose 5-3 at Emley, but none of the other teams below them could make any headway. A point at home to fellow strugglers Bamber Bridge on April 13th finally guaranteed safety, and the season mercifully drew to a close with a home draw against bottom club Alfreton Town. The Crown faithful had witnessed just seven league and cup victories at the Crown all season, the lowest for fifteen years.

Whalley was prepared at least to hold up his hand and admit that he had made some poor appointments, and he remained in credit with the Crown faithful for the obvious strides the club had made off the pitch during his time in the chair. At the end of April, the steel framework to hold the new roof was hoisted into place by a crane. The structure towered over the old John Duckworth stand and represented a significant move towards not just a Conference-standard ground, but one that could conceivably host Football League games.

The season ended with hopes that the club had finally drawn a line under this most disruptive of seasons as Billy Rodaway was unveiled as the new Accrington Stanley manager. Eric Whalley said he could have filled the vacancy twenty times over with the interest shown by people contacting the club, but he had stuck to his guns by approaching someone he thought would have a lasting effect on the club:

> "We have gone for someone who we think has the
> experience at every level both at Football League
> and non-league. This is a long-term appointment
> and we hope it brings some stability to the club."

Rodaway had been an assistant manager for seven years, and now declared that he was ready to have a go in his own right. At least this time the new manager had been given every chance of putting together the team he wanted well before pre-season. The dismissals of Allan and Greenwood had been disastrously timed as both had encumbered a new manager with the underperforming squad of his predecessor. And since most clubs began with large squads that were then pruned, September and October was not a buyer's market, and anyone recruiting at this point had to be quick and astute in spotting the few decent players released by the bigger clubs.

With the new stand now complete and looking very impressive, the club announced a deal with the Daniel Thwaites brewery company, who had agreed to pay a five-figure sum for the naming rights. Once again, the club showed a profit on the year, underlining the success of Whalley and the board in both attracting more money into the club and carefully controlling spending. With all Conference ground requirements now met and the club in the black, there would now be nothing to stop Stanley making the move to nationwide football. Whalley had delivered on his side of things – the hope now was that he had chosen the right man to deliver on the pitch.

Billy Rodaway wasted little time in signing some of the players that he hoped would bring promotion, one of whom was a stocky goalkeeper by the name of Jamie Speare, signed from Bury. Rodaway also hired Ian Britton as his assistant and Greg Abbott as player-coach. Of the contract players at the club, only Darren Quick (who had requested a transfer under Tony Greenwood) was retained. Players released included Jez Baldwin and Peter Smith.

By the eve of the season, Rodaway had signed a full team of new recruits, and in response to the loss of Brian Welch with a broken arm in one of the last pre-season friendlies, the manager pulled off a nifty bit of business with the signing of striker Billy O'Callaghan.

An unwelcome reminder of the previous season's problems came on August 14th, when the club was hit with a suspended £5,000 fine from the FA for their disciplinary record of 70 cautions and nine red cards. It could have been worse – at the hearing, the FA took into account Stanley's argument that a team fighting relegation was more likely to accumulate bookings for fouls and tackles, but the authorities condemned the number of incidents of dissent, abuse, foul language and arguing with the referee after games.

Eric Whalley argued that a team's discipline reflected that of the manager:

> "I think, really, the lack of discipline of the five people who managed the side last season has been shown up. It was pathetic to say the least. I don't have worries about this season because Billy Rodaway is known for being a disciplinarian."

Rodaway confirmed that he would clamp down on dissent, but another attempt to instil a more professional approach caused dissenting voices among the fans. After losing the opening game at home to Colwyn Bay, Stanley faced a midweek trip to Chorley and Rodaway was shocked to discover that the supporters were allowed to use the team coach to get to and from the games. As far as Rodaway was concerned, the dressing room and the coach were confidential areas for the manager, coaches and players, so he announced that supporters would no longer be allowed to travel with the team. He stressed that it was a matter of professionalism and nothing to do with the conduct of the fans, but his case was not helped by results, with Stanley on the wrong end of a 4-0 hiding at Chorley and yet to win a game. A letter in the *Accrington Observer* indicated that the Crown regulars remained far from convinced that Rodaway was the man to steer the club towards better times:

> "Mr Rodaway has asked the supporters to be patient, but I last saw the team win a league game at Boston on February 28th. Since then the team have played ten matches without a win and quite frankly with the current team I can't see where the next win will come from. As has been the case in

the past, good loyal players have been allowed to leave the club while the manager has brought in inferior replacements."

The first league win finally arrived on September 15th, when two strikes from Billy O'Callaghan gave Stanley a 2-1 win at Leigh RMI, and this was followed four days later by an equally impressive 3-1 win at Stalybridge. The team were then unlucky not to collect all three points in a goalless draw at home to Chorley, but a 2-0 defeat of a decent Guiseley side on the Saturday made for ten points out of 12, an unbeaten run of six games and hopes that the side had turned the corner.

It proved, however, to be a deceptive purple patch of form, for by mid-November, the team were still looking for their fourth league win. Stanley had lost six consecutive league games and were bottom of the table. There was absolutely no doubt this time that the club was in the thick of a relegation battle.

In the midst of these woes, news first emerged that the Conference was thinking of setting up a second tier. It seemed fanciful to suggest that Stanley would be able to survive at a higher level when they faced relegation from the NPL, but at a Supporters' Club meeting on October 5th, John DeMaine confirmed that the club would accept an invitation if one was made, and revealed that the club had spent close to £200,000 on the ground since Eric Whalley had become chairman. It was an eye-opening amount of cash to be mentioned in the same sentence as Accrington Stanley, and stood in stark contrast to the baffling lack of success on the field in the same period.

With his team in the bottom four, Billy Rodaway was a man under pressure, but he was still talking a good game in the pages of the local press, arguing that Stanley just needed a result to start the confidence flowing again. On November 14th, Stanley at last recorded their fourth league win with a 2-1 defeat of Gainsborough, but a tough home fixture followed at home to leaders Altrincham, and a resounding 4-1 defeat was the prelude to a disastrous

December. Stanley took just one point from five games, and dropped to the bottom of the table once more.

Black humour was the order of the day for one scribe, who wrote to the local paper with a question for Rodaway:

"I recall that the manager intended Stanley to be in the top eight teams by Christmas. Would Mr Rodaway kindly tell the long-suffering Stanley fans which Christmas he is referring to?"

Publicly, the club gave their full backing to the manager, but the situation clearly could not be allowed to continue. The beginning of the end for Rodaway was a 2-0 defeat at Spennymoor on December 12th, after which striker Brian Welch went to the press with serious allegations about the way the club was being run. In the position of having to defend their manager, the club accused Welch of behaving like a spoilt kid, but the player's revelations could not be ignored. Welch charged that the set-up at the club was "shocking and totally amateurish", and that the training arrangements were pathetic: "You'd get better organised teams in Sunday league football."

Welch was quickly moved on, but his intervention, in tandem with the team's inability to win a game, quickly brought things to a head. The final humiliation came on Monday December 28th, when Stanley were thrashed 5-0 at the Crown by Bamber Bridge in front of 538 spectators. The game was sweet revenge for Bamber Bridge's manager Tony Greenwood, back at the club where he had won the NPL title, but it was the end of Billy Rodaway's tenure at the Crown after just seven months.

Rodaway, to his credit, took full responsibility for the situation. He had brought in 24 players, so he could hardly deny that the board had backed him all the way, and they had been the players he had wanted. He admitted that he was embarrassed by the way his team had performed and that he had left the club in a shambolic state.

In a further disclosure, it was revealed that the complaints of Brian Welch were far from those of a petulant child, since Rodaway had been holding midweek training sessions in

Merseyside and been picking mainly players based over there. Even the *Accrington Observer* could not avoid the conclusion that the whole Rodaway episode was a severe embarrassment to the club, which had now got through six managers and caretaker managers in just 16 months.

Two days after sacking Rodaway, Stanley approached Wayne Harrison to offer him the manager's job. Harrison had been credited with turning around Bamber Bridge from a similar situation the year before after being appointed in November 1997 with the club bottom of the NPL.

Harrison had been controversially replaced by Tony Greenwood that summer, and had gone to Blackpool to work at their youth academy. He agreed to join Stanley and his brief was clear – to repeat the great escape that he had engineered the year before at Bamber Bridge. Whalley told the press:

"Wayne went to Bamber Bridge when they were in trouble and kept them up. I knew he was looking for a job and we asked if he could bring players in immediately and he said he could. We could not lose in the situation we are in. It needed sorting out quickly because time is moving on."

Harrison revealed that the legend in non-league circles was that the managerial position at Accrington Stanley was one of the hardest in the business, with the incumbent having to deal with high expectations and a volatile crowd. In Harrison's favour was the fact that he could not possibly have inherited a worse situation. The 2-0 home defeat to Winsford on January 2nd meant Stanley had won just four of their 24 league games and were now well adrift at the bottom, with gates having thinned to a hard core of around 350.

A letter in the local paper pointed the finger at Whalley, charging that he had prioritised the ground rather than the squad, with the club not offering the wages to bring decent players to the club:

"For all the ambitious talk from the boardroom, Stanley are trying to achieve the impossible on a shoestring budget. Unfortunately, the only mira-

cles produced in football today are usually the result of large amounts of money invested where it
counts – on the field. Until the sort of money required to attract quality players is made available,
it is doubtful whether any manager could succeed
in raising Stanley from their imminent position of
obscurity."

It sounded a little harsh, and a letter the following week
defended the chairman on the basis of what he had done to
the ground and the facilities, but this didn't really address
the point made in the original letter.

In fact, Whalley would later admit that some of the
managers were chosen on the basis that they agreed to
work with relatively small budgets:

"You can make bad appointments, and you've got to
hold your hand up sometimes and say that it was
the wrong appointment for the club, even though it
was made in good faith at the time. Some appointments were made for financial reasons, which you
realise you can't do to get a decent manager, and
you have to hold your hands up and say you made
a mistake."

But even if the budgets varied depending on the manager,
it remained the case that Allan, Greenwood and Rodaway
had each recruited a set of players who were simply not
good enough to compete at the top end of the NPL.

Harrison himself brought in some new faces, but
immediate form showed no improvement – in fact, one of
the lowest points of the season arrived in Harrison's sixth
game in charge when the team lost a 2-0 lead at Darwen in
a Lancashire Junior Cup quarter-final tie before going out
3-2 after extra time, this to a team three divisions below
Stanley.

Hope was raised briefly in mid-March after a couple of
wins, but in reality Stanley never looked like battling their
way out of the relegation places. The team was spirited
and worked hard but, Billy O'Callaghan apart, the squad
lacked the quality to put the results together that were

required in the situation. The form of O'Callaghan was the one consoling feature of the season. He was a quick, wiry striker with an instinctive sense of where the goal was, and as the season approached its final phase, he was well on the way to 30 goals.

With relegation looking almost certain, the board faced some searching questions. In the *Accrington Observer*, John DeMaine refused to concede that all was lost and rejected the claim that a parsimonious wage policy was to blame:

"We will pay out more this year in wages than we will ever have done before. Just because it hasn't worked out doesn't mean to say that we haven't spent money."

He did, however, admit that they persevered too long with Billy Rodaway, and the poor season had affected the club in other ways. The chair of the Supporters' Club, John Russell, announced that the organisation would fold at the end of the season unless more people became involved. It was a shame for stalwarts like Russell to see interest ebb away. He had been behind the first regular and organised travel scheme for Stanley fans to attend away games, the infamous, boozy 'Russ Bus', a development that had reflected the emergence in the early 1990s of a small group of never-miss younger supporters. These fans offered noisier and more colourful support than the older generations at the Crown, and also contributed to the emerging fanzine culture with their own effort, *The Barber's Pole*.

On April 13th, Stanley rallied from 2-0 down to force a 2-2 draw at Winsford, but this was a must-win game, and results elsewhere confirmed Stanley's relegation to the First Division of the NPL after eight seasons in the top tier. Though the damage had been done before Christmas, the chairman sounded unimpressed with the form of the team under Harrison, telling the local press after the Winsford game:

"His position is not under discussion at this moment in time, but once again if it had not been for O'Callaghan we would have been convincingly beaten. You have to question whether all the players were playing as if they were scrapping against relegation. We have been relegated, and in truth, we deserve to be."

Relegation was a huge blow for Whalley. He had prepared Stanley for Conference football with a very considerable investment in the ground and the facilities, and now found the club headed in the other direction. Interested parties elsewhere also thought the time was ripe to test the chairman's resolve. The *Accrington Observer* of April 9th reported that investment banker Ilyas Khan, an Accrington-born resident of Hong Kong, was to pursue a "hostile bid" to buy a majority shareholding in the club.

Khan was already a shareholder to the tune of £13,000, but he now claimed to have offered £750,000 for Whalley's sixty per cent stake in the club. Khan also criticised the commercial operation at the club, maintaining that Stanley were not making nearly as much money from their unique name and history as they ought to be doing.

In the event, the AGM witnessed no showdown between the chairman and Khan, and the affair did not, in the long run, impair the harmonious working relationship between the two. But it was a reminder that Accrington Stanley, though in one sense a living embodiment of a community, was also a business enterprise that could be bought and sold and invested in as people saw fit.

As John Alty had found, predatory investors had sensitive antennae when it came to detecting vulnerability, and Whalley knew that his position as majority shareholder could be undermined if under-performance on the pitch led to him losing the confidence of the supporters.

On May 7th, the club announced that Wayne Harrison has been given the full backing of the board to build a side to take Stanley back into the NPL Premier Division at the first time of asking, but just three days later, Harrison resigned because of work commitments. There was nothing for it but for Whalley to start the process of finding yet another manager, and he could be forgiven for wondering which way he should proceed. Past achievements did not seem to count for anything, and interviews seemed merely to advantage those who talked the best game. Targeting individuals who seemed a good bet had proved to be equally as perilous.

But the non-league network was, and remains, an efficient disseminator of information, and the chairman did not have to wait long before his phone rang. It was Liam Watson, a respected non-league marksman who counted Whalley as a friend. Watson had been on holiday with John Coleman, player-manager of NPL First Division side Ashton United, and the pair had returned to find that Coleman had been sacked by his chairman – a certain Terry Styring.

At Ashton, Coleman had constructed a side in his image – tough, competitive and hard-running – and had been desperately unlucky not to win promotion to the NPL Premier Division. In 1997–98, Coleman's side had gained 87 points, enough for the title in most years, yet had finished third. After another third-placed finish in 1998–99, Styring decided that it was time for a change, and Coleman found himself looking for a new club.

It was through Liam Watson's phone call that Eric Whalley discovered Coleman's interest in the Accrington job, so the chairman arranged a meeting at the Tickled Trout hotel just outside Preston, a long-used border rendezvous between East and West Lancashire. From Whalley's perspective, perhaps Coleman was just what the club needed: a brash Scouser not afraid to ruffle feathers, someone to bring a bit of no-nonsense steel and passion onto the field. Stanley had seen first-hand how difficult a Coleman side was to play against – his Ashton team had muscled Stanley out of the previous season's FA Trophy at the Crown.

One of the Ashton scorers that day was Jimmy Bell, and Coleman turned up for the meeting with Bell, whom he wanted to bring to the Crown as his assistant. Within a short time, a verbal agreement had been made. Coleman and Bell would become the new managerial team at the

Crown Ground on a non-contract basis. On May 15th 1999, the appointments were revealed in the *Accrington Observer* and all involved proclaimed a mutual aim. Said Whalley:

"We have appointed somebody who we believe is the most up-and-coming manager and think he is going to get us promotion in the first year. We are delighted to have got such a high calibre of manager so quickly. He did not need a lot of persuasion to come to Accrington."

For Coleman's part, he knew what was expected:

"The brief is the club doesn't want to stay in the First Division too long and I am looking forward to the challenge of getting what I missed out on with Ashton. I know it is a bit of a cliché, but Stanley are one of the biggest names in the First Division. But a name won't get you anywhere in a league. It is what happens on the pitch that matters. What I want to do is get the club up to its potential. I think everybody expects Accrington Stanley to be near the top of the table and I expect no different."

No club relegated from the top tier of the NPL had ever managed to regain its status at the first time of asking, and there was nothing to suggest that Stanley were equipped for the task. The club had been left with just a handful of players and even fewer established performers. From their base in Merseyside, Coleman and Bell had three months to recruit a first team squad and – an altogether more difficult proposition – to generate among the new players the team spirit and collective understanding that could make them genuine title contenders. A challenge it most certainly was.

Chapter Seven

1999–2006
The Triumph of Hope

JOHN COLEMAN GAVE the impression of a man determined to prove himself in the managerial chair. His sacking at Ashton United, a club with an historically modest record, had followed two seasons of achievement there, including two NPL First Division cups. But now Coleman was in the hot seat at a club that saw its rightful place much higher up the non-league ladder, and expectations were high.

At least the new manager could not do much worse than some of his predecessors. For a club that had made its ambitions so obvious and made such an investment in its surroundings, Accrington Stanley's recent record on the pitch was not far short of disastrous.

The club now found itself back in the division of which it had been an inaugural member in 1987, a decline that had been mirrored at the turnstiles, where gates had slipped from the several hundred that regularly turned out to watch the Phil Staley sides to the diehard core of 350.

Under Eric Whalley, the club seemed able now to weather these struggles without impending crisis, but all the same, the chairman was desperate to regain a place in the NPL. All talk of Stanley in the Conference sounded absurd if the club was not even in the feeder division.

For Coleman, it meant taking that extra step that he had been unfortunate not to make with Ashton United and guide Stanley to promotion, and he started as if he meant business by ordering the players in for pre-season training in the last week of June, earlier than would normally be the case. He told the press:

> "We have to be able to compete fitness-wise. I have been in the First Division for two-and-a-half years and no one will roll over and die for you. Every game you win you have to earn. If we can compete on a level par with teams in terms of fitness then that bit of quality we are trying to bring to the club will make a difference."

Coleman had been making enquiries for over a month, and there was already reason to be impressed by the new manager's powers of persuasion. The first signing to be announced was that of Mark Shirley, a left-sided player who could operate either in midfield or on the wing. Non-league observers knew that Shirley was good enough to be a full-time professional, and the player himself had recently rejected a move to Conference side Rushden & Diamonds. It was an encouraging sign that Coleman was able to deliver the quality players the club needed.

Shirley was quickly followed by another playmaker, Jay Flannery, and two recruits for the midfield engine room, Mark Brennan and Steve Carragher. When left-back Steve Hollis and centre-half Robbie Williams arrived, a pattern was beginning to emerge – Coleman was gathering around him those players he knew and trusted from his own experience.

Most came from Merseyside, and both Brennan and Hollis had played for him at Ashford. Though Williams was at amateur Liverpool club St Dominic's, Coleman had spotted him at a reserve team game at Ashton United and had been impressed by the young defender.

The capture of towering centre-half Jonathan Smith from neighbours Great Harwood was at least a sign that Stanley had not abandoned the locality completely when it came to recruiting players, and the manager also retained a select few from the previous season. As a striker himself, Coleman could not ignore the superb achievement of Billy O'Callaghan in winning the NPL Golden Boot award for the league's top goalscorer, and most of the defence were also given a chance, including goalkeeper Jamie Speare, Mark Howard, Ged Walsh and Paul Tomlinson.

The side that emerged for the pre-season games was thus a mix of the old and the new, but what immediately took the eye was the high-tempo, attacking style that Coleman wanted to employ, and particularly impressive was the 1-0 defeat of Conference side Southport. With the opening fixture looming, the manager had problems with injuries and some suspensions carried over from the previous season, so he returned to Ashton and made late offers for striker Mark Ceraolo and midfielder Brett Baxter, as well as signing another creative midfielder in Russell Payne, who arrived from Congleton Town.

There was clearly going to be an unavoidable period of settling in. The team which ran out for Coleman's first league game in charge, away at Lincoln United, contained just two ex-Ashton players and included nine debutants, with Jamie Speare and Ged Walsh the only ones to have played for Stanley before. A sign that Coleman did not see inexperience as a problem was evident in the central defensive partnership of Robbie Williams and Jonathan Smith, and with Mark Shirley down the left and Jay Flannery down the right, there was plenty of attacking width.

Hopes were high, but things started poorly. The team lost to a late goal at Lincoln and then, in perhaps the worst performance of the season, were defeated 2-1 at home by Trafford in front of just 334 spectators, a game that also saw Robbie Williams sustain an injury which would keep him out until the New Year.

Frustrated with how things had started, and mindful that too many points could not be dropped in a league that a team invariably needed over 80 points to escape, Whalley sanctioned further signings. Coleman returned to Ashton United with a cheque for £6,000 for the services of speedy striker Gary Williams, and also signed centre-half Karl Bell and right-back John Doolan from the same club.

Though the squad now had a healthy contingent of

Coleman's ex-Ashton players, Gary Williams was actually a local lad, raised in Burnley and a pre-season hopeful at the Crown in 1995, when Stan Allan decided not to take him on. That Coleman felt he needed a striker was due to the regrettable problems he was having with Billy O'Callaghan, for although Billy was struggling for fitness with a problematic hamstring, there were also rumours that his relationship with Coleman was not an easy one.

O'Callaghan's future at the club became a matter of further speculation when Gary Williams made a sensational debut at Burscough, running on to a long ball down the right and neatly lobbing the 'keeper from the edge of the box after just eleven seconds of play. Sure enough, after the defeat of Netherfield Kendal at the Crown on September 3rd, Coleman publicly criticised O'Callaghan, and by the end of the month he had been sold to Prescot Cables.

The game at Burscough seemed to crystallise some of Stanley's problems in this opening period of the season. They enjoyed a good deal of possession and looked good on the ball – Hollis, Shirley, Payne and Flannery were clearly far better players than any other recent manager had managed to attract to the club.

But Stanley found it difficult to kill off games. They were by far the better side at Burscough, who had a decent team themselves, but Stanley could not find the second goal and surrendered two points to a late header from a set-piece.

At times, it looked as though Stanley had cured themselves of these exasperating tendencies, but the problem would then re-emerge. An impressive 2-0 win at Harrogate was followed shortly after by a 1-0 reverse at the hands of a poor Netherfield Kendal side, and when, on October 2nd, Stanley lost 1-0 at Bradford Park Avenue, they remained ninth from bottom of the league having lost five of their first ten games. Since promotion winners rarely lost more than seven or eight games during the season, Stanley's position already looked bleak.

An indication, though, of what the team could do when

it fired on all cylinders came on an extraordinary October afternoon at the Crown when Stanley put ten goals past Lincoln United, a game in which seven Stanley players scored, one of whom, Gary Williams, netted four. The win caused such a stir that an additional 100 people turned up for the midweek fixture at home to Workington Town, and again Stanley excelled in a 4-1 win.

Hopes that the team had left their inconsistent ways behind were again put on hold as the side fell to a 2-1 defeat at Farsley Celtic, making it six wins and six defeats from 15 games. Another good home win against Stocksbridge Park Steels on the last day in October had Coleman in a confident mood, however. He told the *Accrington Observer* that they had only themselves to blame for not being higher in the league, having played most teams off the park, but he admitted that the side's tendency to concede bad goals through poor defending needed to be addressed. Coleman revealed that his weekly team meetings were exercises in positive thinking, stressing to the players that they were a lot better than the table suggested.

Mark Shirley, for one, concurred. He told the local paper:
"I didn't envisage us being in this division for anything more than a single season, and I don't see any
reason why we can't go up."

Shirley also revealed that he had moved down two divisions to Stanley from Morecambe because of the type of football he knew Coleman would look to play, as well as the sales pitch from Eric Whalley, who convinced the player that the club was going places.

That optimism seemed well placed as the holiday programme loomed, with Coleman demanding a promotion push and setting the team a target of 80 points. They got a break at Belper with a winner deep into injury time, and a 2-1 win at home to Ossett Town elevated them to sixth before yet another setback derailed the charge. On December 18th, Stanley fell meekly to a 1-0 defeat at Workington Town, but worse was to follow in the Christmas game at the Crown.

In what was billed as a must-win game against promotion-chasers Radcliffe Borough, Stanley again misfired in front of goal, with Gary Williams enduring his sixth game without a goal. The same could not be said of Radcliffe's Paul Mullin. The ex-Stanley reserve team player led the line superbly and scored two as the visitors came away with a 3-1 win in front of 687, the biggest Crown attendance of the season so far.

Stanley remained in sixth, but were 12 points adrift of the second promotion place with just one game in hand. Their playing record stood at ten wins and eight defeats from 23 games, and any cold assessment of Stanley's position would have concluded that promotion was highly unlikely. To reach the manager's target of 80 points, the team would have to accumulate 45 points out of the available 57 – in other words, 15 wins in the remaining 19 games.

The form of his two main strikers was another problem for Coleman. Mark Ceraolo had not scored since early November, and Gary Williams was also suffering. Williams had blasted 18 goals from 30 games, a record that had ignited rumours about a move to a bigger club, but the speculation about an imminent transfer seemed to affect the youngster. Coleman had few options up front other than to play himself or Jimmy Bell, but his reasoning that Williams was too good a player to fire blanks for too long was soon borne out.

There was at least one advantage to the position that Coleman's Stanley found themselves in at the turn of the year. Having to win most of the remaining games, there was nothing for it but to attack. This was Coleman's preferred mode anyway; not for him the idea of nicking a goal and then defending it. So it probably helped that the first three league games of the New Year were difficult fixtures at Congleton, Trafford and Chorley, places where teams might normally be a little cautious. Instead, Stanley went there looking for goals, and in each case emerged with a wildly entertaining victory: 3-2 at Congleton, 4-2 at Trafford and 3-2 at Chorley.

Gratifyingly, Gary Williams was back on the score sheet

with five goals in these three games, but his re-emergence quickly precipitated the long-rumoured bid, and when it came, Stanley could not turn down the money on offer. The interested party was Doncaster Rovers, and the resurgent Yorkshire team proffered £60,000, which Stanley accepted. It remains, at the time of writing, the biggest fee Stanley have ever received for a player.

With Williams' exit inevitable, Coleman wasted little time in submitting a £10,000 bid for Paul Mullin. It was an emphatic amount of cash for the NPL First Division and Stanley envisaged few problems, but they had reckoned without Mullin's sense of loyalty. With Radcliffe challenging strongly for promotion, Mullin turned down the move back to the Crown.

Coleman's 'Plan B' was to pair himself up front with Mark Ceraolo, and to draft in yet more attacking flair by playing Flannery as well as Payne and Shirley. This was now a side designed to go forward, keep possession and open up defences, but it left a minimal amount of defensive cover in the middle. It did not seem to matter. Harrogate were walloped 5-0 at the Crown, and though the sending off of goalkeeper Speare at Whitley Bay stopped the winning run, Stanley still fought back from a goal down to earn a point that saw them up to fourth.

By the middle of February, the Christmas pessimists were being forced to think again, and not just because of Stanley's unbeaten run. With some of the Gary Williams money still available to the manager, Coleman went to NPL side Runcorn and paid £10,000 for striker Liam Watson, and also recruited another front man, Gerrard Courtney, on a free from Southport. It was a real statement of intent from the club at a pivotal moment of the season: if they had to win all their games, then they would find the personnel to do just that.

If any doubts remained about the feasibility of promotion, they were dispelled on February 19th. With Watson making his debut, Stanley went to mid-table Eastwood Town and crushed their opponents 7-1, with Russell Payne outstanding in his play-making role; elsewhere, leaders Witton Albion and second-placed Burscough both lost. Stanley were now just six points from the promotion places with two games in hand, having taken 25 points out of a possible 27 since the turn of the year.

Stanley ended February riding their luck with a 2-1 defeat of Bradford Park Avenue in front of 738 at the Crown, a game that saw Avenue leading, and then missing a late penalty. Coleman was much happier three weeks later when he made his first visit back to Ashton United, with Stanley earning a hard-fought 2-1 result.

What loomed now was a series of games against teams either vying with Stanley at the very top, or lying just outside the promotion race. On March 24th, Stanley travelled to Witton Albion and shared a point in a 0-0 draw, the second such result between the teams that season, but there were fewer excuses for the goalless draw at home to mid-table Chorley the following week.

The first of two crunch ties came on April 8th, when Stanley entertained leaders Burscough. By now, the town had very much tuned in to Stanley's brave assault on promotion, and a crowd of 912 turned up to see the clash. With ten minutes remaining, Stanley found themselves 2-0 down and staring disaster in the face, but a goal from Jonathan Smith set up a frantic finish, and Coleman himself completed the comeback with an emphatic half-volley. Stanley left the field to resounding applause and with the players euphoric at having rescued the situation, but the reality of the two dropped points was that there was now little margin for error in the remaining five games.

Two scrappy encounters against Stocksbridge Park Steels and Ashton United were both won, before a huge game at Radcliffe Borough on the Easter Monday. Both teams needed the win to stay in touch with the leaders, and by the hour mark it was Radcliffe who looked the more likely winners – not only were they one goal to the good, but Stanley had lost both Watson and Coleman to injury.

On 67 minutes, Stanley went 2-0 down, but pulled one

back five minutes later through sub Jimmy Bell, and just four minutes later, a towering Jonathan Smith header brought the teams level. Stanley now scented blood and were being urged on by hundreds of travelling fans, but it was still anyone's game. With ten minutes left, Paul Mullin looked to have restored Radcliffe's lead, but his effort was dramatically ruled out for offside.

With just two minutes remaining Steve Carragher scored the third, and Stanley held on for a famous 3-2 victory. The comeback represented yet another twist in a wildly unpredictable and highly dramatic series of events. It was barely believable, but after losing eight games before the year was out, Stanley had now gone four months undefeated; they had twice found themselves two goals down against promotion challengers, and on both occasions they had survived and emerged afterwards still in the promotion race. All this, reasoned the Stanley fans, had to count for something.

Stanley had two home games left. On Monday May 1st, Belper Town visited the Crown, and in front of 1,826 fans, the highest league gate at the Crown for eleven years, four superbly crafted and executed goals saw Stanley to an emphatic 4-1 win. It was a performance reassuringly free of any sign of promotion jitters, but victories for the top two sides, Burscough and Witton Albion, meant that Stanley's work was not yet complete. Three points from the last game of the season, at home to Farsley Celtic on May 6th, would see Stanley to the top of the table on goal difference.

The supporters were confident, reasoning that such a stout-hearted team as this Stanley side would not survive everything and get this far only to throw it away at the death. But for John Coleman, it was a testing time. He had been here before, only to have his promotion hopes dashed at the last, and had faced hoots of derision when insisting at the turn of the year that the team could still win promotion. The portents now favoured Stanley. One more decent performance at the Crown would see them home, but this measured assessment did nothing to relieve the tension.

It was also a huge game for Eric Whalley. He too had suffered the brickbats of fans, those who questioned why the team had so conspicuously failed to match the improvements he had made to the Crown Ground. Now there was the chance for Stanley to regain their place in the NPL Premier Division and use the momentum to have a tilt at the Conference the following year. It was, in short, a glorious opportunity to put Stanley on an upward curve again.

The club appealed for as much support as possible, and the town responded as a record Crown and NPL First Division attendance of 2,468 turned up on a warm, sunny day to cheer Stanley on to what everyone presumed would be a win and promotion. As things turned out, the team took a while to stamp their authority on the game, but once Jonathan Smith had opened the scoring with another brave and forceful header, the result was never in doubt. John Coleman added a second, and Mark Shirley a late third with a quality finish.

With their 3-0 victory, Stanley had clinched the NPL First Division title with 84 points and ended the season with a 19-match unbeaten run. When John Coleman had set the promotion target of 80 points, he had actually underestimated what would be required. That the team had gone on to surpass the manager's task reflected nothing but credit on everyone involved. They had won 15 and drawn four of their last 19 league games and in so doing had overhauled a deficit of 15 points on eventual runners-up, Burscough.

With 96 goals, Stanley were easily the division's highest scorers, but Gary Williams remained the only Stanley player on the individual charts, with 17 goals. The rest were shared around the team, with the manager himself scoring 11 times in the league. There was one other landmark for Coleman during this season, and that was his 500th non-league goal, which came in an FA Trophy tie at NPL Premier side Leek Town, which Stanley won after a replay.

His approach to the cups was another evident aspect of Coleman's management that stood out from some of

his predecessors. Having won two NPL First Division
league cups at Ashton, he valued the benefits to team spirit
and confidence that a medal brought. It was no surprise,
therefore, to find Coleman playing his first choice team as
Stanley embarked on their NPL League Cup campaign in
September, and an additional incentive was the fact that
Stanley had been drawn in a group with NPL Premier
Division sides Stalybridge and Droylsden. As far as
Coleman was concerned, here was an opportunity for his
team to prove to themselves what he was trying to drill
into them at team meetings – that they were good enough
to compete at a higher level.

Having defeated both Stalybridge and Droylsden, they
went on to win the second group stage, defeating two
more Premier Division sides in Hyde and Bamber Bridge
– the latter being the side who, eleven months previously,
had humiliated Stanley 5-0 at the Crown. Though Stanley
eventually lost in the semi-final to Worksop after a penalty
shoot-out, for Coleman it was a useful exercise in educating
the squad about the approach that he expected from them:
that every game was an opportunity for them to improve
themselves as players.

The season did have one sad footnote, and that was
the death of Bill Parkinson, the man who fronted the
public campaign to re-establish Accrington Stanley in the
summer of 1968, and who would become the new club's
first chairman. He had also served as a councillor for
more than 30 years, and was the last mayor of Accrington
before the reorganisation that created the Borough of
Hyndburn. Parkinson spent his whole working life in
Accrington and was, in sum, a model citizen who would,
no doubt, have been thrilled at the way John Coleman's
side had stormed to the title.

For the manager himself, his first season at Accrington
Stanley could hardly have had a more satisfactory finale,
though the roller-coaster ride on the way there had been
difficult to cope with at times. Seven years later, reflecting
on his time so far at the club, John Coleman still rated the

swinging fortunes and high emotion of the 1999–2000 season as the highlight:

"Nothing will ever match the Farsley Celtic game. No matter what I do in my life, nothing will match that for the sheer tension and drama over the weeks building up to that one game which we needed to win to clinch the title."

The top tier of the NPL was new territory for John Coleman as a manager, but he expressed no doubts publicly about the ability of his title-winning squad to compete. It was announced that the squad would more or less be kept intact. This revealed for the first time a key Coleman principle, and one that he would have reason to apply again in future seasons – that players who had proved themselves at one level deserved the chance to prove themselves at a higher level.

In fact, so rigidly was this rule enforced during the 2000–01 season that Coleman attracted some criticism for what was perceived to be an excess of loyalty to his squad. For though many Stanley fans mused on the possibility of Coleman taking Stanley straight through to the Conference, this turned out to be the classic season of "consolidation" at a higher level with what was virtually the same set of players.

Though there was far less transfer activity than usual at the Crown during the close season, one highly significant addition to the squad was striker Paul Mullin. With Radcliffe Borough having failed to win promotion the year before, he now took the chance to move up a division, though not before Stanley had paid out a club record fee of £15,000. Both Coleman and Bell were registered as players, but both knew that they could not play on a regular basis any more. Mullin was a classic centre-forward, a target man who could hold the ball well, but he was also an astute reader of the game, someone able to slip a marker or vary his runs into the box. It was a lot of money for Stanley to pay for a player, but Mullin would prove to be one of the very best signings made by John Coleman.

If transfer activity was well down on the norm, the Crown Ground itself remained in the throes of transformation. This time, the club had received the go-ahead to extend the new seating area so that it ran the full length of the pitch, and work began almost immediately on the new section which ran from the clubhouse to the dressing rooms. One project not authorised, however, was the plan for an all-weather training pitch behind the ground. Residents' complaints about the proposed floodlighting were upheld by the council, though this was just the first skirmish over the issue.

Stanley kicked off the campaign at Leek Town with a side containing nine of the regulars from the previous season. Only Wayne Maddock – a defensive recruit from Bamber Bridge – was making his debut, in the place of a suspended Steve Hollis; also in the team was the familiar figure of Paul Burns, starting a second spell at the club. Things began well with three wins, including a midweek defeat of Altrincham at the Crown in front of just over 1,000 spectators. Though the 22-match unbeaten run was brought to an end on the August Bank Holiday Monday at Barrow, the 2-1 defeat of Runcorn on September 6th in front of another decent midweek crowd of 856 sent Stanley to the top of the league.

Another victory looked likely when Stanley went into a 2-0 lead at home to Worksop in front of another healthy gate of 929 on the following Saturday, but the first sign of the defensive uncertainties that would plague the team through the campaign became evident in the second half when Worksop blitzed Stanley with four quick goals. After the game, which ended in a 4-3 defeat, Coleman admitted to that familiar managerial problem of keeping everyone happy, with the likes of Robbie Williams, Steve Caswell and Mark Brennan in the reserves and unable to get a game.

A vacancy was created with the loss of striker Liam Watson, who returned to Runcorn for a similar fee to that which brought him to the Crown. Coleman responded by buying back Gary Williams from Doncaster for a reported fee of £25,000, making him both the most lucrative and expensive player in the club's history. Observers reasoned that Williams' pace and strike-power would complement Mullin's aerial prowess, but the manager had, in fact, tried to sign Williams before he moved in for Mullin, only for the player to decide to stay and battle for his place; it had not, however, worked out for him.

The realities of life at the higher level now started to reveal themselves to Coleman and his players. After shipping two goals at Hucknall, Stanley found themselves unable to find a way through an uncompromising home rearguard. The *Accrington Observer* noted:

"There are few easy pickings in this league, and you
can't claw back two goals deficits as regularly as
they managed to do in the previous year."

The inference was that Stanley got away with defensive frailties the previous year because of the standards of defence they themselves faced, and the point was only reinforced when Stalybridge arrived at the Crown on September 23rd and became the second team in a fortnight to hit four past Stanley at home, winning 4-1 in front of another excellent crowd of 935. For Karl Bell, one of the defenders that day and the recipient of one of the 'player of the year' awards just a few months previously, it was the end of his Stanley career.

League form was maintained reasonably well after these two shocks at the Crown, with Stanley powerful enough to take points from the weaker teams in the division. After 17 games, they were fourth, but already a long way behind leaders Emley, and were also out of the FA Cup after being thoroughly out-hustled at Bedlington Terriers, losing 5-2.

Coleman's frustration at his team's inconsistency surfaced after the 2-0 defeat at Runcorn on November 25th. The manager had tried a sweeper system, but when the second opposition goal went in, he reverted to a more attacking formation, and Stanley threatened much more. The fans who had travelled to the game were not impressed and thought that Stanley should have been more adventurous, but Coleman argued that Stanley had to tighten up and stop losing the ball so easily.

It was the beginning of an exasperating period for Coleman, who caused a shock by announcing that the entire squad was up for sale. After emotions had cooled down, Coleman retracted the statement, saying that he was merely angry at the poor performance and wanted to give the players something to think about, but the ploy misfired.

Stanley embarked on a poor run of form that lasted through the Christmas period and into the New Year, which included heavy defeats at Emley, Stalybridge and Lancaster, with the last performance being described by the manager as the worst of his managerial career.

By the time Stanley emerged out of their torpor with a league defeat of Gateshead on February 6th, all hopes of promotion were long gone, and the managerial team admitted that they were now planning for the following campaign, which was being touted as a push for promotion. Some fringe squad members were released, and Coleman made an important acquisition in Simon Carden, an attacking midfielder signed for £5,000 from Radcliffe. Coleman maintained that his squad were better than their league position implied, but he conceded that he needed to strengthen key areas.

A sign of how badly Stanley were playing at this time was a match report in the *Accrington Observer* after the 1-1 draw at home to basement team Frickley Athletic on February 10th, played in front of just 511 spectators. Reporter David Hinksman wrote:

"While no one expects Stanley to win promotion this season, their present position suggests they should see off the likes of Frickley without too much difficulty. However, this was a side that lacked hunger, a team comfortable with their league position, under no pressure from relegation, lacking any real promotional aspirations, content to do just enough to maintain their Premier League status next season. In brief – complacent. Perhaps talk of a push for the Conference next season should be put on ice until this season's campaign is completed and the players can get back to the task of giving value for money in the here and now."

These were very tough words from the local paper, and perhaps a little harsh, for Coleman had indeed resorted to a more attacking line-up in the hope of a decent run-in to the season. He found places for three attackers in Mullin, Ceraolo and Williams, and also put Carden and Payne in the midfield to provide further options up front.

In truth, Coleman had every right to be disappointed with some of his forward players, especially Gary Williams, whose four league goals were a poor return on the manager's investment. When Jimmy Bell scored at Marine on March 20th to earn a 1-1 draw, it was Stanley's first league goal in a month, and the team shipped another five at Altrincham five days later. When Hucknall came to the Crown for the next league game on March 27th, only 319 fans turned up to see an out-of-sorts Stanley fall to a 2-1 defeat.

Elimination from the President's Cup at Blyth, and with it the last hope of any silverware for the season, made it six games without a win, and Coleman drew a line in the sand. He told the *Accrington Observer*:

"There will be players leaving, I am sure they will accept that. It isn't easy because a lot of them have become friends over the years. The bulk of the squad have had a good chance, but we know the season overall hasn't been successful enough."

So far, John Coleman had adhered to the traditional non-league template of the manager who moved from club to club with a core of trusted players. He had been loyal to a fault to the Ashton lads who had helped him to his first managerial league title, but now the manager was being pushed another stage along. His first Stanley squad had proved themselves as a decent NPL side – as he indeed had insisted all along – but now Coleman had to go beyond that. He had to build a Conference side to get out of the NPL.

Stanley ended the season in ninth after a strong finish of four wins out of five, the best run of the season, including a satisfying 2-0 win at Worksop to end the campaign, but Eric Whalley confirmed in the local press that Stanley were looking to sign three or four quality players and to have a real go at the Conference. Indeed, an important element of the club making concrete moves towards fulfilling the aims and ambitions that had been long stated was the relentless focus of the chairman, who refused to let anyone at the club, manager included, live on the fat of the progress made.

Whalley had also ensured that the surroundings of the club mirrored those ambitions, and the season had seen rapid strides towards the completion of the stand extension. After receiving planning permission in June, by December the steel framework was in place, by which time the Conference authorities had again indicated that the Crown, with a few minor adjustments, would be fit for their league. In the middle of February, with much of the brickwork completed on the extension, Stanley received confirmation that they had been awarded a grant of £82,000 from the Football Stadia Improvement Fund, the amount they had applied for. The grant would cover the cost of roofing the new stand and upgrading the terracing. A pleased Whalley diplomatically told the local press:

"This grant means that we will be more or less past the Conference stage of the pyramid, facilities and ground wise. We are very lucky in Lancashire because the County Council have backed us and been enormously helpful. I'm confident that Conference football is not too far away, and Football League status is the next thing after that."

In the world of the Football League itself, both Bury and Blackpool had reason to raise a glass to Stanley. In December, the Crown Ground had hosted a fundraising match for Bury, who were in the midst of a financial crisis, and had also organised an auction of memorabilia. By the end of the season with all donations in, Stanley had raised £8,500 for the Third Division club. Elsewhere, ex-Stanley striker Brett Ormerod had an afternoon to remember at the Millennium Stadium, where he scored for Blackpool in the play-off final to help his team to a 3-2 victory and promotion to the Second Division. Ormerod had been one of the undoubted heroes of Blackpool's campaign with 20 league goals, and he was suddenly one of the hottest properties in the lower divisions. Stanley could be forgiven for being distracted by Ormerod's progress, for there was the tantalising possibility that he might be on his way to bigger and better things, in which case Stanley could claim twenty per cent of his value.

As Stanley went through their pre-season programme, the reshaping of John Coleman's squad was perhaps less radical than many people expected, though the manager and chairman were frustrated by what they saw as players using the interest shown by Stanley to negotiate better deals at their current club. Neither were the bigger clubs enticed by cash in the same way that NPL clubs were. An enquiry to Conference side Morecambe about the availability of Phil Eastwood found the value of the striker soaring overnight. Whalley was not impressed:

> "His price suddenly became five figures. I have some good friends at Morecambe but they can whistle for that kind of fee. We won't be held to ransom or pay more for players than we believe they are worth."

On July 20th, Coleman at last landed one of his targets with the acquisition of 29-year-old striker Lutel James from Bury. James was Manchester-born but had played for St Kitts, so the club made a big noise about having persuaded an international player to move down three divisions to play for Stanley. In reality, James had struggled to break into Bury's first team and had a more realistic pedigree in non-league, where he had played at Guiseley and Hyde. All the same, James' pace and skill gave the impression of someone who had underachieved by not playing Conference football.

With the season almost underway, Coleman made further signings, all from Football League clubs. Right-back Peter Cavanagh, released by Liverpool, was snapped up after playing well in a couple of pre-season friendlies, and also impressing was midfielder Steve Flitcroft, just released by Blackburn. Another right-back, Paul Howarth, was signed from Shrewsbury.

It was thus a familiar-looking Stanley that lined up for the opening game at Gainsborough, with just three of the new men, Cavanagh, Flitcroft and James, given starts. The opening games, however, did not go well, with four defeats in the first six games, including an initial 5-2 hammering at Gainsborough and an equally poor 3-0 defeat at Colwyn Bay.

One of the conundrums that Coleman was grappling with was how to accommodate three front men, and he did so at first by playing Gary Williams in a wide role on the right, but the player was far from happy with this. After the defeat at Colwyn Bay, a result that left Stanley in a lowly 17th position, Williams unwisely went to the press with his grievance, telling the local papers that he did not think the squad was good enough to go up given the start that the team had made.

For Coleman, this was both embarrassing and unacceptable. He dropped Williams, at which point the player handed in a transfer request, which was accepted. The manager again had the right to feel that he had been let down. Coleman had arranged a summer spell in the USA for Williams to play for the New Jersey Barons and regain his match fitness. It was not so much the criticism that had stung Coleman but the fact that it was made public. His comments had, said the manager, upset a lot of people around the club.

The Triumph of Hope

With Williams sidelined, Coleman was at least able to settle on James and Mullin up front, but the manager was again frustrated by the inconsistency of his side, and particularly by the persistence of defensive gremlins. The 3-2 home defeat to Whitby Town on September 22nd had the manager fuming: "We conceded the first goal after trying an offside trap we hadn't even practised!" Little wonder that the *Accrington Observer* compared Stanley to Kevin Keegan's Newcastle United side – dynamic going forward but calamitous at the back.

By the end of October, Stanley were well adrift of the promotion race and Coleman had started to look around for reinforcements. Midfielder David Robinson was acquired for £4,000 from Runcorn, and the first mention was made of Mike Marsh, the ex-Liverpool schemer who now plied his trade in non-league and who had helped three teams on to greater things.

Coleman quashed the Marsh rumour, telling the press that the player had retired after years of injury problems, but the manager quietly kept on the case.

The squad evolved a little more with the release of two more players from the class of 2000, Mark Ceraolo and Jay Flannery, and another, midfielder Brett Baxter, was the subject of a bid from Chester City. The club professed themselves sorry to lose Baxter, but Chester had offered him full-time football and the player wanted to try his luck, so he moved on after playing just short of 100 games for Stanley.

The loss of two central midfielders and a striker left the squad looking a little thin, but it did at least lessen the manager's selection problems, and it was at this point in early November, with the team virtually picking itself, that form began to turn. On November 10th, Stanley travelled to a very good Vauxhall Motors outfit and returned with an excellent 2-1 win, and not even an injury to Paul Mullin in the following 7-0 demolition of Castleton Gabriels in the Lancashire Junior Cup could halt the team's progress.

Although Coleman had few other options up front than to pair Mullin and James, he improvised for the next game, at Droylsden, and this minor selection crisis opened the door to a new phase of the season in which Stanley's form and confidence would burgeon, and which would lay the foundations for more trophies. With only James available, the manager tried a 4-4-1-1 formation. His idea was for Robinson and Flitcroft to hold the middle, and to use the wing play of Payne and Shirley to get round the back of the home defence, with Simon Carden deployed in the attacking midfield 'hole'.

It worked like a dream. Carden had been a fairly prolific scorer from midfield at Radcliffe, but it is doubtful whether he had ever scored four in a game before as he did at Droylsden. Stanley came away with a 5-1 victory, and though Mullin would soon return, Carden's attacking instincts remained, with Coleman happy for the midfielder to venture forward at every opportunity.

Despite a harrowing exit from the FA Trophy on penalties at Altrincham, where the home side's Ian Craney missed his spot kick but then got the opportunity to retake it, Stanley's league form continued apace. On December 8th, Stanley played so well in their 5-1 demolition of Bradford Park Avenue that *Accrington Observer* reporter Jim Wilkinson mused on the possibility that Stanley could still win the league.

To do this they had to catch the division's newcomers Burton Albion, and though another satisfying league win at Hucknall on December 15th moved Stanley into a solid third position, Burton remained some eight points clear, having started the season with a string of impressive results.

The acid test of Stanley's progress thus came when Burton, with both Nigel and Brian Clough on the team bus, arrived at the Crown on December 22nd. Victory was vital if Burton were to be overhauled, and when Jonathan Smith rose majestically to head Stanley into a 3-1 lead with less than ten minutes remaining, the win looked on. Burton, however, rallied, and with the help of a penalty that had Coleman raging afterwards, they pulled the game back to 3-3. The crowd was 1,251, the biggest league gate at the Crown since the Farsley Celtic game.

Though the loss of the two points was a blow, Stanley had already received an early Christmas present – and it was no trifle. The rumours about the transfer of Brett Ormerod to a Premiership club had been circulating for a month or so, but only at the start of December did anything concrete materialise. The interested party was Southampton, and the fee was something around £1.5 million.

According to the strict terms of the sell-on clause inserted into the Ormerod deal between Stanley and Blackpool, this would have meant a £300,000 cheque in the post to the Crown Ground. This was serious money, in a different league to the few thousands that the club was used to exchanging, but Blackpool understandably wanted to extract as much money as possible from the deal themselves.

After reports of prolonged haggling between the clubs, a deal was finally announced in the *Accrington Observer* of December 17th. Since Blackpool were being paid the £1.5 million in instalments, Stanley had settled for a reported £200,000 to be paid immediately. There were also a few other add-ons, such as Stanley being given first option on players released from Bloomfield Road. In a statement that seemed to suggest that the main parties to the deal had viewed Stanley's claims as impedimental, Whalley said:

"There is no way that we wanted to be an obstruction to the deal and we have done this mainly to help Brett achieve his lifelong dream. He came here on £40 a week, and he's a great example that you can bounce back."

Eric Whalley told the press that most of the money would go on the Crown's facilities, but the windfall clearly represented an opportunity to strengthen the team with one or two careful acquisitions, and Coleman immediately tabled a £10,000 bid for Burscough striker Lee McEvilly.

Although Burscough had accepted an earlier offer of £7,500 from Cambridge United, with the deal later breaking down, they now turned down Stanley's higher bid. Neither Coleman nor Whalley was impressed, with the chairman insisting that it would be Stanley's final bid.

Having let the leaders Burton escape with a point, and with a number of cup ties now interrupting the league schedule, Stanley's league form suffered a dip through January and February. They did, however, make progress in the two cup competitions in which they maintained an interest, and Coleman made a point of insisting in the pages of the *Accrington Observer* that he was taking the cups seriously.

In the Lancashire Junior Cup (now known as the Marsden Trophy after the sponsor), following kind pairings against Castleton Gabriels and Atherton Collieries, Stanley faced a quarter-final at home to Conference side Leigh RMI. In the NPL League Cup, the team had emerged from the convoluted group stages to a tough quarter-final tie at home to Emley.

The Emley tie, played on a Saturday, January 25th, attracted nearly 600 to the Crown, and it saw the debut of Steve Halford, whom Coleman had just signed from Chester City. Halford was a no-nonsense centre-half who immediately commanded a first team position, and the partnership he forged with Jonathan Smith in the middle of the defence made for a consistent and stable back four for the remainder of the season – good value already from the first investment of the Ormerod money. The back four – with Peter Cavanagh and Barrie Hart in the full-back positions – was now almost completely remodelled from the previous season.

Stanley defeated Emley 1-0 with a Russell Payne goal, before a Paul Mullin double won the Lancashire Junior Cup tie. Leigh RMI played their full-strength side, but a brilliant first-half display from Stanley gave them the advantage, and they defended stoutly for a well-deserved 2-1 win.

League defeats against Hucknall and Runcorn ended any lingering hopes of promotion, and so the Lancashire Junior Cup semi-final at Burscough on Tuesday February 19th offered one of Stanley's last routes to a meaningful season's end. On a horrible night of wind and cold, driving rain, it was Stanley who played the better football, and a moment of real quality from Gary Williams won the tie. With the 90 minutes all but up, Williams teed up the ball from 25 yards and sent a sublime, curling effort beyond the 'keeper.

For only the third time since their revival in 1968, Stanley had reached the Lancashire Junior Cup Final. That Gary Williams at his very best had got them there was merely a source of frustration and puzzlement for manager Coleman. He knew Williams was gifted, but it was a talent that showed itself only sporadically. Within a month of providing this great highlight, Williams was sent out on loan and would not play for Stanley again.

Also leaving the club at this time was Mark Shirley, whose Stanley career had been blighted with a cruciate knee injury. Even so, he had played his full part in the 2000 promotion, and those who saw Shirley take command at Radcliffe with Stanley 2-0 down and facing disaster were in no doubt about what a great player Shirley was and how much he might have achieved at the club without the constant injuries. He left with the thanks and best wishes of everyone at the Crown.

On March 9th, Stanley overcame the tenacious challenge of Trafford at the Crown, 2-1, to book a place in the NPL League Cup Final, a game that saw the home debut of another recruit, midfielder Andy Proctor, who had impressed all season at neighbouring Great Harwood Town.

Earlier in the season Proctor might have struggled to get a game, but Stanley's poor disciplinary record meant that the team was hit with a number of suspensions. Proctor took his chance and performed so well that Dave Robinson was hardly missed, and the local youngster would become a key player in the seasons to follow.

The defeat of Trafford boosted the team's league form, and confidence was high going into the first leg of the League Cup Final at Bradford Park Avenue on April 10th. It was to be a highly dramatic evening. It started with a red card for goalkeeper Jamie Speare after he handled outside the area. Full-back Barrie Hart went in goal, but he was sent off just before half-time for what most observers thought was an accidental collision. Peter Cavanagh went in goal, and nine-man Stanley held out comfortably until the last minute when they conceded a goal that Park Avenue hardly deserved.

An enraged Coleman pointed out that Speare and Hart would now miss the Lancashire Junior Cup Final, which was probably the biggest game since the Farsley Celtic clash, for this was the premier cup competition for the area's non-league sides and had a history almost as long as the organised game itself.

On Wednesday April 24th, several hundred fans from Accrington made their way to Christie Park, Morecambe for what was the new Stanley's third Lancashire Junior Cup Final appearance, where they faced one of the less competitive Barrow sides of recent years.

Paul Mullin gave Stanley a first-half lead, but after looking comfortable for most of the half, the result was again thrown into doubt when Peter Cavanagh was sent off just before the break. John Coleman reacted by stringing five across the middle for the second half, and the ploy worked well, with Stanley easily containing Barrow. The ten men even finished the stronger of the two sides after Simon Carden had scored a second just after the hour.

The game finished 2-0. It was Stanley's first Lancashire Junior Cup win since their reformation in 1968, though the old Stanley had won the same trophy as a Lancashire Combination side in 1921.

Less than a week later, Stanley went for the NPL League Cup with the second leg of the final against Bradford at the Crown. After surviving for most of the first leg with nine men and no goalkeeper, Stanley fancied their chances in the return, and a large and expectant crowd of 1,107 turned up for the occasion.

Somewhat predictably, Bradford Park Avenue played far better than they had in the first leg, but Stanley made the breakthrough in the second half through Paul Mullin to level the scores on aggregate. The visitors continued to match Stanley, however, and came close to winning the cup when a late effort came back off the Stanley bar. With the teams unable to produce another goal between them, the cup was decided by a penalty shoot-out. With home advantage perhaps counting for something, Stanley converted all their penalties; when Speare saved a Bradford Park Avenue effort, it meant that Stanley had won their second piece of silverware in a week, and the first league cup for the club since the days of the Lancashire Combination.

Monday May 6th saw the final action of the season. As NPL League Cup winners, Stanley travelled to newly-crowned NPL champions Burton for the Peter Swales Challenge Shield. There was some needle between the clubs as a result of their league encounters. At Burton, Coleman was on the field as a sub and with Stanley chasing the game had tried to pick up a prostrate Burton player who he thought was time-wasting by feigning an injury. This provoked a clash with another Burton player who was booked as a result. The Burton crowd turned on the Stanley manager with venom, and he later claimed to have been hit by a missile thrown from the crowd.

After the 3-3 draw at the Crown just before Christmas, Coleman had invited further hostility by suggesting that the referee had been over-generous in awarding Burton a late penalty. All this made for a vibrant atmosphere as Stanley took on the champions in front of 1,005 fans, and since Coleman had decided that this would be the occasion of a rare appearance, he started on the subs' bench.

With Stanley a goal down, the manager brought on himself – much to the derision of the crowd – but Coleman silenced them by heading a 93rd-minute equaliser from a

Simon Carden corner, and made it quite clear to the Burton fans how much he had enjoyed the goal. Stanley again converted all five penalties in the shoot-out to win 5-3 and seal a satisfying treble.

The silverware represented yet more achievement for Coleman and Bell. Though promotion to the Conference had remained out of reach, the experience of three triumphs in a short space of time was a tremendous confidence boost for the squad and renewed the winning culture at the club established with the title win in 2000. In addition, it underlined the next step for Stanley. After this, nothing but promotion to the Conference would do.

It is fair to say that Stanley had never before challenged seriously for the NPL title. The best finish for the club in this division remained the sixth place and 73 points achieved by Phil Staley's 1992–93 side, and they had never really looked like going up. The sixth place just achieved by John Coleman's team represented something very close to that, but now Coleman planned for a further push, and he was aided by the greater financial stability at the club.

The state of the NPL league table at the end of the season also offered some hope for the following campaign. The traditionally dominant teams at this level were, for various reasons, going through difficulties. Barrow and Altrincham were suffering from financial problems, and Marine and Runcorn were going through lean periods.

Coming down from the Conference was a demoralised Stalybridge Celtic, who had failed to survive even one season at the higher level. So unusually, none of these big non-league outfits were in a particularly strong position, and of the teams who had finished above Stanley during the previous campaign, none could be said to be 'bigger' clubs. In other words, brewing on the horizon was a perfect storm for Stanley to make the Conference, and the season had barely finished before John Coleman made an unmistakable statement of intent. He announced that ex-Liverpool midfielder Mike Marsh would be playing for Stanley the following season.

Marsh had retired early from the professional game after too many injuries had left him unable to cope with the rigours of full-time football, but he had made a real impact in semi-professional circles. At both Kidderminster and Boston, Marsh had been instrumental in their step up to the Conference and then the Football League, but halfway through his second season at Boston, he had suffered further injury and had effectively retired. This was when Coleman made his first, unsuccessful move, but now, after six months of rest, the player was refreshed and feeling more positive about the game, and Coleman persuaded him to come to the Crown Ground for one season to help Accrington Stanley achieve their dream of promotion to the Football Conference. It was quite a way to begin the summer, and it sent the Stanley fans away dreaming of what was to come in August.

One part of the team that Coleman did not have any worries about was the strike force. Paul Mullin had ended up with 34 goals for the season and Lutel James with 23, so the club moved quickly to quash rumours in the local press that James was leaving. There had been a brief falling-out between James and the club at Christmas over a disciplinary matter, and fans feared that the rumours might have been the result of another disagreement, but Eric Whalley told the press that James was a key player and was going nowhere, and nothing else was said about the matter publicly.

The defence remained an area that the manager looked to strengthen, and despite the form of the Halford–Smith partnership at the end of the previous season, in mid-July Coleman announced the signing of Mark Sertori from Altrincham, a 34 year-old centre-half with more than 380 Football League appearances.

The manager explained that his centre-halves, Williams, Smith and Halford were young lads, and Sertori would bring some experience to the back four. With left-back Barrie Hart also absent with work commitments, Coleman made a rare signing of a local lad in Barry Shuttleworth, who had Football League experience at Blackpool and Rotherham.

On the eve of the season, the manager sounded happy that the squad had fitted together well, and pre-season results included a 2-0 defeat of Burnley Reserves and a 4-4 draw against a Blackburn XI. The *Accrington Observer* reckoned that it was an "open secret" that Stanley were going all out for promotion, and Coleman himself professed a cautious optimism:

"Everyone is bullish and optimistic at the beginning and we are no different than anyone else. But I can detect that the players have more confidence in themselves and each other this time around. They have more belief. It was clear last season that we conceded far too many goals. The arrival of Stevie Halford stopped the rot and he and Jonathan Smith finished the season really well. Add Mark Sertori to that equation and I think we will be very difficult to score against."

A late addition to the squad was winger Dean Calcutt, signed from Bradford Park Avenue for £5,000, who took a place on the bench for the opening game on Saturday August 17th at home to Runcorn. Just 602 turned up, a disappointing response to the club's attempts to reach a higher grade of football.

Despite being reduced to ten men, Stanley outplayed Runcorn in the second half and deserved their 2-1 victory, and on the Tuesday they won by the same score at Colwyn Bay, this after being a goal down with time running out. It was a decent start in terms of results, if not performances, but a thoroughly comprehensive 3-0 win at Marine on August 24th was far more convincing. Stanley looked the part that afternoon, and the gate for the following home fixture against Frickley was much improved, helped along by a 'kid for a quid' scheme.

Talking about wanting to win promotion is somewhat

different to dealing with the pressures of achieving it. Perhaps one of the reasons why the town did not immediately flock to the Crown in their thousands was that they had heard such ambitious platitudes from the club before. As far back as the ill-fated 'All the Way' campaign of 1988, Stanley had been trying to woo the townsfolk with what had proved time and again to be mere wishful thinking.

This is not to criticise Stanley's attempts down the years to entice more people to the Crown; a decent level of support is the prerequisite of progress for all but the most well-funded clubs. But it might explain why it took a while for the gates at the Crown to grow to the levels one might expect of a successful NPL side. But once Stanley had extended their winning run to five games with defeats of Frickley and a decent Harrogate Town side, there was real reason to hope that, at last, they were genuine title contenders.

The midweek visit of Vauxhall Motors on September 4th was a real test of Stanley's mettle, for they were far more dangerous an outfit than the works-team moniker suggested. More than 1,000 turned up for the game, all but a few from Accrington, the first four-figure midweek league gate at the Crown since the visit of Altrincham in August 2000. They watched an absorbing game, won 2-1 by Stanley, with both goals from Lutel James.

Even better was to follow on the Saturday when Stanley went to Stalybridge, just down from the Conference and one of the more fancied teams. Coleman's men demolished them 4-1, and another old foe, Barrow, were seen off, 2-1, the following Wednesday at the Crown in front of 1,334. Droylsden were next up, and Stanley again prevailed 2-1 for their ninth straight win.

They came within ninety seconds of a tenth at home to Emley on September 21st, but a late penalty earned the visitors a point in a 1-1 draw. Emley were a decent side, but more frustrating was the 2-2 draw at newly-promoted Ashton United three days later, with Stanley contriving to lose a 2-0 lead.

Having been given byes in the early qualifying rounds of both the FA Cup and FA Trophy, it was only at this point, during the last week in September, that Stanley had to break off from their league programme to start a cup campaign. In little over five weeks, they had rattled through a quarter of their league schedule, eleven games, and had surpassed all expectations by winning nine of them and drawing the other two. It left Stanley four points clear at the top of the league. After a break for the FA Cup, another crunch league game loomed when second-placed Burscough visited the Crown, and 1,455 turned up to see a thriller. After a goalless first half, Burscough hit Stanley with two goals shortly after the restart, but Calcutt quickly grabbed one back before a Simon Carden hat-trick sealed the game for Stanley. It had been a scintillating spectacle of quality attacking football from both sides, and the win extended Stanley's lead to seven points.

With promotion most definitely on, chairman Eric Whalley sanctioned more signings. Stanley already had a substanial squad, which had enabled the team to maintain form in the face of injuries, but now Coleman looked to make further reinforcements. Central midfielder Michael Knowles arrived from Morecambe, and the club made yet another bid for a high-profile veteran professional, this time Kevin Gallacher. Coleman had already failed to land Kevin Ball, and 18 months before, the club had even made an enquiry about David Ginola. Coleman was forced to deny that the club were doing it merely for the publicity, but nothing came of the Gallacher approach.

The attitude of the club was now clear, however. Now that promotion was most definitely a possibility, no reasonable expense would be spared to see them through. The chairman was most definitely not amused, however, when Stanley went out of the FA Cup at Harrogate Town. With a tie at Eastern Counties League minnows Wisbech Town in the final qualifying round for the winners, it represented a chance lost for a first round appearance and £30,000 in prize money.

The Triumph of Hope

The loss to Harrogate on October 15th – the season's first defeat of any kind – was the first indication of a problem that was about to take hold and provide the first minor crisis of the campaign – poor away form.

The first league defeat of the season arrived in the sixteenth game at Frickley on October 26th, and another quickly followed at Barrow, where Mark Sertori was sent off. Having seen Lutel James also dismissed in the home game with Colwyn Bay the previous month, Coleman expressed his dismay at the team's indiscipline, which brought suspensions at a time when the team was already missing key players through injury, including Marsh and Smith, who had hurt his knee at Barrow.

The Barrow defeat saw Stanley's lead reduced to just one point, with Bradford Park Avenue the nearest challengers, and for the first time there was a sense that the team was vulnerable. To Stanley's advantage, three home league games followed, and with them the chance to push ahead again. Unsurprisingly, the first of these against Gateshead was tense and scrappy, and there were only 606 there to watch it, but Stanley came through 2-1. Much better performances followed in wins against Stalybridge (4-1) and Hucknall Town (2-0), so much so that a confident *Accrington Observer* reckoned that the team was on its way again.

However, Stanley could not shake off their indifferent away form. Elimination from the League Cup at Barrow was followed by a poor performance at bottom club Hyde United, where a last minute Lutel James penalty rescued a point in a 3-3 draw. An incandescent John Coleman made his thoughts quite clear to the players after the game. Still unhappy with some aspects of the team's play, Coleman announced to the press that he would be releasing some fringe members of the squad to make way for more signings:

"We are always keen to strengthen things and perhaps after half a season we need to freshen things
up. I personally believe we will never be in a better

position at this stage to go on and win promotion
and we have to do what's best for the club."

Something working out in Stanley's favour was that
no single club was emerging as a serious challenger. A
couple of days after the draw at Hyde, second-placed team
Bradford Park Avenue suffered a 7-1 defeat, confirming
suspicions among the non-league cognoscenti that they
were not serious challengers to Stanley. Of the division's big
beasts, only Barrow were showing any kind of consistency,
and they remained well adrift of Stanley. The analysis
was clear enough: the title was there for the taking bar a
collapse in form.

The convincing 4-1 defeat of Ashton United at the
Crown on December 4th sent Stanley ten points clear at
exactly the halfway stage, and there were no complaints
about the point earned at Emley a few days later. Talking
to the *Accrington Observer*, Whalley dispensed with the
usual caution in looking ahead to the further steps that the
club wanted to take in the future:

> "There's no point in saying 'Don't talk about
> promotion' because it is no longer a myth, it's
> something which could soon become a real-
> ity. We have basically given John and Jimmy
> carte blanche to bring in whoever they feel we
> need. It's been disappointing not to make more
> progress in the cups, but we aren't as desperate
> for the money that generates as we are to win
> the league.
>
> The ultimate plan is for the club to go full-time
> in terms of playing staff. The costs are obvious-
> ly proportionally higher in the Conference, but
> so are the rewards. Our support is solid, things
> have taken off incredibly on the commercial
> side and the profile of the club has never been
> higher."

Coleman did some good business before the holiday
programme with the signings of Andy Gouck, a beefy
midfielder who came in on loan from Morecambe, and

Rory Prendergast, a left-sided wide player who cost the club £7,500 from Bradford Park Avenue.

Of the holiday programme, the bizarre Boxing Day pairing of Stanley and Whitby Town on the North Yorkshire coast was ideal ammunition for Whalley's keen populist touch. It was the first season that the FA had compiled the fixtures rather than the NPL, and the chairman was in no doubt as to what had happened:

> "They must think we're round the corner from each other! I've complained in no uncertain terms about this, it's a farce. I often wonder if they even know where the teams are. There are plenty of teams in the league in the Manchester area so why they should go and do this is unbelievable. It's just not on. They've cocked it up."

In the event, the holiday games at Whitby and Burscough were postponed because of frozen pitches, but the fixture at the Crown on December 28th went ahead. In front of 1,068, Stanley efficiently overcame Gainsborough Trinity, 3-0, to go 12 points clear, with only Worksop and Vauxhall Motors able to catch up if they won their games in hand.

John Coleman expressed himself satisfied that he now had the best squad in the division, but remained concerned about the continued difficulties away from home, where Stanley struggled to impose themselves. Just before Christmas, a third league defeat had been suffered at Hucknall, and the team had put in a very limp performance in their FA Trophy defeat at Tamworth.

As if to emphasise the analysis of their manager, the January 11th trip to Gateshead turned into a strange and worrying day. After an hour of play, Stanley held a 1-0 lead and looked in control of the game, but a Gateshead equaliser prompted a catalogue of individual errors in the Stanley defence, and Gateshead ran in another four goals for an emphatic 5-1 defeat of the league leaders.

Perhaps sensing that he had already criticised the defence at length on other occasions, the manager remained publicly calm, dismissing the result as a one-off and vowing that it would not affect the team. No doubt, though, that Coleman had words privately, for the Gateshead result made it four draws and four defeats away from home since the win at Stalybridge, four months previously.

The team had a point to prove, and they did this emphatically with a 5-0 defeat of Marine at the Crown the following Saturday, and then successfully began the defence of the Lancashire Junior Cup with a 2-0 defeat of Conference side Southport. But the key result of the month arrived on Saturday January 25th, when Stanley travelled to Burscough and, at last, won away from home, grimly hanging on to a one-goal advantage in the face of a strong second-half performance from the home team.

Though the result did not extend Stanley's lead or take them past a certain staging post, the relief of finally leaving a ground with a win had a definite impact on morale. Seven days later they travelled west again for a league fixture at Runcorn, and this time Stanley were more commanding in registering a 2-0 win. Runcorn manager, ex-Stanley player Liam Watson, was in no doubt about what he had just witnessed, telling the press:

"If there's a better side in the division then I haven't seen them. They can only lose the league them-selves now."

John Coleman evidently thought that his side's early-season momentum had now returned, so he set a target of eight wins from the remaining 14 games to secure the title. The manager also rationalised the squad, releasing a number of players including two summer signings he had earmarked as central performers, Sertori and Shuttleworth. Though still inexperienced at this level, Smith and Halford had made the centre-half berths their own. Another local youngster, Andy Proctor, was the recipient of admiring reviews, and the side had also benefited from the return of Mike Marsh from injury.

Harrogate Town once more provided tough opposition in the league encounter at the Crown on February 8th, but Stanley's spirit again proved the decisive factor as the home side came from 2-1 down to win 3-2. Far more impressive was Stanley's third successive away league win at Worksop Town on February 22nd, where two Lutel James goals contributed to a handsome 4-1 win. Worksop had remained one of the few clubs with a remote chance of catching Stanley, but this result ended those hopes.

A 3-2 win at home to Blyth Spartans moved Stanley 12 points clear with 11 games remaining, and another win at Lancaster on March 15th extended that lead to 14 points. Stanley were running away with the NPL title and the club now started to make preparations for life in the Conference. An indication of the higher profile that the club could expect in nationwide football came with the visit of the *Football Focus* cameras to record a short film for the Saturday lunchtime show, and the deal that the Conference held with Sky was already established, meaning that Accrington Stanley would at some point be involved in a live game on television. The consequences of impending Conference status were thus both astonishing and exhilarating. It was hard to credit that in little over three years the club had gone from playing Stocksbridge Park Steels in front of less than 250 to having to plan for nationwide football in front of the television cameras.

Promotion to the Conference had, of course, still to be won, but Stanley were now playing with the confidence of a team that knew they were easily the best in the division. Further excellent away wins at Whitby and Blyth left Stanley with the opportunity to clinch the NPL title at the Crown on April 12th. Altrincham were the visitors, and 2,263 spectators gathered in the mood for a party. Stanley did not let them down: a 3-1 win sealed promotion.

The reaction of the club was that the Conference was just the beginning of something much bigger. In February, Eric Whalley had already revealed plans for a £400,000 stand along the Whinney Hill side of the pitch. Faced now with the reality of promotion, the chairman made it clear that the aim was to gear the entire club towards being a full-time operation, and then to move on to higher things.

In setting John Coleman the target of a play-off place for the following season, the chairman said:

"We now have to prepare to become a professional club, possibly with a full-time professional squad in a couple of seasons. The sort of gate we got on Saturday makes a big difference to the finances, and promotion will lead to other opportunities."

Whalley's words were a reminder that although Stanley had expanded their operations since going up to the NPL, the extra few thousand pounds of gate income on a regular basis made quite a difference to what they could achieve as a club. It was easy for the fans to slip into the complacent idea that the Brett Ormerod money would sustain them, but ground improvements would be needed for the Conference, as would a higher wage bill; future accounts would reveal that the wages to maintain this squad in just the NPL had incurred a loss on the year of £48,000. Further progress still very much depended on support through the turnstiles.

Stanley rounded off their season with a successful defence of the NPL Challenge Shield they won at Burton the previous season with a 2-0 defeat of Marine at the Crown. The club received their second civic reception in two years, and Hyndburn Borough Council cemented what appeared to be a developing relationship with the club by entering into negotiations for a three-year shirt sponsorship deal.

Those familiar with the way John Coleman operated were not surprised to hear him insist that most of the players who had served him so well would be given a chance in the Conference. He told the local press:

"It is very important for us to keep a large proportion of the squad which won us promotion because our team-spirit was first class and I want to keep that."

Mike Marsh and Russell Payne left the squad. Marsh had been worth every penny, directing the play from the midfield and guiding the younger players around him with a calm authority. Payne, too, had served the club with distinction and left the Crown with two league championship medals, having been one of the key players in the 2000 side. To replace Marsh, Coleman had lined up another experienced midfield anchorman in Paul Cook, an old friend who had just finished his contract at nearby Burnley.

The Cook deal was announced in May, but the manager was going to take longer to make further additions. He had to spend carefully. His was a part-time squad in a league where well over half of the teams, 14 out of 22, were full-time. There was every possibility that Stanley's players would have to take half a day off work to travel south and play midweek against a team of professionals. The challenge could not be overestimated.

Both the potential and the weakness of Stanley's position were seen when their opening game at Aldershot was chosen by Sky to be the first live Conference transmission of the season. The television company had been attracted by the historical angle of two former league clubs, and both clubs received a fee, which though modest for the away team was compensated for by the exposure that the game would provide, it being beamed around Europe as well as the UK.

But it also meant a Sunday afternoon kick-off and a late night arrival back home for the Stanley players, and then two days' work before the first scheduled home game on the Tuesday against Leigh RMI. Mindful of this, Eric Whalley contacted the Conference and received permission to play the Leigh game on the Wednesday, giving the players an extra 24 hours to recover, but it would not always be the case that games could be rearranged in this way for the benefit of the part-time players.

With pre-season well underway, another sign of Stanley's elevated status was the multinational profile of the triallists at the club, with a Nigerian, Iranian and a German hoping to win deals. This was a period of considerable rationalisation among Football League clubs hit by wage inflation and a reduction in television money. Many were stripping their squads, and it was estimated that there were around 800 players out of work. John Coleman looked to use this to the club's advantage by avoiding transfer fees; in a pre-season game against Radcliffe, the manager introduced an entirely new team at half-time in order to see as many triallists as possible in action.

Definitely joining the club was another ex-Burnley professional in Gordon Armstrong, and Lutel James had agreed a new two-year deal. He and Paul Mullin had formed a highly complementary partnership up front, with the two of them bagging 66 goals between them in the previous campaign. Regrettably leaving was Simon Carden, who preferred the guarantee of first team football at Radcliffe. His 37 goals from 113 midfield starts was a strike-rate most forwards would be happy with, and he had played a full part in Stanley's three cup triumphs of the 2001–02 season.

Burnley brought their first team squad to the Crown for a pre-season game on July 30th, and their presence attracted enough visiting fans to revise the Crown's attendance record to 3,035. With the Aldershot game on the horizon, Coleman finally made his choices and, among others, signed goalkeeper Jon Kennedy. Even so, 16 of the 22-strong squad were players retained from the previous season.

On the eve of the Aldershot game, the manager expressed what most Stanley fans felt – that it was a testing, but exciting, step into the unknown. Many hoped that Stanley would do well, but fans were just as ready to accept the possibility that the team might struggle. The experience of other clubs did not seem to hold any concrete clues either. Some recent NPL champions had flourished. Part-time Leigh RMI, for example, had achieved a superb fifth place in their first Conference season in 2000–01. Others, though, had not competed – both Altrincham and Stalybridge had come straight back down.

In such a mood of excitable uncertainty a good contingent of Stanley fans made their way to the first game of

Stanley's nationwide football life at Aldershot on Sunday August 10th. This also happened to be the hottest day on record, with temperatures nudging 38 degrees. More than 3,500 had packed the Aldershot ground, and the teams made a grand entrance to a tumultuous noise. It seemed as if Accrington Stanley had finally 'arrived' in the wider world of football – playing outside the north of England, television cameras on cranes and around the touchline, press photographers everywhere, a packed and voluble stadium – and Coley in a collar and tie.

The game was a close affair with both teams coping remarkably well with the sweltering conditions. An early Aldershot opener was cancelled out by a textbook volleyed finish from Andy Proctor, but disaster struck as half-time approached when Jamie Speare was adjudged to have handled outside the area. The referee had little option but to send him off, and Jon Kennedy's first touch of the ball in a Stanley shirt was to retrieve it from the net after a well-executed freekick. Stanley pushed Aldershot back in the second half, but could not find the equaliser.

After the midweek Leigh game attracted just over 2,000 to the Crown, the police asked Stanley to start segregating the fans, a wise move, for the following Saturday around 800 Shrewsbury Town fans swelled the gate to a record 3,143. The resounding 4-1 defeat of Leigh was a huge relief after the disappointment of the opening game, but Stanley were more diffident against Shrewsbury and lost to an 81st-minute goal.

This was the occasion of Coleman's first real outburst of the season – not so much for the defeat, but for the perception that his side had shown Shrewsbury too much respect and had been intimidated into playing without their usual passion and will-to-win. It was a good lesson for the players that their manager would not permit them to develop an inferiority complex in the higher league. They either competed or they were out – as Coleman pointed out, there was no shortage of out-of-work players looking hungrily for a contract.

329

The Shrewsbury manager Jimmy Quinn thought Coleman was being harsh, and the Stanley boss later admitted that he had perhaps gone too far in his criticisms, but it was a good marker for any players tempted to think that they could use the higher standards as an excuse to shrink from the battle. The last thing Coleman wanted was for Stanley to become mired in a long fight to haul themselves away from the foot of the table.

Things were to get worse before they improved. On August 23rd, Stanley sunk to a disappointing 2-1 defeat at Forest Green Rovers, which made the 1-0 victory against Scarborough the following Monday all the more of a relief. In a gee-up to his striking pair, Coleman went on the record as saying that the team was not converting enough chances:

"Paul and Lutel were head and shoulders above the rest of the strikers in the NPL, and now, in the Conference, they are in with a lot of other good strikers."

The point was, in fact, a wider one to the whole team. Rather than just Mullin and James, they all needed to move out of what had become, by the end, a comfort zone in the NPL.

The team responded well, and Stanley embarked on a run of unbeaten games that saw them rapidly move out of the relegation zone and up towards the contest for the four play-off places. Gritty draws at Tamworth and Barnet were followed by three wins, including the first away victory at Dagenham & Redbridge.

This east London ground held painful memories for Coleman and Bell. They had gone there in February 1997 with Ashton United for an FA Trophy quarter-final tie, and had suffered the agony of losing to a last-minute penalty. Jimmy Bell went so far as to call it his worst moment in football, so there was no mistaking the satisfaction that the pair derived from Stanley's 1-0 win. It was perhaps all the sweeter for how it was achieved, with a determined defensive display after Stanley had been reduced to ten men.

Discipline was, however, an emerging problem. Andy Proctor's first-half dismissal at Dagenham for two bookable offences was the fourth red card of the season in just the ninth game. Paul Cook had gone at home to Scarborough for two similar transgressions, though less forgivable was Dean Calcutt's sending-off at Tamworth after just 28 minutes for dissent, conduct which took a while to be forgiven among the Stanley faithful.

By October 11th, and the 3-1 defeat of Farnborough Town at the Crown, Stanley's unbeaten run had been extended to ten games. The team were in sixth position with 23 points from 14 games, and the atmosphere around the club and the fans was much more settled. Those uneasy early-season questions had been answered: Stanley would survive their first campaign in the Conference without too much trouble, and the play-offs remained a possibility.

Attention now turned to the FA Cup, in which Stanley had been given a home tie against Leigh RMI, already decisively beaten at the Crown in the league. James and Mullin again met the manager's challenge to take their chances with a goal apiece in a 2-0 win, a result that put Stanley in the first round proper for the first time in ten years. It was also John Coleman's first such tie as a manager, and Stanley were given an attractive home game against Third Division Huddersfield Town.

What was a decent draw suddenly became a great one when the BBC phoned up and told a delighted Whalley that they had decided to televise the fixture live on the Sunday afternoon. One could see why, as Huddersfield were in the middle of a poor run and Stanley in the middle of a good one; it had the makings of an upset.

There was some disquiet over Huddersfield's allocation of 393 tickets, clearly not a lot for a club with an average home gate of 10,000, but it escalated into a wider row when it became clear that Stanley would not sell out the home part of the ground. With space for well over 1,000 fans left unsold, the club suggested that they could allocate a terrace behind the goal to Huddersfield fans and thus allow far more of them to see the game. It seemed an entirely reasonable plan, but it was rejected by the police. The television fee received by Stanley of £50,000 more than compensated for the loss on the tickets, but it was something that the club set about ensuring would not be repeated.

On the day, 3,129 attended the game, the third gate above 3,000 during the season. Played on a grey, slightly misty afternoon, the game was uneventful even after the visitors had been unluckily reduced to ten men before the half-hour. It was looking like they would achieve their aim of a goalless draw when Coleman replaced Paul Cook with Andy Gouck. It seemed like a shoring-up exercise, but with just seconds remaining, a ball cleared from the Huddersfield lines fell to Gouck outside the box, and the sturdy midfielder connected perfectly with a volley that screamed into the net. It was a great strike in any company, but the context of the match made it one of the great Crown Ground moments – up there with John Nuttall's goal in the 1970 Formby game, Paul Beck's hat-trick against Gateshead, and Jonathan Smith's header against Farsley Celtic.

There was hardly time to restart the game. Stanley were in the second round for only the second time, and the win was the club's first against Football League opposition. Of the following day's headlines, the *Sun's* 'Fat'll do nicely!' probably took the honours, and Gouck had to endure more than one photo-shoot with a tray of pies.

Not that anyone minded. The win had earned £12,500 in prize money, enough to cover the loss on the 1,000 unsold tickets, and Gouck's moment of glory had been watched by two-and-a-half-million viewers.

A month of Conference fixtures lay ahead before the second round tie at Second Division AFC Bournemouth, and Stanley initially continued their good form. Promotion contenders Hereford were seen off 2-0 at the Crown, but then six bookings in a physical 2-1 defeat at Stevenage prompted the FA to issue Stanley with a £1,000 fine. Coleman argued that his players were still adapting to the stricter refereeing in the Conference, but the manager also knew that this side to Stanley's game had to improve, if only to reduce the number of suspensions.

There was cause for concern when, on November 22nd, Stanley suddenly fell to their heaviest home defeat since the days of Billy Rodaway, 5-1 against Telford, and things did not look as if they were about to improve when, with newcomer Ged Brannan in midfield, the team found themselves 3-1 down at Chester three days later. Stanley rallied to force a fine draw, and the recovery was emphasised on the Saturday with the 2-0 defeat at the Crown of another strong side, Barnet.

With confidence restored after a minor wobble, Stanley went down to Bournemouth for their tough FA Cup second round tie. An early Paul Mullin goal was the ideal start, and though Bournemouth had more of the possession from that point on, Stanley made them work hard for their openings. Just short of the hour, Bournemouth finally equalised, but a desperately tired Stanley hung on bravely for the draw. Around 400 travelling fans in a crowd of 7,551 cheered their side off proudly. Bournemouth manager Sean O'Driscoll said: "Every Conference side is now organised and professional, and Accrington are no different."

Except that Stanley were newly-promoted part-timers who had now ventured into new territory. For the first time as a non-league club – and not since 1961 as a town – Accrington were in the hat for the third round of the FA Cup.

Stanley's pairing with Second Division Colchester United was something of a disappointment, but at least it was a home draw that gave the club a chance, and soon there was another phone call to dispel the gloom – not the BBC, but Sky this time, with the news that they had chosen the Bournemouth replay to be shown live. Furthermore, the BBC would show extended highlights, bringing in a total of £90,000 in further television revenue.

The replay took place on Monday December 15th, and Stanley had to contend with a number of injury and suspension problems. Jonathan Smith had picked up another knee injury at Bournemouth and was now a long-term casualty, Brannan was cup-tied and Steve Hollis suspended. Nonetheless, it was a closer game than some might have suspected, and as it progressed, this time it was Bournemouth who started to look the more ragged.

After 120 goalless minutes in which Stanley had matched their opponents in every way, the tie came down to a penalty shoot-out. John Coleman bravely did what he thought right and replaced the unlucky Jamie Speare with Jon Kennedy for the penalties, though the change made no difference in the end. After successful spot-kicks from James, Prendergast, Flitcroft and Cavanagh, Bournemouth's Karl Broadhurst missed his team's fourth penalty, and Paul Howarth calmly slotted home Stanley's fifth to win the tie. It was a great moment for Howarth, a good player who had been at the club for over two years with little opportunity to play regularly.

Stanley were now in the somewhat other-worldly position of challenging for a play-off place to return to the Football League, and also contemplating their forthcoming FA Cup third round tie. They were truly remarkable days, and the team showed little sign of letting up, rounding off a spectacular calendar year with two league wins at Leigh and at home to Morecambe, the latter game being played in front of 2,928 spectators.

Saturday January 3rd 2004 remains in the Accrington Stanley record books (at the time of writing) for this was the day that the biggest Crown Ground crowd of 4,368 watched Accrington Stanley in the third round of the FA Cup. Like Huddersfield before them, Colchester came to the Crown with the primary intention of not being beaten, and they succeeded in stifling Stanley's attacking prowess.

Another moment to remember followed on the Monday lunchtime with Stanley in the draw for the last 32, but again there was some disappointment when Stanley were given an away tie at Coventry if they won their replay. This took place at Layer Road on January 13th, and it was a game of some drama.

After going behind in the 11th minute, Stanley thought they had a certain penalty ten minutes later when James was clipped in the area by Colchester 'keeper Brown. The anger at the referee's decision to play on simmered until half-time, when John Coleman approached the officials to enquire about the decision.

He spent the second half in the stand, but it made no difference as Stanley outplayed Colchester and came within inches of an equaliser, only for Calcutt's effort to be cleared from the line. Colchester added a second against the run of play in the 86th minute, and though Mullin nodded a reply in the 89th minute, it was the end of Stanley's great FA Cup adventure.

Interviews after the game betrayed an air of disbelief that they had lost a game in which they had enjoyed so much possession. The players were adamant that they had been denied a blatant penalty, and both Mullin and Prendergast insisted that Stanley would have gone on to win the game if Calcutt's effort had gone in. It exemplified the fine team spirit and will-to-win of the players.

What had taken its toll, however, was the gruelling January schedule of playing both league and FA Cup games. As well as the two high-tempo clashes with Colchester, Fleetwood had taken Stanley to extra time in the Lancashire Junior Cup, and by the end of the month, the team had played eight games in 24 days.

Though the club would retain their interest in the Conference play-offs until the end of February, there was no denying that the verve of the forward play had been dulled by fatigue.

Coleman tried to pep things up by taking the long-admired forward Lee McEvilly on loan from Rochdale, but the final two months of the season saw the team gradually slip down to mid-table. In the *Accrington Observer* of March 5th, few disagreed with Lutel James when he told them:

"I think we are only struggling now because we are all so tired. You can see it in the play, we look jaded.

It is hard when lads are working full-time and then training and playing. And it is going through the whole team. I think the season has just caught up with us."

One who did disagree was John Coleman, who was unconvinced by the notion of fatigue and became increasingly frustrated by results, but after the 1-0 defeat at Hereford on March 13th, he admitted that the play-offs were now out of reach and gave the team the target of a top eight finish so as to qualify for the following season's LDV Trophy, which would pit Stanley against Football League opposition.

The issue of the players' ability to last a full season of nationwide football was pertinent for another reason, and that was the announcement that Stanley were going full-time from July 1st 2004. Home gates were averaging 1,800, and the money from the cup run was estimated to have been as much as £230,000. The club's accountants told Whalley there would never be a better time to go full-time, with enough in reserve to fund a couple of seasons – enough to launch an assault on promotion and assess the viability of the project.

With the benefit of hindsight, the move to full-time football appears just another decision in a series of well-planned moves to restore Stanley to the Football League. At the time, however, the announcement was greeted with trepidation by many of the fans. Perhaps more than anything, the potential consequences of the move going wrong were the major concern. Though they trusted Whalley implicitly with the finances, full-time football did not come cheaply; it represented easily the biggest step yet for a club that had already taken a number of leaps and bounds in the last few years. In a nutshell: were Stanley ready after just one season in the Conference?

John Coleman, himself putting his professional teaching career on hold to take the plunge, was sure that it was the right thing to do:

"Personally I think it has got to be all or nothing.

If we go full time, we all do, the whole staff – me,

Jimmy Bell, and the players, and we'll be speaking to them over the next month. Things are in place to do it, and it is just a case of agreeing it with the players who we want to keep. It will certainly be better for coaching as it has been restricted in the winter months, and to iron out one or two things on the field. I think we will benefit a lot, although we have done well as a part-time club this season."

In making the official announcement, Eric Whalley also made the case from a football point of view:

"On 1 July 2004, Accrington Stanley will become a full-time club again. We are in negotiations with somebody so hopefully, in July, we will have our own training facility. If you look at the Conference, it is virtually two leagues. There is the top half who are all, bar Aldershot and ourselves, full-time. The bottom half are all part-time. I'm not saying you can't do it as a part-time club, but it is a lot harder."

There was also the fact that part-time Conference clubs often struggled after the adrenalin rush of that first season travelling round the country and playing in new venues. By going full-time for the second season, Stanley were at least doing something to raise playing standards and expectations. Goalkeeper Jon Kennedy, who had experience of full-time football at Sunderland, approved the move and was certain that it would raise standards:

"It is a different kind of tiredness when you go to work during the week and play Saturdays and train twice a week than when you train full-time. We will be a lot sharper and should be stronger mentally."

Stanley ended the season in tenth position after winning just four of their 18 league games after the Cup exit at Colchester; they also lost to Morecambe in the final of the Lancashire Junior Cup. The squad had clearly run out of steam, and now the manager had the task of negotiating contracts with those he wanted to keep. The club immediately released six players, including Dean Calcutt, who rejected the terms he was offered. Another to leave in similar circumstances was Jamie Speare, who felt that the club had made him a derisory offer in the light of the financial commitments he had. He told the *Accrington Observer*:

"I am sick and a little confused. I just couldn't accept the offer. I didn't feel I was asking for a lot, just enough to meet what I have to pay out every month to cover giving up my job at the bank. It would have been impossible."

It was a regrettable end to Speare's distinguished Stanley career after six seasons and exactly 300 appearances for the club. Coleman admitted that it had been a tough decision, but revealed that there were even question marks about the retention of Jon Kennedy, who, along with Peter Cavanagh, had won an England non-league cap during the season:

"They are both good keepers and Jamie especially has been a brilliant servant to the club. But they would both need to improve if they are going to stay. We have got to improve all over the park. The one thing that stands out is that we have conceded too many goals."

There was, inevitably, some financial brinkmanship going on, with the club asking for some financial sacrifices from the players, and some of them holding out for more money. In the wider game, finance remained centre stage and the Conference was not immune. Both Telford United and Northwich Victoria were in serious financial trouble, and Exeter had attracted a great deal of criticism by going into administration and then threatening legal action against the Conference if they deducted points. The league backed down rather than risk losing the case, and the other Conference clubs had to pay a share of the legal bills, with the cost deducted from sponsorship income; it cost Stanley around £25,000. Essentially, it was not an easy time for a lot of clubs, and that Stanley were thriving in the midst of this and actually going full-time – at an estimated additional annual cost of £200,000 – was testament to how well the club continued to manage their finances.

Careful husbandry of resources appeared, alas, somewhat lacking at Hyndburn Borough Council. After just one year and £15,000 of the three-year shirt sponsorship deal, the council cancelled the deal in the light of debts totalling £1.8 million. The club was disappointed to find itself in the middle of some party political points-scoring. But in an attempt to put a brave face on the row, the club and the council publicly signed a 'partnership accord' to show that the split had been amicable. The club found another shirt sponsor as local retailers Oswaldtwistle Mills quickly agreed a deal.

John Coleman wasted little time either in revealing his first signing for the new campaign in mid-May: striker Lee McEvilly. The manager had indicated he was a definite target since he did not see either Lutel James or Paul Mullin as "out and out strikers". All the same, the established front pair had done well, with Mullin scoring 29 goals in total, and James 22 goals, which seemed to compare favourably to McEvilly's 25 goals in 85 appearances for Rochdale.

May also saw a casual and inauspicious mention of the player who would make perhaps the greatest impact at the club of any recent recruit: Ian Craney. Just voted the NPL player of the year and in line for a call-up to the England non-league side, Craney had been the subject of a £5,000 bid from Stanley and was rumoured to be keen on the move because of the opportunity to go full-time. Altrincham unsurprisingly rejected the bid. Coleman acidly commented:

"I don't think we will go back with a bigger offer as you don't have to pay transfer fees so much at lower levels anymore. We gave them a good sell-on clause of 50 per cent. If they change their minds then they know where we are."

But Craney was too good a prospect to ignore. In early June there had been reports that Stanley had gone back with an improved offer, with Craney again keen, but that the clubs had been unable to agree a fee, with Whalley accusing the NPL club of upping the asking price at a late stage in negotiations. Finally, at the end of June, Coleman got his man in a deal worth around £15,000. Craney told the press:

> "It was good to know the manager rated me so highly to keep chasing me and it has given me a confidence boost. I enjoyed my time at Altrincham, but sometimes you have got to move on."

With his pursuit and eventual capture of Craney, Coleman had shown again why he was more than fulfilling Eric Whalley's description of him as one of the most up-and-coming young managers in non-league. The fee was not exactly a giveaway, but neither was it a gamble with the club's money, for Coleman was sure that in Craney he had an attacking midfielder with massive potential given coaching and the fitness that full-time training would provide. Indeed, as the players of Accrington Stanley prepared to clock in for their first day's work as professional footballers, hopes were high that improvement would be both universal and decisive.

On July 1st 2004, Accrington Stanley returned to the fold of professional football clubs for the first time since that frost-laden Tuesday morning in early March 1962, when the last set of Stanley professionals had arrived for work to be told that the club had resigned from the Football League. It was quite an emotional morning at the club's training headquarters at Wilson's Playing Fields in Clayton-le-Moors as the players arrived.

The squad was not yet complete, and the move to full-time football was proving a difficult decision for some. Jonathan Smith, having requested to juggle training with his job at Hyndburn Sports Centre, was told to make a decision one way or the other, and Steve Hollis was also reluctant to give up his coaching job at Liverpool FC's academy. In the end, the lure of becoming a full-time

Stanley player proved enough for Smith to take the plunge, but though Hollis remained registered with Stanley, his decision to stay at Liverpool effectively ended his Stanley career after 157 appearances. On his eventual departure from the club, Hollis told the *Accrington Observer*:

> "What has struck me most is how much the club has changed in the time I have been here. It's everything – the facilities, the ground; the club has gone full-time and hundreds of players have come and gone. One achievement that sticks in my mind is winning the NPL First Division title. I know everyone says it, but that is when it all started for the club."

New signings included central midfielder Steve Jagielka, but Coleman's attempts to sign a first-choice goalkeeper were frustrated when his preferred target could not obtain a work permit. With the new season just days away, Jon Kennedy re-signed. Looking ahead to the new season, there was no mistaking Eric Whalley's expectations:

> "We want to win the league. There is no point resting on our laurels. There is no problem with finance, we can fund a return to the Football League, so we are forever looking forward. We have a big plan here. We have gone full-time and we don't just want stability, we want to go up and we should improve on last season. We have quality players here, we have signed more and we want to win the league. That is not putting the manager and staff under any pressure, but I want to win it."

One area that definitely needed improvement was Stanley's disciplinary record. Whalley had been summoned to an FA hearing during the previous campaign after the team had reached 60 yellow cards and 10 reds. On that occasion the FA had given the club a chance by suspending a £10,000 fine, but things failed to improve conspicuously. The team ended the season with 15 dismissals, and the FA issued a £2,000 fine, and kept another £5,000 fine suspended.

Stanley began the season well with four of August's five league games being won. There was an especially fluent performance at Morecambe, where a spectacular strike by Ian Craney helped Stanley to a 2-1 win, though this was followed by a disaster at Stevenage where the team were simply blitzed in the first half under a barrage of crosses and long shots.

The team came back from the 5-0 mauling to defeat newly-promoted Crawley at the Crown, but a worrying sign was that the 1,270 gate was well down on the 1,800 average of the previous season. The club also lost Steve Halford to a stress fracture of the leg, and were forced to recall Jonathan Smith from a loan spell at Barrow for the game at Dagenham on September 11th.

Hopes were again raised by the stunning 5-0 demolition of Dagenham, but it was not enough to instil the confidence to sustain a prolonged run. A poor Leigh RMI side were unconvincingly beaten 2-1 at the Crown, with the three points lifting Stanley to second in the table, but the team then lost a 3-1 lead and surrendered two points at Northwich Victoria in midweek.

With Halford out for some time and the manager not convinced that Williams and Smith were the right central defensive duo, further signings were bound to be made, and they arrived in late September. Mike Flynn, a vastly experienced central defender, was signed from Blackpool, while Chris Butler was a young left-back just released by Liverpool. Flynn went straight into the side, but a home defeat to Gravesend and then a very poor performance in losing at Farnborough on October 2nd hinted at serious problems, in spite of an unexpected victory at Bradford City in the LDV Trophy.

The team was not helped by a shocking accident on the training pitch that saw goalkeeper Jon Kennedy break his leg after falling awkwardly, and Rory Prendergast was also lost for three months with a hernia. Full-time employment obviously did not provide any insurance against injury, and the rhythms and routines of daily training made for something of a learning curve for Coleman and the players. There were bound to be teething problems. Nonetheless, the manager had expected more fulsome benefits than he had found so far, and, to his credit, he did not shirk from the responsibility that he had to put the problems right. He told the local press:

> "There is no getting away with it, it is a slump. It's worrying because we have got quality here. We have been doing everything right – we get looked after, we are professional, and now we have to work that bit harder. We have raised expectations and it is hard to lower them. We got to second in the league and raised the expectations of everyone, but I am no different. I have high hopes and, at the moment, we are underachieving."

A 4-0 defeat at Scarborough on October 23rd could not be interpreted as anything else, and was the prelude to activity both inside and outside the club. A letter in the *Accrington Observer* asked precisely what improvements full-time football had brought to the club, and, in his weekly column in the paper, anonymous Crown regular 'Red Herring' called the performance at Scarborough an "amateurish and disorganised shambles".

Someone else not impressed with the way things were turning out – although this time from a more personal perspective – was Lutel James. Shortly after the defeat at Scarborough, where James stayed on the bench for the duration, he submitted a transfer request which was accepted by John Coleman. It was not the first time that James had asked to leave, nor was it the only occasion that he had revealed his grievances in the pages of the local paper, but this time Coleman was in no mood to argue. James told the *Accrington Observer*:

> "I know now I am not going to get in the team again and I am in a no-win situation, so I have to leave, I have to be playing regularly. John has got his team – and I am not a part of it."

Coleman insisted that James was wrong with his

analysis and that he did not hold anything against him, but the manager felt that it was in the best interests of the club for James to go if he wanted away. It was a regrettable end to his Stanley career after 170 games and 83 goals. Together with Paul Mullin, he terrorised NPL defences for two seasons, and the partnership adapted well to the Conference. James remains the most complementary striking partner that Paul Mullin has played with.

To round off one of the more trying weeks of John Coleman's Stanley career, his team then lost 2-0 at home against Leigh RMI in the fourth qualifying round of the FA Cup. With Leigh propping up the Conference, it had not been too much to expect Stanley to advance to the first round again, and there were serious words spoken after the game, both in the dressing room and the boardroom. The club had lost £10,000 in expected prize money at a stroke, and potentially much more, with the FA Cup easily the most lucrative competition they were allowed to enter. More letters appeared in the local press. One stated of the FA Cup exit:

"Despite being a team of part-timers, Leigh were yards faster and played better football than we did. Now we are getting the familiar moan from John Coleman about getting fresh players. How many more players is he going to sign? There are enough players if he would play them in their proper position. The wage bill must be colossal."

Others took the longer-term view and defended Coleman's record and the stability he had brought to the club. One wrote:

"I would like to remind all the Coley bashers of the directions to Stocksbridge, for that is how far we have come and where we could go back to without a steady, long-term manager. Now we are in a bit of a sticky patch, the chap needs our support."

These sentiments were echoed by club captain Peter Cavanagh who issued a strong rallying call to the players to extract themselves from the doldrums. In a gesture not publicised at the time, the squad voluntarily took a collective pay-cut to reimburse the club with the £10,000 that would have been won had they performed against Leigh. It was an unusual example of a squad of players being prepared to shoulder their responsibilities to the club beyond the immediate events on the pitch, and the gesture was appreciated by those whose task it was to find ways of maintaining the club's income.

Another pointer that things might not be quite as bad as results suggested was the experience of the players who continued to train full-time with Stanley but who played at the level below. Both Smith and Flitcroft had gone to Conference North side Barrow on loan, and both had shone among the part-timers. Improvements were being extracted from full-time training, even if some of the squad members from the NPL title-winning side would prove ultimately to be just short of the grade at the top end of the Conference.

Another cause for continued hope was the state of the league table, for the early indications suggested that the Conference was a close division. No elite group had broken away at the top, and for all of Stanley's problems, their first victory in over a month, at lowly Northwich Victoria on November 13th, moved the team back into third place. It was all very close. A much sterner test followed at league leaders Barnet, and Stanley flunked it, never really getting into the game and ending up well beaten 3-0.

The inconsistency continued through to the New Year. Wins against Canvey Island and Leigh were offset by defeats against Forest Green, Carlisle and Dagenham, the last at the Crown in a game where Stanley drew a blank from 21 efforts on goal. Jimmy Bell's after-match comments sounded more than a little exasperated and hinted at an increasing impatience with the forward line:

"We just need to string a run of wins together. We know we are one of the better teams in the league, but we are just so inconsistent. John is a great be- liever that things will change if you work hard. I am a little more pessimistic and think we may have to change things, but if we bring in another striker, we lose what Paul Mullin and Lee McEvilly give us, and the same goes for the defence. Teams are coming to Accrington, playing negatively and trying to hit us on the break – and it is working. We are falling for the sucker punch time and time again and it has to change. It is just so confusing."

One could see the source of Bell's bewilderment, for just as soon as Stanley appeared set to make a decisive move for the play-offs, form tailed off and they slipped back. An excellent victory at Halifax on January 3rd was a case in point, with the team managing for the first time that season to win after going behind, and they followed up with a 2-1 win against Farnborough that took them to fourth in the table. With the possibility of consolidating a play-off place with a decent run, the team then turned in a very poor performance in losing 1-0 at Tamworth. Jimmy Bell again sounded as though the management team were not sure what to do next:

"It looks like the lads are tired but we have tried everything, we have given them quite an easy week but we still looked jaded. Just everything seems to be going against us, and if Lee is not scoring then it is not going to be our day."

Once again, the team rallied. After a morale-boosting 1-0 win in the Lancashire Junior Cup at Morecambe, three points at home to Scarborough put Stanley up to sixth, and then came a real boost with a hard-fought 2-1 win at Exeter. This performance was more like it. Stanley were clinical with their few chances and utterly committed throughout, with the team defending their narrow lead for the last 35 minutes. When Stanley then thrashed league leaders Barnet, 4-1 at the Crown, they went second in the table with just 11 games remaining. The sequence was enough to win John Coleman the manager of the month award for February.

Home draws against Forest Green and Halifax, and then defeat at Carlisle on March 12th, had the fans wondering whether the team had again lost its way, but victories against Morecambe and Canvey sustained hopes that the play-offs were still on, particularly due to the character of both performances.

At home to Morecambe, Stanley cancelled out an opening goal for the visitors, but were then reduced to ten men when McEvilly was sent off before half-time. Facing an uphill task in the second half, Stanley played with a purpose and chased the win, and were rewarded for their approach when a Paul Mullin goal secured all three points.

Another two goals from Mullin secured victory at Canvey Island. The managerial team were particularly happy with the professionalism of this display. Stanley finished two chances clinically, and maintained their shape and composure to keep a satisfying clean sheet. The six points gained lifted Stanley into the final play-off place with seven games remaining, and saw Paul Mullin up to third in the divisional goalscoring charts with 17.

As well as Mullin was playing, the manager by this time had made a couple of moves to bolster the forward line that suggested he still was not happy with the firepower at his disposal. David Brown arrived from Hereford, and Gary Roberts was signed from League of Wales side Welshpool. With Brown, the manager was able to take advantage of the fact that the player, still living in the north-west, had fallen out with Hereford boss Graham Turner over his training schedule and had not played for Hereford for around a month. Brown, a former Hull City, Chester and Telford striker, was clearly in limbo and needed a way out, and once Hereford agreed to cancel his contract he was free to move to Stanley.

The arrival of Gary Roberts was less heralded. The manager commented that he would give the wingers some competition, but for some time there had been strong rumours that Rory Prendergast had been the subject of a bid from Bristol Rovers and was looking for a move to a Football League club. The consensus of the fans, with whom Prendergast was popular, was that being ambitious and well capable of playing at a higher level, the player would move on. There was also some uncertainty about the situation with McEvilly, who was dropped at Canvey in favour of Brown.

That there were some problems within the camp seemed to be borne out by the events that followed. With Stanley in the final play-off position, a solid run to the end of the season would have seen them reach their target, but the team lost a 2-0 lead at Burton to draw 2-2, and then conceded another two goals at York and did well to come back for a point. Both games represented ground lost, and, if the events at Crawley were anything to go by, the snapping of Coleman's patience with his regulars.

At Crawley, a bewildered group of Stanley fans scanned the team sheets to find that Craney, Prendergast and Jagielka had all joined McEvilly on the subs' bench, and that Danny Alcock had been preferred in goal to the fit-again Kennedy. This bizarre formulation produced a terrace rendition of "We've got the best bench in the land", and Coleman's replacements, including player-coach Paul Cook, failed to make an impression.

After the game, a 2-0 defeat, Coleman argued that Stanley had played some of their best football of the season in the first half, but no one agreed with him. In truth, it had been a depressingly poor showing just when Stanley needed a win to hoist themselves back into the play-off places. Even the normally irrepressible Stanley Ultras gave up and sat out the final twenty minutes in silence.

The Ultras had been formed earlier in the season partly in response to declining gates at the Crown, but also as part of a wider movement to create more noise and spectacle at football games. The Ultras have made quite an impression with their banners and drums, and goodness knows what sort of noise they would make with a roof to amplify their efforts. But the gates were both a worry and a disappointment. After averaging close to 2,000 the previous season, they were now hovering around the 1,400 mark, probably a little below what the club had budgeted for.

The Crawley defeat heralded the end of the play-off

aspirations for most fans. With four games to go, Stanley needed a minimum of 10 points and possibly the full 12 to reach fifth place, and the task was not made any easier by events a few days after the Crawley game in a midweek league cup tie at Stalybridge.

Both Prendergast and McEvilly were given starts, but, clearly unhappy at their recent demotions, both expressed their displeasure publicly. Prendergast was hauled off after only 25 minutes after answering back to the touchline, and McEvilly also had some harsh words for the management team during the game. Stanley went out on penalties, but the greater fall-out was from the Prendergast incident, with Coleman taking the unusual step of publicly criticising one of his players in a very specific way:

"Rory's temperament is suspect. There is no doubt he has the ability but Rory needs to concentrate on what he does best – playing football. There are a lot of things going on in his head. He has been at this club the longest he has been at any club, and we have bent over backwards to try and appease him. But this is not the first time this has happened and we have had talks to clear the air. He has touted himself to league clubs and has instructed an agent to get him a move and is not dedicated to Accrington Stanley."

Prendergast was relegated to the bench for the Stevenage game, which was the occasion of one of Stanley's best performances of the year, avenging their heavy defeat at Stevenage with an equally emphatic 4-1 victory.

The result kept Stanley in seventh, just three points from a play-off place, and again had the fans wondering whether Stanley were starting a decisive play-off push or merely prolonging the agony.

It turned out to be the latter, and agony was most definitely the apposite word to describe the defeat at Woking. Stanley dominated the first half and were a goal to the good before a defensive howler gifted Woking an undeserved equaliser on the stroke of half-time. Woking's last-minute winner merely compounded the frustration. The reality was that for all the additional fitness and training, Stanley were just short of being a play-off team; they were too liable to concede goals through momentary defensive lapses, and remained vulnerable at set-pieces.

Six goals shared with Aldershot made for an exciting final home game of the season, but Coleman was sent to the stands for arguing with the referee.

His behaviour was too much for the *Accrington Observer*'s 'Red Herring', who penned a highly sarcastic piece, charging that the manager too often deflected the blame onto the performance of the officials rather than that of the team:

> "I've lost count of the dozens of stone-wall pen-
> alties that we've had turned down. Week after
> week we've had perfectly good goals chalked off
> by match officials hell bent on undermining our
> promotion chances. Of course, you won't hear any-
> one at Stanley complaining.
>
> "Critics will point to a catalogue of individual er-
> rors; and, at times, breathtaking defensive disor-
> ganisation and a staggering degree of inconsistency
> as reasons for our missing out on the play-offs. But
> I know better!"

Coleman maintained that his team had underachieved in missing out on the play-offs, but he admitted that the defensive aspects of Stanley's play needed to improve if they were to be serious contenders in the Conference:

> "We have conceded too many goals, and a lot of
> them have been individual errors. You can't chal-
> lenge for honours if you are going to concede 58
> goals in the season. We have got experience at the
> back, but it is not just the defence; you have to de-
> fend as a team. At the moment, the way we defend,
> it means it is in the lap of the gods."

This pointed to defensive signings, and one defender on the way out was Jonathan Smith. In a nice touch, Coleman handed the captain's armband to Smith for the Lancashire

Junior Cup Final, Stanley's third county cup final in four years. Without playing a full-strength side, Stanley had disposed of Atherton LR, Morecambe and Bamber Bridge, and now faced Burscough in the final over two legs. Stanley won 7-0 on aggregate and it was a measure of the progress made at the club that the trophy was viewed as just a consolation prize.

It was nonetheless a fitting end to Smith's Stanley career of 250 appearances and 29 goals. He had been a key figure in the 1999–2000 side that had defied the odds to win the NPL First Division, the foundations upon which the club had based their later progress up the non-league ladder, progress which Smith himself enjoyed. At one stage, rumours were strong that Oldham Athletic were planning a bid for him. It was rare to see Smith outjumped at a corner, whether defending or attacking, and residing within those 29 goals are some precious memories – headers against Radcliffe and Farsley Celtic were vital moments in the 1999–2000 promotion – and alongside Steve Halford, Smith formed the defensive partnership at the heart of the 2002–03 promotion-winning side as well. Smith was a genuine terrace hero, and hundreds turned out for his pre-season testimonial game to say thanks for everything he had done for the club.

The immediate post-season was notable more for the players leaving the club than those joining. The club's first season of full-time football had been borne with falling gates and hardly any additional income from the cups. The messages emanating from the Crown suggested that Coleman had little money to play around with, and the club appealed for more of their regulars to buy a season ticket in order to fund the push for the Football League. Whalley openly admitted that he was a little disillusioned with the falling attendances.

For Coleman, it meant that another careful pruning exercise had to be done in the knowledge that he might not be able to afford the replacements he would like. The manager released four others in addition to Smith, including Lutel James and goalkeeper Jon Kennedy; Steve

Halford went on the transfer list. Recent signings Roberts and Brown were tied into longer deals.

Coleman then got a break – and some additional spending power – when Wrexham made an offer for Lee McEvilly. The deal was quickly concluded. The striker was keen to make a return to the Football League anyway, and though he had weighed in with 16 league goals, his display of dissent at Stalybridge had not been appreciated by the managerial team who placed much store on the togetherness of the squad. Just a couple of weeks later, the uncertain future of another dissident was solved when Blackpool tabled a bid for Rory Prendergast. Again, the deal was quickly concluded, and the two moves – both rumoured to be in the low five-figure range – gave Coleman a little more ammunition to bring in the players to move Stanley that additional stage forward.

It was no secret that Eric Whalley was expecting nothing less than a play-off place. A season of settling in to the demands and routines of full-time football was fair, but all the indications were that the attractions of Conference football alone were not enough to sustain Accrington Stanley as a full-time operation, with few of the southern teams who dominated the league bringing any kind of support to the Crown. Stanley simply had to launch a serious promotion bid.

In April, as Stanley's play-off hopes faltered, Mike Flynn had defended the players in the local press, arguing that it was too much to expect dramatic progress right away:

> "What we have got to remember is that this is the first season as a full-time professional club. A lot was expected, but a lot of the players haven't done this before and have had to adjust mentally and physically. It has been hard, but the players will only get better for it."

If incremental improvement was the more realistic way of understanding the impact of full-time football, as Flynn suggested, then the only hope was that enough of it would accumulate in time for Stanley to justify the costs.

The Triumph of Hope

The pre-season of 2005 was both testing and intense. Stanley invited no fewer than four Football League clubs to the Crown. All were from the top two divisions, with Stanley avoiding defeat only against the highest ranked, Premiership side Wigan Athletic. Of the numerous triallists hoping to win a contract, those emerging with deals included goalkeeper Stuart Jones, central defender Michael Welch, full-backs Leam Richardson and Danny Ventre, and striker Andrew Mangan.

They joined earlier recruits Andy Tretton and Anthony Barry, and what was noticeable was the youth of the new recruits. Ventre, Barry and Mangan were teenagers and not expected to be first team regulars. Gary Roberts was only just out of his teens, and the rest of the squad, too, were relatively young. Mike Flynn was the squad's bona fide veteran, and even those in their mid-twenties counted among the older players.

Coleman certainly could not be accused of denying the kids their opportunity, and there would be no shortage of youthful enthusiasm among the troops. As Stanley prepared to kick off another campaign with a home game against Canvey Island, John Coleman told the *Accrington Observer*:

> "I wouldn't be in the league if I didn't think we could win it. I was talking to the players about teams whose ambitions are to finish in 12th place. I can't understand wanting to exist at a club that doesn't want to win the league. I know everybody can't win the league, but I think we are capable of mounting a challenge. Our focus this year is not to concede as many goals, and that should reflect in the whole team, not just the defence."

Surprise starts for the opening game were Welch in defence, Barry in midfield and Mangan up front, with Cavanagh, Proctor and Brown on the bench. The season's pledge to tighten up at the back seemed to be evident in the first two games, which were both won 1-0, but the aftermath of the second win, at Altrincham, provided Coleman with his first major problem.

It emerged that goalkeeper Stuart Jones had been signed on a non-contract basis due to a long-standing ankle injury, which he had aggravated in the pre-season friendly against Wigan. After struggling through the first two fixtures, he retired from the game, his ankle unable to take the punishment of professional football. Jones's retirement gave Danny Alcock his chance, but in a stroke of terrible luck, he broke an arm in a midweek reserve game in which he was only playing to sharpen up for the Saturday.

The club was forced to hurriedly register their youth team 'keeper, Martin Fearon, on Conference forms before the weekend game at Cambridge United, while Coleman sent out an SOS for a loan 'keeper.

Darlington offered one of their custodians, Bertrand Bossu, who duly played at Cambridge, but he made such a howler in conceding the opening goal that there was little regret when Darlington quickly recalled him.

Stanley returned from the university town without honours after a 3-1 defeat, and the team then struggled to find much rhythm in going down 2-1 at home to Exeter on August 27th, a game that saw the debut of the season's third goalkeeper, Darren Randolph, a burly Irish youth international who arrived on loan from Charlton. This time the portents were much better. Randolph was a presence in the box, had a huge kick, and in the second half made a flying save that put to rest any questions about his agility.

One question that did remain, however, was that old one about Stanley's defence. On August 29th they let slip a 2-0 lead at Scarborough to draw 2-2, and nearly did the same at home to Woking on September 3rd. This time, however, they repelled Woking's late efforts for an equaliser and hung on for the 2-1 win.

Despite the three points, John Coleman bemoaned the fact that Stanley continued to make life difficult for themselves. Both Scarborough and Woking had been outplayed, only to be let back into the game by poor defending. The manager was, however, much happier with the attacking prowess of the team, with Brown, Roberts and Craney all working hard to support Mullin up front. It was a pity, though, that so few people were bothering to watch them.

Attendances had been a source of unease from the opening day of the season, when just 1,012 had turned up for the Canvey Island game, the lowest attendance in the Conference. But Woking represented a trend the club could not afford to let continue. For the first time in the Conference – indeed, for the first time in over two-and-a-half seasons – fewer than 1,000 people attended a league game at the Crown.

Whalley responded by offering free entry for a child accompanied by an adult for the next home game, against Crawley. The gate did improve to 1,365, but this was still a relatively poor turnout, far less than the average of 1,800 in the first Conference season, and only just within range of the 1,500 that was thought to be the barest of break-even levels.

These troubles on the attendance front ironically coincided with the first signs that Stanley were putting together a serious promotion challenge on the pitch. The team had gone to Burton Albion and won there for the first time since Coleman's now-legendary salmon-like leap in the NPL Challenge Shield, with goals from Brown and Mangan giving Stanley a 2-0 win.

Home victories against Crawley (4-2) and Aldershot (3-2) followed, and when Stanley went to Dagenham on September 24th and successfully defended a 2-1 lead, the five straight league wins had catapulted Stanley to third place, behind favourites Exeter City and newcomers Grays Athletic, who remained unbeaten.

The club had lost Andy Tretton and Andy Proctor, both requiring knee operations, but Coleman had strengthened in the midfield area by signing a player who had impressed on a week's trial. He was Romuald Boco, a French-speaking Benin international.

Though Boco was signed up initially for just three months, there was already something of a buzz about this new recruit, with Whalley telling the local press that Boco had the potential to be "one of the biggest signings the club has ever made".

Other additions to the squad included Andy Dibble, who joined primarily as a coach, though he also registered as a player. Paul Cook's contacts in the professional game landed full-back Phil Edwards on loan from Premiership side Wigan. Leaving to find regular first team football was Ged Brannan.

Coleman introduced his new signings gradually, with Boco most often a second-half substitute, and detectable in the manager's pronouncements was a new-found confidence. A 3-2 defeat at Morecambe on September 27th was Stanley's first in six Conference games, but they had been reduced to ten men after just five minutes and had competed well throughout. Coleman told the *Accrington Observer*:

> "The difference between this season and last season is that we have the belief in ourselves. We are a good side and we now believe it. And it means we will take setbacks in our stride, unlike last season where we may have got nervous."

October was to put Coleman's theory to the toughest of tests. The root of the problem was the loss of goalkeeper Randolph for a couple of weeks while he played in an international tournament. In his last outing before leaving, Randolph helped Stanley defeat Hereford 2-1 at the Crown, a result that lifted Stanley a place to second.

The key decision was whether to find another 'keeper or to use Dibble. The goalkeeping coach had vast experience, and Coleman opted to take advantage of this. The month's troubles started at Stevenage in Dibble's first game. At half-time, things looked to be going Stanley's way. Jagielka had given them a 1-0 lead, and Stevenage were down to ten men, but once the home side had equalised after Dibble had deflected a strong cross-shot into the path of an oncoming attacking player, Stanley were simply over-run. In front of a large and hostile home crowd, it was a depressing experience for both players and fans, with Stevenage running out 3-1 winners.

Three days later the team were eliminated from the LDV Trophy at Rotherham, though again it was an agonising affair. Stanley were 3-2 ahead with just seconds of extra time remaining before conceding an equaliser and then going out on penalties. Rotherham boss Mick Harford conceded that the best team lost, and quipped half-seriously that he would want to avoid Stanley in the FA Cup.

Harford was, however, jumping the gun, for Stanley's FA Cup fourth qualifying round tie at home to Conference North side Worcester City was next up. On paper it looked relatively straightforward. Worcester were next to bottom of their league with just one victory all season, but Stanley were sluggish, and once Worcester had managed a second-half equaliser to cancel Gary Roberts' effort, the visitors defended stubbornly to take the tie to a replay.

The return, played just two days later, was a disaster for Stanley. After taking an early 2-0 lead, Stanley conceded two goals in the last 15 minutes of the game to go out 3-2, with Worcester's winner arriving in the 88th minute. As had happened the previous season, Stanley had seen £10,000 in prize money snatched away by a team they should by rights have easily beaten.

It did not exactly help Whalley's mood that a first round tie against minnows Chippenham Town awaited the winners, which represented a rare chance to progress serenely to the second round.

The defeat at Worcester was a drama that turned into a crisis. It was a source of embarrassment that there were 400 more spectators at Worcester for the replay than there had been at the Crown for the first tie, but that would have been tolerable if Stanley had gone through. As it was, gates were worryingly mediocre, and the bank account now remained untroubled by the FA Cup for two seasons.

There were also question marks on the field. Mike Flynn, one of the few fit centre-halves at the club, remained unused on the bench, and Stanley worryingly ran out of steam at Worcester, with the part-time side clearly ending the stronger outfit. To the club's credit, none of these questions were shirked, though the club obviously preferred to do their blood-letting behind closed doors. Flynn's decision to air his grievances in the local paper heralded the end of his Stanley career, with Coleman sending him to Hyde United on loan.

Eric Whalley assured the fans that the Rotherham or Worcester defeats did not imperil the season's plans since they did not budget for any cup income. Coleman argued that injuries had played their part in the poor run, though the manager also conceded that it had been unfair to ask the 40-year-old Dibble to play four games in ten days; he should instead have looked for another 'keeper.

Within the club, the defeat had a more resounding impact. No one was left in the slightest doubt that form had to pick up, or things would change. In response to the fatigue of the players, the club doctor, Dr Joyce Watson, suspected that the players were not recovering quickly enough after games due to their nutritional intake. Dr Watson, who had a professional interest in sports nutrition, had instituted a rehydration system during the FA Cup run in 2003–04, when the players were part-timers. The feeling then was that it had helped the recovery process greatly, so now Stanley re-introduced the same system. The club also accepted an invitation from a hypnotherapist, Lesley Graves, who, like Dr Watson, offered her services free of charge, and again some players felt that the hypnotherapy sessions had helped them. It was just another step in the club learning how to be as professional as they could possibly manage on the resources that they had.

Having had five days in which to rehydrate and recover from the trauma at Worcester, Stanley's Conference clash with York on the following Saturday, October 29th, was a crucial game. York were one place above Stanley in the league, so it was a chance for Coleman's troops to make headway against one of their main competitors.

Randolph was back in goal, and Phil Edwards made his Crown debut. If Stanley had any doubts, they hid them well with a brave and positive performance in front of 2,193 spectators. Goals from Roberts and Mullin saw Stanley home 2-1, and now they had a week off before the biggest test of the season so far, a much-anticipated clash at unbeaten Grays Athletic.

In the best tradition of the football cliché, Grays were being heralded as the 'surprise package' of the Conference, having equalled the league record of 15 unbeaten games from the start of the season in their first Conference campaign. The reality was a little less romantic. Though the club had indeed enjoyed a rapid rise up the non-league ladder, they arrived in the Conference as a full-time, well-funded outfit, helped by their position in a large and reasonably affluent catchment area.

All the same, Grays' progress had taken most pundits by surprise. Sky decided that the clash was worthy of their cameras, and so the kick-off was moved to 12 noon. In front of the television cameras, Stanley walked out in T-shirts bearing the face of Anthony Cavanagh, brother of full-back Peter, who had tragically died after being attacked in a Liverpool bar. The death had affected the squad, especially those close to Cavanagh himself, and the players had determined to use the shock and sadness of events to the best effect on the field; they wanted to win for their team-mate.

And win they did. Paul Mullin put Stanley ahead only for Grays to equalise. But then Steve Jagielka scored and Stanley hung on for the remaining 25 minutes, with the fans heaving a collective sigh of relief when Phil Edwards deflected a goalbound shot onto the bar.

Although the defeat of Grays was Stanley's third win from their last four Conference games, it was from this battling performance that significant reserves of belief and confidence were mined. This wiped the slate clean of Stevenage and

Worcester and left something to spare. Stanley had gone to the division's form team and deservedly become the first side in 65 games to leave with a win, and in the process had confirmed their own title-chasing credentials.

That other people believed in the challenge of Accrington Stanley was an important development. In football as in politics, observations make an impression, and then impressions take shape as perception, from where it is only a short road to fact and then truth.

No football pundit asked to name his or her most-fancied Conference side now omitted Accrington Stanley. The professional certainty of these paid observers of the game that Stanley were on their way back to the Football League quickly moved from perception to fact. And when a group of players are constantly told that they are among the best – if not the best – in their division, then they gradually come to believe it themselves.

It was Stanley's luck also that the victory at Grays was followed by four consecutive home league games, partly as a result of re-arranging fixtures after cup commitments. Coleman was now concerned to maintain focus. Stanley's emergence at the head of the Conference was attracting welcome media attention, but the team had too often in the past let situations like this slip. None of the four sides due at the Crown were anything better than mid-table, and so the manager made it quite clear what was expected: four wins, nothing less.

Club captain Peter Cavanagh echoed the sentiment with a steely confidence:

> "The Accrington Stanley of old would beat Grays and then lose to Forest Green. But we are all confi-dent that this is a new Accrington Stanley. We have done better against the lower teams and we've con-tinued our form against the top teams."

Cavanagh's faith was well placed. Forest Green – so often one of the 'lower' teams against whom Stanley struggled – were never allowed to settle, with Boco particularly impressive when he came on shortly before half-time. Goals from Jagielka and Roberts saw a solid Stanley collect three points with a 2-0 win. The next game, at home to Southport on November 26th, was the last for Darren Randolph, who had served the maximum three months on short-term loan. This time Stanley were more emphatic victors, winning 4-0 in front of 1,630 spectators.

The third of the four home games, against Altrincham on December 3rd, saw the debut of Stanley's new 'keeper, Rob Elliot. Like Randolph before him, Elliot was a Charlton Athletic youngster on a month-long loan. This was a hard-fought affair, but Stanley again prevailed, with a Gary Roberts free kick the only goal of the game. The win moved Stanley a point clear at the top of the Conference with 13 wins and 41 points from their 19 games, and that was extended to four points following the 2-0 defeat of Kidderminster on December 10th.

The team had delivered exactly what John Coleman had asked for and more – the four wins had been achieved without conceding a goal. The quiet euphoria around the squad was, however, tempered by the reaction of the town, for the gates had actually gone down since the Southport game, and the average for the season so far stood at just 1,389, far lower than the averages for the previous two seasons.

The club decided to ventilate their thoughts on the issue in as clear a way as possible. In the *Accrington Observer* of December 16th, both the chairman and the manager asked the readers whether they wanted a club at all. An online poll had indicated that the four home games in as many weeks so close to Christmas was simply too much money for some people at £12 a time, but others pointed to the poor facilities at the ground, such as the lack of covered terracing, as a reason for attendances declining in the winter months.

John Coleman pointed out that he was doing everything he could from his side of things, and that the lack of support undermined his efforts to motivate the players:

"I am devastated by the crowds. We have won four

home games on the trot, but with every win we lose 100 fans. The Accrington public need to ask themselves if they want a professional club in this area. We have had some good times since I have been here and all the time it has snowballed and got bigger so I don't know if we have reached saturation point. I would hate to see what the attendances were if we were third from bottom."

Eric Whalley was less apocalyptic, but made the entirely reasonable point that the facilities were as they were because of the resources of the club, which in turn were determined by levels of support:

"If we want to progress we have got to have the support. I am not pleading poverty, we are not skint, but it is a huge season for us, we are doing so well, and we want the people of Accrington to get behind us."

The feature provoked a flurry of responses. Of those offering constructive suggestions, some pointed out that there were few incentives or concessionary deals from the club. Others thought that the club could do more to promote a family-oriented atmosphere on match days. Among the less helpful suggestions was the usual point about the expense – that an adult bringing two children has to pay £26, and would not get any change out of £30 once drinks and a programme are added. While this was undeniably the case, it seemed to merely confirm Coleman's suspicion that too many were not all that bothered about status and would be happier paying a fiver, even if it meant watching Stanley in the North West Counties League.

The unbeaten run of league games, going back to that grim afternoon at Stevenage, was only just maintained at Halifax on Boxing Day, where an 88th-minute Gary Roberts' free kick rescued a point in a 2-2 draw, but the sequence had also seen the manager settle on his preferred defensive line-up. The back four of Edwards, Richardson, Williams and Welch now had a decent run of games behind them, and Rommy Boco had also earned a midfield starting berth alongside Barry and Craney.

The settled line-up at least eased slightly the pressure on John Coleman when it came to reinforcing the squad during the January transfer window. Whalley had promised to fund a transfer, and with Proctor still two months from fitness, Coleman professed the need for more midfield bodies. But he did not have to rush to get someone in, and instead ensured that Edwards, Ventre, Barry, Welch and Richardson were all tied up on longer deals. In the case of Phil Edwards, it spoke volumes that he was prepared to leave a Premiership club for Stanley. He told the local paper that it was a no-brainer – Stanley had given him regular first team football and he loved the atmosphere in the squad.

Leaving the holiday period, Stanley remained two points clear at the top of the Conference with between one and two games in hand on those below them. But two difficult away fixtures loomed that demanded very different qualities. At Canvey Island on January 7th, Stanley brilliantly neutralised the pace and width of the home forwards by playing possession football, with two quick and clinical attacks of their own providing the decisive moments. At Tamworth three days later, the physical challenge was more to the fore, but again Stanley were equal to it, closing ranks once Ian Craney's second-half strike had established a 2-1 lead.

These two wins on the road extended Stanley's lead from two to six points, and this failure of the chasing pack to keep up with Stanley's relentless progress was a trend that enabled them to build a considerable cushion between themselves and the rest. John Coleman admitted that Stanley would never have a better chance of going up, while Jimmy Bell rejoiced in the win at Tamworth, Stanley's first there, and some compensation for a 4-1 mauling in the FA Trophy a few years before that still rankled.

Of the FA Trophy, John Coleman insisted that Stanley's progress was a matter of genuine importance as he had never won the competition, but the performances of the team suggested otherwise. They were very lucky to escape from Carshalton Athletic with a 2-2 draw after equalising deep into injury time, and then an equally insipid performance at Worksop saw them go out on penalties. In the light of their league performances, it was difficult to believe that it was the same team, for by the time of their FA Trophy exit on February 7th, Stanley had taken a huge stride towards the Conference title at Exeter.

This game, played on the night of Monday January 30th, was the biggest of the season yet, a clash between the top two Conference teams, played in front of 4,624 fans and televised live on Sky. Stanley went into the game eight points ahead of Exeter, and knowing that a win would put them into an almost impregnable position.

Gary Roberts opened the scoring again and then made it 3-0 after Boco had scored Stanley's second, and though Exeter scored and then had a great chance for a second, Stanley fully deserved their 3-1 win. There was still a long way to go, but the result – and the 11-point lead – was quite a statement to the rest of the league.

Both Craney and Roberts had been outstanding at Exeter, and these two players had also been at the centre of speculation about imminent moves into the Football League. Coleman insisted that the squad would remain intact, but with the January transfer window almost over and no sign of any departures, midfielder Anthony Barry accepted a last-minute move to Yeovil for an undisclosed fee.

Coleman admitted to being tremendously disappointed, both personally and for the team. The manager had given Barry his opportunity in the side when the player himself had expected to be on the fringes of the first team, and now they had to face the run-in without a valued member of what had become a tightly-knit group.

In response to the loss of Barry, Coleman made a quick move for Burton's right-sided wide midfielder Andy Todd, a summer target. At 26, Todd became one of the older members of the squad. A few days later, midfielder Mark Boyd became the final recruit, having been released by Gretna.

With all the transfers done for the season, the net result was that Coleman had made the squad younger, hungrier and perhaps slightly easier to man-manage. Those who had challenged the authority of the manager, either in the press or on the pitch, had been moved on, as had the older squad members unable to get a game. Many of the younger ones had been released from League clubs and yearned to prove wrong those who had rejected them. The departure of Barry remained the only chink in the armour of the squad's spirit.

The home game against Dagenham on February 11th was Stanley's first league encounter at the Crown for three weeks, and the club was heartened by the 2,156 gate, a big improvement on those depressing pre-Christmas crowds. They witnessed a tough battle, goalless for the best part of an hour, but Boco's opener for Stanley stung Dagenham into action. They pushed Stanley back in search of an equaliser, and only the shot-stopping prowess of Rob Elliot preserved Stanley's lead, and, ultimately, the three points. Similarly, the 3-1 win at Gravesend & Northfleet six days later was another hard-fought game that could have gone either way, with Elliot again outstanding.

Three days later, Stanley faced another key game, at home to Morecambe, who had moved into second place. Another decent crowd of 3,041 gathered at the Crown, in spite of the game being televised. It was yet another uncompromising clash, won by two moments of inspiration from Andy Todd and Paul Mullin. Though Morecambe recovered to test Stanley in the second half, the energy levels of the Stanley youngsters remained impressive. The 2-0 victory sent Stanley 13 points clear at the top.

After the high of the Morecambe performance, played under the lights in front of a big crowd, came the following Saturday's game at home to Burton. Stanley's performance could not have contrasted more. They were lethargic and bereft of creativity, while Burton played their passing game with fluency. Had the visitors been more ruthless in front of goal, they would have sealed the game long before the end, but Stanley clung on to parity until the closing moments when Paul Mullin's second goal of the game stole the points, 2-1.

Though it is almost always the case that a successful side has the ability to scratch a win from the flattest of performances, the Burton game was the shrill alarm that jolted the squad back to reality. In the light of this performance, Coleman instituted a media ban, for the previous few weeks had seen the club's training ground in Barnoldswick the consistent destination of the nation's television cameras and journalists, all wanting a piece of the remarkable Accrington Stanley story. From now on, the team would knuckle down beyond the glare of the media circus and focus on the next game only; anyone mentioning promotion in the earshot of the manager or the chairman was fined.

Those behind the scenes at the Crown, however, could not put the blinkers on. Promotion was very much on, and now the question of preparing the Crown Ground for League football became the priority. As early as mid-November, after the win at Grays Athletic, the County Council had held a meeting with the club's architect and chief executive about the long-discussed roof for the Clayton end terrace.

The council encouraged the club to move from thinking about individual development projects to a wider, more long-term view about the Crown's development given the possibility of League football. And when, in early February, Football League officials themselves visited the ground, it became clear that significant sums had to be spent on infrastructure if the Crown was to be fit for purpose. The ground needed better segregation and more turnstiles, CCTV and a police control room, upgraded floodlights and PA system, and a first aid room for spectators. None of this came cheaply, and with the investment needed immediately there was no time to apply for a grant that might otherwise have covered some of the costs. Inevitably, the money earmarked for a popular project like the

Clayton terrace roof was needed urgently elsewhere. Chief executive Rob Heys told the press:

> "To put a roof on would cost over £100,000 and we are again entering the unknown if we do make it into the Football League. We have to be careful, but as soon as the necessary work for promotion to the Football League is completed, our attention will return to covering the terrace."

On the pitch, a desperately scrappy game at Crawley was illuminated by yet another quality Stanley finish, this time from Gary Roberts, who curled in a beauty from 25 yards. It was enough for the win, but it was not pretty. Much more reassuring was the 4-1 midweek win at Aldershot on March 7th.

The Aldershot result made it ten consecutive victories, and the only other team now in sight of Stanley were Hereford United, on a decent run of their own. The next game, on Saturday March 11th, saw Stanley visit Edgar Street, with Hereford manager Graham Turner admitting his side had to win to stand any chance of catching Stanley.

It was another highly eventful game, but one which left neither side satisfied. The magnitude of the occasion clearly had a greater affect on Hereford, as Stanley continued where they had left off at Aldershot, playing composed football in front of a 4,497 crowd. After an hour, Stanley had carved out a 2-0 lead and looked in control, but fortunes swung as the game approached its final quarter. Stanley full-back Danny Ventre was adjudged to have handled in the area. He was sent off, and though Elliot blocked the resultant penalty, the rebound was bundled in. Stanley continued to defend hardily, but deep into the six minutes of added time, Hereford equalised.

It was a decent result for Stanley on paper, but the manner of it felt like a defeat. The draw also dashed Stanley's hopes of equalling the Conference record of 11 straight wins, but it was hardly a disaster. While John Coleman criticised the referee at Hereford for what he saw as blatantly wrong decisions, he had no complaints about the 2-0 defeat at Southport on March 21st. Stanley were well below their best, and the manager was aggrieved to have lost the record of scoring in every game, especially given Ian Craney's late miss from the penalty spot.

It was a rare blot on Craney's copybook. The midfielder had enjoyed an outstanding season, unsettling defences with strong runs from midfield, and maintaining his form through the season, one of the main targets he had set himself. Craney made up for his transgression at York the following Saturday. This was another tough encounter for Stanley against a team challenging for the play-offs. Stanley found themselves 2-1 down at half-time, but in the second half they embarked on another irresistible period of attacking football, scoring three goals without reply.

The win at York, in front of 3,912 which included around 400 from Accrington, sent Stanley 14 points clear with just six games remaining. There was little point in denying that promotion was virtually sealed, but the 3-2 home defeat to Grays on April 1st was the signal for the biggest Coleman blasting of the season. He kept the players in the changing room for some time afterwards, and by the time he left, none were in any doubt about the standards he expected from the final few games of the season.

Though the players knew the dangers of complacency, they still struggled to rediscover the attacking rhythm last seen at York. A scrambled Andy Todd goal rescued a point at Forest Green, but results elsewhere at least brought the end game in sight. If Stanley won at Woking the following Saturday, April 15th, they would win the Conference and secure automatic promotion to the Football League.

It was a relief to finally arrive at the point where the club could face squarely the prize that they had sought for so long; the endless permutations were over. It was a simple case now of winning at Woking and grasping their historic reward. Stanley had always found Woking a difficult place from which to leave with a result, but the context of this game was entirely different to those of the previous two seasons. Stanley were on the very point of an historical achievement; Woking, unusually for them, had not even an outside chance of the play-offs, only the opportunity to spoil a party.

The game was hardly likely to be a classic, but the occasion ensured high drama. Stanley's breakthrough came, as it had done the previous season, courtesy of a first-half Paul Mullin goal. Stanley negotiated the rest of the first half without incident. But in the second half the home pressure paid off when Paul Mullin was adjudged to have handled, and a penalty was awarded. As the Stanley players protested, news came through that Grays had gone ahead. A win for Grays and a point for Stanley was one of the few outcomes that would deny promotion. As he had done consistently through the season, Elliot guessed right and parried Justin Williams' penalty, but the big striker stroked home the rebound. Woking began their celebrations, but the referee quickly intervened. He had spotted an encroachment and ordered the penalty to be retaken. Williams again placed the ball low to Elliot's left, and again Elliot guessed right and parried the ball. This time, the young 'keeper blocked the rebound as well, and Stanley scrambled the ball away.

For the Accrington fans at the game, these had been moments of almost unbearable tension. But at last the referee brought proceedings to an end, and the pitch was engulfed by celebrating Stanley fans.

Hundreds had travelled down from Accrington, among them some of the stalwarts from the early days: Tony Clements, who for season after season sat on the Stanley bench as trainer and physio (legend has it that the players would walk miles for one of Tony's leg rubs); Harry Stevenson, who helped knock together the old Crown Ground shed using roof trusses and railway sleepers; and Jack Barrett, who famously walked to Liverpool to raise funds for the new club and served on the committee for many years. For these people, and for many more unsung heroes who had quietly worked for the club without fanfare or reward other than the pride it gave them in supporting their town team, this was a remarkable and emotional moment. It was just a pity that not everyone who had contributed could be there to join in the celebrations.

Victory at Woking allowed the team to relax and celebrate their achievement with the fans at the final two home games of the season. John Coleman characteristically demanded results, and in front of more than 3,000 fans on both occasions, Stanley duly registered two wins. The 1-0 defeat of Scarborough was a scrappy game in difficult conditions, but the team turned in a much brighter second-half display to beat Tamworth, 2-1.

Ten days later, the last action of the season saw more than 1,000 turn up for Paul Cook's testimonial game against a Burnley XI. Though Cook had been rarely used on the park in the previous two seasons, his experience and contacts in the professional game had been crucial to the relatively smooth transition of the club in catering for a full-time playing squad. Cook knew what was essential and what the club could afford to ignore, and his contacts opened previously inaccessible doors – such as the Premiership training facilities in London that Stanley enjoyed before southern-based games.

Cook was but one working bit of many in the enlarged and sleek machine that Accrington Stanley had become by the time of their Conference triumph. It is worth reflecting on how far the club has come in those seven years since John Coleman arrived at the Crown Ground. How exactly had the club managed to go from the 334 people who watched his first game in charge at the Crown, to the 4,000 or so who were predicted to watch the first League game?

Much credit has to go to the managerial team and to John Coleman in particular. Football might be a simple game, but it is played by eleven highly complex creatures, each of which is motivated to give of their best by different needs. It is in the face of these unavoidable tensions that a manager must try to forge togetherness, and it takes a certain type of leader to persuade a group of players that each ought to support the other, because the reasons for each doing so will be motivated by different concerns.

Ask any number of Accrington Stanley players the secret ingredient in John Coleman's alchemy and they will tell you the same thing: team spirit. But the reality behind that uncomplicated, well-worn notion is that someone is dealing with a shoal of human relationships within which individual contrariness must be carefully handled and harnessed in the right direction. Coleman's impact at the Crown indicates that he is a particularly adept manager of men who can make football enjoyable for each squad member, a virtue that helps to attract players and keep them at the club. Many who have moved on from the Crown have done so reluctantly.

Coleman has also been an astute judge of a player. Each of his three title-winning teams has been quite different – but in each case the players who won the promotion were first given a chance at the higher level. Those not deemed to be quite up to standard were moved on when replacements were found who were deemed to offer that little bit more. It sounds a simple formula, but it demands much of the manager. Better players need convincing that the club is a good bet career-wise, and those players whom the manager wants to keep also have to be prepared to stay in the face of more competition for places. It speaks volumes that so few players have left the Crown of their own volition since John Coleman arrived. Stanley fans who remember seeing a new team each season appreciate that this is not as easy as it sounds, and have especially appreciated the stability that Coleman has brought to the playing staff. For the manager himself, it is a matter of loyalty. Of the 67 players to have made more than 100 first team appearances for the club, nearly a quarter have done so in the past seven years – a span which makes John Coleman by some distance the longest-serving Accrington Stanley manager.

This gives us cause to reflect on the role of Eric Whalley. As chairman, he has not been immune to criticism and charges of interference, something he found intolerable when he was on the managerial side of things. But Whalley's relationship with Coleman is clearly well established and full of mutual respect. The passion they bring to their respective roles means clashes are inevitable, but the appreciation that each holds for what the other has done at the club now seems to outweigh any immediate disagreement. While the manager has delivered League football, Whalley has invested heavily to make sure that the ground is ready to host it. Not without reason is it described as a unique relationship.

The move to full-time football also placed a burden on those working at the club. It was not just the players but the entire organisation that had to shift from its part-time habits. From an employer of no more than two or three members of staff, Accrington Stanley suddenly had more than 20 employees who had to be paid all year round, not just for the nine months of the football season.

The money from the 2003–04 cup run gave the club a financial cushion that made the initial move to full-time football less of a gamble, but it remained a big step and a big responsibility.

What has been crucial is the value that Accrington Stanley has extracted from the additional income that has come their way. Let us assume that, firstly, the Brett Ormerod transfer money was used both to complete the work that made the Crown a Conference ground and to fund the extra bit of quality in the squad that brought the NPL title; and secondly, that the FA Cup money underpinned the move to full-time football. This means that from around £500,000 of additional income for which the club could not have budgeted, Accrington Stanley have extracted two league titles, two promotions and full-time football. It represents a remarkable return on what, in the context of the wider football world, remains a modest amount of money.

As well as these wider points, there have, of course, been factors specific to each season, and the Conference triumph was no different. John Coleman pointed to the

fixture anomaly after the Worcester FA Cup game that
gave Stanley four home games to get the Cup defeat out
of their system and generate some momentum in the
league. Paul Mullin, too, pointed to the nadir at Worcester
as a significant moment, but he also revealed that feelings
were imparted and possibly some grievances cleared up,
which seemed to galvanise the team:

"The turning point was the Worcester defeat in the
FA Cup. We were so down after that and there were
a lot of words said by the team and the staff which
needed to be said. Then we had York straight after
and it was a massive game for us to win. And since
then we haven't looked back. The team spirit and
the confidence has grown and it is just a winning
mentality."

Central defender Michael Welch, credited by Ian Craney
for marshalling the defence into a more coherent unit,
pointed to some different moments on the field. He
thought that the early win at Altrincham, where the team
had not played well but dug in and nicked a late winner,
was an early boost to the self-belief of the team.

Both Halifax games, in which Stanley rescued points
after being behind, were also big results, as was the point
earned at home to Stevenage after being reduced to ten
men early in the game. Welch pointed out:

"I don't think we would have drawn that game
in the first couple of months of the season and it
showed how we had developed as a side."

Paul Mullin's observation about the previous year's
squad also seemed to offer an illumination about the
development of the promotion-winning team:

"There were a lot of characters in the team. You never knew what Dean Calcutt was going to do next,
and Steve Halford was not the most normal bloke I
have ever met. We were probably not as talented in-
dividually as we are now, but we had a great team
spirit. I think we were horrible to play against."

That is, Stanley triumphed because they had found

the right balance between the ability of those who could produce moments of individual brilliance and those whose greater value lay in the graft of tackling and harrying. Stanley remained a horrible team to play against, but they now coupled that with a much greater ability to hit teams with unpredictable moments of creativity.

And there are probably 101 other things to consider – the fact that the team did not rely on a single goalscorer must have counted for something. Mullin was again the leading scorer, but goals were both created from and finished by many different sources, with Roberts and Craney also reaching double figures for the season. The youth of the squad had its benefits as well, especially in the tremendous energy levels at places like Exeter and Gravesend, where Stanley repelled the siege tactics of the home side; and what about the cool head of Rob Elliot when faced with a penalty?

They have all had their part to play – and perhaps this is the best way to think of it, of a club comprising of a couple of dozen individuals, all with a job to do, and all doing it to the best of their ability. And of course there is luck. Even if every manager in the Conference had made exactly the right decision at exactly the right time, one team would still be the champions and three would be relegated. Anyone who watched through their fingers at Grays Athletic when a last-minute volley skimmed Phil Edwards' head, hit the bar and then looped out of play will tell you that you do not win league titles without, every now and again, having the unpredictable bounce of the slippery sphere go in your favour at the right time.

As the promotion celebrations died down, those at the Crown began a long summer of hard work to ready the ground for the new Football League season, but the first problem soon emerged. In June, the club learned that police advice to the Football League resulted in the home fixtures of Burnley and Accrington Stanley coinciding.

This was precisely the thing that Eric Whalley did not want, and he had said as much to the Football League. If

Stanley's fixtures had to coincide with one of their local rivals, then it made more sense for it to be Blackburn Rovers. As a Premiership team in Europe, Blackburn's Saturday schedule would be heavily disrupted, something Stanley were in an ideal position from which to benefit, and it was thought that far more 'floating' fans drifted between Burnley and Stanley.

The police argued that since the same division of the force covered Blackburn and Accrington, their resources would be stretched in the event of, for example, a Stanley game on the Saturday and a big Blackburn game on the Sunday. Both Burnley and Stanley complained about the decision, with Whalley estimating that it could cost the club £70,000 and force them to move games to a Friday night. At the time of writing, there are signs that a compromise may be reached, with the Football League agreeing to look at ways of alleviating the problem.

It was, however, a thought-provoking start to Stanley's latest venture into the Football League, not least because the incident was a ghost of problems past and a reminder of the challenges that endure.

Some things have changed since 1962. Unlike its predecessor (and most current Football League clubs), Accrington Stanley is not in debt. Although the club is ambitious, it is also sensibly run and has a keen nose for the commercial opportunity, even renaming the Crown Ground for sponsorship purposes. Merchandise is now shipped worldwide. The squad enjoys good training facilities in a private and rural setting under the supervision of a stable and well-established managerial and coaching team. All this is testament to the hard work and good business sense of those who work in and around the club.

But some facts of existence cannot change. History and circumstance is not on the side of the small, community club. The old realities of Accrington's size and location remain – and to overcome these challenges, the club has to hope that the people of Accrington have reflected on the harsh lessons of the past: that to abandon or ignore

Accrington Stanley is to imperil it, and that to merely wish the club well is neither here nor there in the carnivorous world of football. If Accrington wants its Football League club to survive, its people have to go to the Crown Ground and lend their support.

Hope is a good philosophy for the football fan. It tells us that although we cannot expect anything by right, and that we will from time to time suffer despair, it is worth trusting in life all the same. Hope does not prevent us from being prepared for the worst, and it guides us through the disappointments that we know are ahead. Accrington Stanley could flourish in the Football League, but it may also be the case that Stanley's return is only fleeting. A hopeful attitude would enable us to meet both eventualities in the same way, for hope rests not on a need for success or status, but on a conviction that, despite setbacks, justice will be done.

It was in a spirit of hope that George Goodwin wrote his letter in the summer of 1968, and that Bill Parkinson called the meeting in Bold Street WMC. Hope fuelled Dick Briggs as he laboriously dug through the Crown Ground clay, and spurred on Jack Barrett as he walked to Liverpool.

Eventually, the hope of those citizens who created Accrington Stanley in 1968 and nurtured the new club through its early years has been vindicated and the injustice of 1962 has been addressed. Their efforts now stand as a shining example of what can be achieved – and also of how the town should now respond to what they have done. But no matter what happens to Accrington Stanley hereafter, their 38-year journey back to the Football League will always stand as the remarkable and inspiring triumph of hope.

ACCRINGTON STANLEY CLUB HONOURS

Lancashire Combination champions
1973–74, 1977–78

Lancashire Combination Challenge Cup winners
1971–72, 1972–73, 1973–74, 1976–77

Lancashire Combination League Cup winners
1971–72

George Watson Trophy winners
1971–72, 1974–75

Cheshire League Second Division Challenge Shield winners
1979–80, 1980–81

Cheshire League Division Two champions
1980–81

John Duckworth Trophy winners
1985–86, 1991–92

North West Counties Division One runners-up shield
1986–87

Lancashire U18 Youth Cup winners
1989–90; runners-up, 1990–91

North West Alliance Cup winners
1994–95

Anglo-Barbados Cup winners
1994–95

Northern Premier (Unibond) First Division champions
1999–2000

Lancashire Junior Cup winners
2001–02, 2004–05; runners-up 1983–84, 1996–97, 2003–04

Northern Premier (Unibond) League Challenge Cup winners
2001–02

Peter Swales Challenge Shield winners
2001–02, 2002–03

Northern Premier (Unibond) Premier Division champions
2002–03

Football (Nationwide) Conference winners
2005–06

APPEARANCES AND GOALS
1970–2006

Darryl Adams	298 - 17	Stuart Illingworth	222 - 129
Dave Baron	303 - 39	Lutel James	170 - 83
Paul Beck	300 - 135	Steve Lampkin	109 - 5
Jack Brydon	129 - 80	Ian McCrae	124 - 22
Glyn Burr	169 - 7	Dave McDowell	240 - 62
John Blackburn	198 - 40	Dave Mooney	339 - 13
Andy Bondswell	109 - 39	Chris Molloy	118 - 1
Mark Brennan	131 - 13	Rob Mulloy	148
Paul Burns	128 - 23	Mick McHugh	134 - 8
Kevin Bradshaw	109	Paul Mullin	314 - 158
Simon Clarke	122 - 8	Benny Newell	212 - 9
Simon Carden	113 - 39	John Nuttall	107 - 29
Peter Cavanagh	218 - 14	Stuart Owen	103 - 14
Ian Cookson	125 - 2	Dave Parr	226 - 86
Mark Ceraolo	107 - 34	Russell Payne	196 - 20
Charlie Cooper	136 - 14	Steve Parry	286 - 108
Alan Davies	301 - 146	Bernard Poole	133 - 4
Dick Ellis	233	Rory Prendergast	110 - 19
Martin Eatough	110 - 8	Darren Quick	208 - 15
Tony Farrell	129	Neil Rowbotham	276 - 5
Mick Finn	222	Lee Rogerson	138 - 15
Jay Flannery	103 - 10	Colin Smith	100 - 55
Steve Flitcroft	116 - 11	Jonathan Smith	250 - 29
Chris Grimshaw	363 - 56	Jamie Speare	300
Steve Guest	100 - 7	Duncan Seddon	104 - 6
Jim Howley	187 - 23	Kevin Twinney	190 - 4
Steve Halford	116 - 7	Dave Tattersall	106 - 2
Dave Hargreaves	355 - 316	Keith Walkden	182 - 19
Dave Hindle	100 - 15	Ian Wilcox	343 - 18
Mick Higgins	109 - 4	Mel Widdup	209 - 31
Ashley Hoskin	143 - 31	Brian Welch	163 - 44
John Hubberstey	172 - 10	Gus Wilson	113 - 12
Bernie Hughes	136 - 41	Robbie Williams	267 - 5

INDEX

383